GUERRILLAS

Journeys in the Insurgent World

JON LEE ANDERSON

ABACUS

First published in the United States by Times Books,
a division of Random House Inc., in 1992
This edition published in Great Britain as an Abacus original in May 2006

A CIP catalogue record for this book
is available from the British Library.

ISBN 0 349 11885 X

Typeset in Garamond by M Rules

Printed and bound in Great Britain by
Clays Ltd, St Ives plc

Abacus
An imprint of
Time Warner Book Group UK
Brettenham House
Lancaster Place
London WC2E 7EN

www.twbg.co.uk

Jon Lee Anderson is the author of *The Fall of Baghdad*, *Che Guevara: A Revolutionary Life*, *The Lion's Grave: Dispatches from Afghanistan*, and, with his brother Scott Anderson, *War Zones* and *Inside the League*. He is a staff writer for the *New Yorker*. He lives in Dorset, England, with his wife and three children.

Praise for *The Fall of Baghdad*:

'Superb . . . this is non-fiction writing of the highest order: acute, laconic, vivid'
William Boyd, BOOKS OF THE YEAR, *Sunday Telegraph*

'In an inspired piece of publishing, Anderson's reporting has been turned into one of the best books likely to be produced about Iraq and the conflict visited upon the country. This is a powerful piece of writing which has marked the Iraq conflict like no other. In Anderson, Iraq has found its George Orwell and there can be no higher praise'
Trevor Royle, *Sunday Herald*

'A great book in the best tradition of reportage, along with John Reed's *Ten Days that Shook the World* and George Orwell's *Homage to Catalonia*'
Sunday Times

'This is the rich, raw material of history – that beguiling but elusive muse – an account by a skilful observer and reporter, and a sheaf of extended testimony about daily life and contemporary attitudes by concerned Iraqis during the historic remaking of their country. Anderson's book . . . is indispensable for understanding what is going on inside Iraqi society today'
Washington Post

'In this measured, keenly descriptive account, hindsight gives way to horror as the early rumblings of war become reality and the city of Baghdad is changed beyond recognition . . . *The Fall of Baghdad* is as current as it is important'
New York Times

'A gripping tale of a country faced with an impending war and a people torn apart. Anderson makes Iraq come alive through his descriptions of everyday life, his visits to local hospitals and the building of friendships with Iraqis. Anderson gives more than just a snapshot of history – he offers a real insight into the turmoil that is now Iraq'
Ireland on Sunday

'An elegantly written account by a reporter at the height of his art . . . An invaluable eyewitness report for posterity'
Times Literary Supplement

For Erica, Bella, Rosie, and Máximo
with my love

Loving as I love this life, poetry, and the people,
how can I not offer up my bones?

– FROM A POEM BY HAROLDO,
A SALVADORAN GUERRILLA

'Haroldo' was the revolutionary *nom de guerre* of Miguel Huezo Mixco, a Salvadoran poet who joined the guerrillas of the Fuerzas Populares de Liberación in 1980. In 1988, while he was still underground, two of Huezo Mixco's poetry collections, *El Pozo del Tirador* and *Tres Pájaros de un Tiro*, were published by Editorial Universitaria in San Salvador. The poems that are quoted in this book and attributed to Haroldo are drawn from Huezo Mixco's *Tres Pájaros de un Tiro*.

CONTENTS

Introduction

If the conditions are right, guerrillas can emerge from within any society. If people perceive themselves to be irrevocably disenfranchised by their government, or oppressed within their country, violence is almost bound to occur. People take up arms for many different reasons, ranging from outrage over economic inequities and social injustices to systematic forms of cultural, racial, and political discrimination.

Imbued as most people in the world are with distinctive credos of tribal, cultural, or national identity, the impulse to repel outside intruders is an intrinsically human response, and there are few things more likely to spark off the spirit of rebellion than a military invasion of one's country by a foreign power.

Guerrilla violence erupted in Iraq within a few weeks of the fall of Baghdad to American military forces in April 2003. By the time President George W. Bush declared an 'end to hostilities' on May 1, the first shots in the Iraqi insurgency had already been fired.

It was probably inevitable. Even if it had been well planned and administered, the American and British-led occupation of Iraq was never going to be warmly received by all Iraqis. Well before the war, there had been widespread suspicion in Iraq about the ultimate intentions of the Coalition. Many Iraqis believed what Saddam Hussein had always warned them: that the West wanted to destroy Iraq's civilization and to steal its oil. This prevailing mood of skepticism combined with other factors to sow the seeds of an Iraqi resistance movement.

Overnight, gun-toting young American soldiers who spoke no Arabic became Iraq's new overseers, patrolling the streets and manning checkpoints. In Baghdad, and throughout the country, they took over Saddam's grandiose palaces and converted them into fortified military bases. When Baghdad's public buildings were looted and burned under the tolerant gaze of the recently arrived 'liberation forces,' many Iraqis, including die-hard Saddam opponents, became angry and resentful. The fact that the Americans had protected the Oil Ministry but not Iraq's national treasures in the Iraq Museum was widely noted, and convinced many that it was part of a nefarious master plan to obliterate Iraq's cultural patrimony. Next, President Bush's newly-appointed viceroy for Iraq, Paul Bremer III, ordered the dissolution of Iraq's armed forces and outlawed the Baath Party, effectively disenfranchizing several million Iraqis and their dependents from any hope of a future place in the vaunted 'new Iraq.'

Simultaneously, thousands of Iraqi exiles and foreign 'contractors' poured into the country, assuming well-paid jobs with the occupation authorities and taking over the grand villas vacated by Saddam's nomenklatura. But there were very few improvements in the everyday lives of ordinary Iraqis. During the long, hot summer of 2003, Baghdad's electricity, which had been damaged in the war, remained largely unrepaired, and much of the city was blacked out for months. Iraq's oil industry was soon up and running again, however, a fact which may have made economic sense, but merely reaffirmed the suspicions of many Iraqis that what the occupation really represented was a wholesale rape of their nation by profiteering outsiders. The Coalition did very little to dispel such beliefs, nor did it effectively address the mounting sense of alienation among Iraq's Sunni minority, who had predominated during Saddam's regime and now found themselves out of power.

The first guerrilla actions against the Americans took place in Fallujah, the Sunni city west of Baghdad. By the end of the year, Iraq's Sunni insurgency was widespread; American troops were doing battle all over central and northern Iraq, and they were taking casualties every day.

In December 2003, eight months after the fall of Saddam Hussein, I met with several Sunni insurgents in a house on the western fringes of Baghdad. My intermediaries were an Iraqi businessman and a friend of his, an unemployed engineer. Both were very critical of the Americans, and had offered to introduce me to the 'resistance.' The meeting took place in the engineer's house. After waving me into his living room, the engineer left the room. He returned accompanied by three Iraqi men. They acknowledged me with nods of their heads, but otherwise their faces were expressionless.

I walked over to greet them. As we shook hands, two of the men smiled and met my eyes with theirs, but the third man seemed uncomfortable, and stared at me with frank distrust. He was stocky, thuggish looking, and appeared to be in his late thirties. He took a seat by the door. The second man looked to be in his early fifties, with silver hair and a mustache, and he wore a felt jacket over a gray dishdasha robe. The other stranger stood out markedly from the other two. He was fair and tall, in his early thirties, and was dressed in a tailored blue shirt with pearl buttons and expensive-looking suede moccasins. He fingered a string of blue prayer beads.

We established the ground rules for our meeting. Each of the men chose a fictitious name for himself in order for me to identify them in my notes. The silver-haired man in the dishdasha asked me to call him 'Abu Ahmed'; the thuggish man chose 'Abu Barwan'; and the tall, fair-haired man with the expensive clothes chose 'Abu Abdullah.'

'Why is there a resistance?' I asked Abu Ahmed.

'The Americans came here by force and as occupiers, so what do you think? They say they will bring democracy, but so far we have not seen any of the things they said they would bring.'

The fair-haired man, Abu Abdullah, interrupted to say that Iraqis were fighting the Americans because they did not believe their declared aims for being in Iraq. He leaned forward and spoke bluntly to me. 'I don't trust you, either, my friend, because imagine if someone from Europe or Mexico came to your country with guns, could you trust them?' I shook my head in what I hoped seemed an agreeable way, but privately I was becoming worried about the turn in the conversation. After a pause, he spoke again. 'But that doesn't mean I will do something against you. You can be from Scotland Yard or the CIA, I don't mind, because we want your countries to have this information.' He continued. 'The killing of Americans in Iraq is normal, my friend. If they weren't being killed it would not be normal, because everyone is against them being here.'

Addressing myself to Abu Ahmed, the silver-haired man, I asked, are you fighting for Saddam?' (Our meeting took place a couple of weeks before Saddam was captured in his 'spiderhole' in Tikrit.) 'No,' he replied. 'I am not a Baathist. I was one of those who was against him before the war, but now, from what I have seen from the Americans, I would put my hand with Saddam Hussein.'

I asked the men about the Americans' plans for a transfer of power to an Iraqi government. If there were free elections, I

pointed out, it was highly possible that the majority population of
Iraq, which was Shia, would form the next government. How did
they feel about that possibility? Would they end their insurgency?

Abu Ahmed took issue with my assertion that there were more
Shiites than Sunnis in Iraq, but sounded agreeable to the idea of a
political compromise. 'If there is an election, and the people choose
anyone from the Shia, I will agree with that, and the resistance
will stop.'

Hearing this, the thuggish man, Abu Barwan, who had said
almost nothing until now, clicked his tongue and shook his head in
disapproval. 'No,' he said. 'This would not be a good thing if the
Shia win. I believe that the resistance will continue, against the
new Shia government, and the Americans.'

Abu Abdullah agreed with Abu Barwan. 'I think the Americans
are confused if they think that this will be a solution to Iraq's problems. I believe it is the wrong solution, and the Americans will be
hated even more. If they give power to Shias because they think
they are more than the Sunnis, this would be unfair to the Sunnis.
The resistance will not stop; it will continue against the Shia and
against the U.S., because the resistance rejects them both, and
doesn't trust either of them.'

'So,' I asked him. 'What is the solution?'

Abu Abdullah replied, 'The solution I think is that the Americans
should go, and before they go, in order to improve their image with
the Iraqis, they should give real power to the Iraqi people. But I think
the Republican Party people of the U.S. are not peaceful people, they
are war people, so I don't know if they will do this . . . I've heard that
democracy is good, in the West, that it fixes economies, and these
things. That's what I've heard, but I don't know. I don't care what
kind of government Iraq has, as long as it works. And here it is all
a mess, and I don't think America knows what it's doing here, or
what its goals are. That's what I think, my friend.'

After a pause, Abu Abdullah added, 'The Americans are losing the war. And I tell you that they will face more losses very soon. Sooner or later, America will lose.'

Abu Abdullah's prediction may well turn out to be accurate. By April 2004, the Americans were facing not merely a Sunni insurgency but a Shiite revolt as well, and that month alone, over a hundred American soldiers lost their lives. A month later, U.S. authority in Iraq was further undermined by the revelations of the abuse of Iraqi prisoners in Abu Ghraib prison. As the violence intensified and the death toll mounted in Iraq, there was increasing talk in the United States and Great Britain of finding an 'exit strategy' for their troops. By then, most Iraqis also wanted them to go.

When I first began exploring the insurgent world for this book, I wanted to understand what it was that makes ordinary people decide to go to war, to make the conscious decision to kill and die for an ideal that exists, at the beginning, at least, only in their own minds. The first step, or so it appeared to me, was the crucial one, because it involved a step across an invisible line into an everyday realm where death, not life, was the greater certainty. It was the consciousness of the undertaking itself, I felt, which separated the guerrilla from the rest of us. As in Che Guevara's famous dictum extolling armed revolutionaries as 'the highest form of the human species,' the guerrillas seemed a distinct kind of man.

In 1967, as a ten-year-old boy, I saw the gritty front-page photograph of Che Guevara on his death bed. The image is now classic: A gaunt and bearded Che lies shirtless on a cot; his torso is riddled with bullets; he is surrounded by his uniformed killers. Before this, I had never heard of Che Guevara or his plan to liberate the Americas with guerrilla warfare. His death was my first awareness that people like him existed, but from that moment on, I was fascinated by the image of the rebel, the guerrilla.

This book is about five groups of guerrillas – the mujahedin of Afghanistan, the Karen of Burma, the Polisario of Western Sahara, the FMLN of El Salvador, and a group of Palestinian boys in Gaza – but it is also about a way of life that, though quite alien to most of us, has aspects that are universal to human existence. Though guerrilla groups are essentially political organizations, I have written about the people within them, not the groups themselves. I have viewed the guerrilla as a global phenomenon, not on a region-by-region basis. I have examined guerrillas as I would any other group of people, taking into account their common concerns about family, religion, economics, society, law and order, and mythology, and how these concerns play a role in their everyday life. I compare the differences and similarities between members of these armies, but most of all I have tried to extract the rich trove of stories all guerrillas hold dear. In the end, I hope I have created a portrait of what it is like to be a guerrilla in today's world.

Guerrillas have become ubiquitous figures, filling our newspapers and television screens with their violent attacks and shouted demands. Their actions and strange-sounding names and acronyms have become quotidian but their motives often remain obscure. At any given moment, there are a couple of dozen guerrilla wars being waged around the world. Some are longstanding ethnic or territorial wars that have been inflamed by the arms and advisers of regional powers, or have hemorrhaged on since the days when they were proxy battlefields of the Cold War. Over time, some guerrillas have become so entrenched that they have assumed the role of de facto governments in their territorial fiefdoms.

In this 'other world,' the presence of arms is not an anomaly but a raison d'être; children are born, raised, and educated in the vortex of war. Guerrillas are people living in defiance of their would-be world conquerors, according to their own laws and beliefs, telling their own stories and legends – making history. But, however well we sometimes understand their politics, the guerrillas themselves remain inaccessible and obscure to most of us. They are strangers seen only in photographs, posed threateningly with automatic weapons, their faces set in fierce determination or masked by scarves.

The inspiration for this book began when, as a young journalist, I reported on the conflicts taking place in Central America. A key moment came in January 1986, when I saw in the New Year with the FMLN guerrillas in El Salvador's Morazán province. Guerrilla-controlled Morazán was only three hours outside the capital, where I was living, but it was a world apart. For some days, I hiked and drove my jeep around the rocky oxen trails, accompanied by these guerrillas, their automatic weapons clacking against the hot metal interior with each bounce and bump. Wherever we went, they seemed to remember places where important events had occurred, events that lived on in their hearts and impelled them to further action. I began to wonder how much more unseen history and folklore these people possessed. I realized that in Morazán I was glimpsing something remarkable – a rebel society living outside its nation's laws. And all I had to do was spin the globe to see that this phenomenon was worldwide; large swathes of territory now belonged not to governments that ostensibly ruled there, but to the political outlaws who were the real authorities.

For this book, I wanted to get as broad a view of guerrillas as possible. To do that, I knew I would have to visit wars taking place in different parts of the world. However, because it was impossible to cover the globe comprehensively, I limited myself to a number of groups that would faithfully represent the modern guerrilla. Even so, it was not my intention that the guerrillas I have chosen would speak for every guerrilla alive today.

First I decided to go to Afghanistan. Not only did I have an invitation from one of the mujahedin groups, but the Soviets had not yet completed their withdrawal from the country, and I wanted the rare opportunity of observing guerrillas fighting against a foreign invader. I went to Kandahar in Afghanistan's southern desert. Afterward I visited the disputed territory of Western Sahara with the Polisario Front guerrillas. This was the most streamlined and 'organized' visit I made. I obtained a visa at the Algerian Embassy in London only after the Polisario had approved my trip, and in Algeria, the Polisario representative met me at the customs desk. This kind of open complicity between a guerrilla army and a foreign host nation is rare. I returned to Afghanistan again to observe the mujahedin's abortive siege of the city of Jalalabad. For a couple of months I stayed in the Pakistani border city of Peshawar and made cross-border trips.

The third place I traveled to was Burma. I had received assurances of a warm welcome in a letter sent to me by an exile politician allied with the Karen guerrillas fighting along the Burma-Thailand border. There, over a three-month period, I made repeated visits to the Karen bases.

Next I went to El Salvador, a country I know quite well, where friends helped me with arrangements to enter the FMLN guerrillas' 'liberated zone' in the mountains of Chalatenango. El Salvador was important to me because the things I had seen there before had provided the genesis of this book.

My final journey was to the Israeli-occupied Gaza Strip, to the Breij refugee camp, a place where I had previously made friends among the militant *shabbab* involved in the intifada there. Some may wonder about the inclusion of the *shabbab* in a book about guerrillas, but they suit my definition of what a guerrilla is: anyone risking his or her life in a struggle to change things, by whatever means are at his or her disposal.

I wrote this book in the present tense, so as to give readers a sense of immediacy about the insurgent world. The people I met and places I visited are described as I found them during my travels, which took place over a three-year period between December 1988 and January 1992.

Like all other things in life, however, wars change over time, and so have most of the situations portrayed in this book. But in the end, this book is not about the particular circumstances of the wars I visited; it is about guerrillas, as they might be found at any time or in any place Above all, it is my hope that it gives the human side of their story, because it is one that could so easily be our own.

GUERRILLAS

ONE

Myths of Creation

In the old days, the unexplored areas of the world were left blank on maps; cartographers wrote the words TERRA INCOGNITA to describe them. Often these were populated areas that had simply not yet been probed by the mapmaking, colonial powers, and so they officially remained 'unknown lands.'

Later, as these lands were surveyed and fell under the dominion of expanding European empires, the blank spaces were filled in, and new colonial boundaries were superimposed on ancient tribal territories and native kingdoms.

Maps have always reflected the conceits of history's conquerors, and the present time is no different. Today, the territories inhabited by guerrillas fighting wars to establish their own visions of life aren't yet included in the pages of modern political atlases. Their borders, if delineated at all, exist only on military charts used by themselves and their enemies. The shifting boundaries shown on these maps are unofficial, even secret, and definitely inexact. And yet they represent a truer reality than those maps showing the counties, provinces, and national borders of the official nation-states.

Throughout the world there are inner landscapes perceived only by the guerrillas and their followers. For them, infinitely dramatic and memorable events – some horrible, some sublime – have occurred in the growth of trees and bramble they call home. So much has happened in the overgrown thickets where human settlements once flourished. Here, there was a battle. There, a guerrilla hero died . . . an enemy column was ambushed . . . a helicopter was downed . . . The sites of massacres are dignified by their loneliness, their silences interrupted only by a raucous cicada or the rustling of birds. Already, the leafy trees and the vines are overtaking the rubble where houses once stood, where a church once ushered the faithful to prayer; the dead lie beneath, unseen.

These are places with the disquieting feel of hallowed ground; in them the guerrillas creep around, speaking in hushed tones. For them, such places are terrible proof of the nature of the enemy – and also a reminder of the price that innocents have had to pay as a consequence for their own presence.

The gods and ghosts of war, its heroes and villains and its moments of daring and defeat – all of the transcendental moments that make up a war's history – are invisible to outsiders, but they inhabit the land in the hearts and minds of the guerrillas and their followers.

Someday, if they ever take power, there will be plaques and statues erected in honor of this ghostly pantheon; there will be monuments in the places where blood was spilled, where one can go in homage to lay a floral wreath and try to imagine what happened. But for now, this living history is still being forged in bloodshed and can only be commemorated orally, in reminiscences told over and over again, passed down to those who are younger. This folklore, this inner landscape of the war, will continue to exist as long as there are guerrillas left alive to remember and recount what has happened. Eventually, the stories will become myth.

All guerrillas have creation myths. To justify killing others, men mythologize the origins of their conflicts, and, as the wars develop, so do accounts of what is taking place. For guerrillas, the resulting folklore satisfies a need to immortalize their actions, to ensure that their own version of history is being told. For their fear is that, living as fugitives, they shall remain forever invisible to the world beyond the battlefields where they fight and die. Just like men looking into pools of water at their own reflections, the guerrillas also have a need to see themselves, to reassure themselves of their own place in time.

Deep in the expanse of the Sahara Desert, a group of guerrillas has perpetuated one of the most unusual creation myths of all: They declare their barren wilderness refuge to be nothing less than a sovereign republic, and themselves to be its government and citizens.

The wall snakes diagonally over a desert ridge a half-mile away. From a sniper's dugout and with a sirocco picking up in the mid-morning heat, it is visible only as an uneven white line against the dun hills. The way it shimmers and winks, the wall might almost be a mirage, like the silvery lakes that beckon repeatedly, only to vanish the closer one draws to them.

This is the front line in the war over Western Sahara, a former Spanish colony on Africa's northwest hump. For nearly two decades, ethnic Saharawis have fought a guerrilla war against the occupying troops of King Hassan II of Morocco. It was he who built this 1,500-mile-long fortified wall around two-thirds of the territory. Relentlessly cutting across the desert wilderness, the wall has transformed this into one of the world's strangest conflicts.

Like the wall, the war itself looms like a tornado at horizon's edge, never completely within grasp; perhaps this is appropriate in a desert without obvious landmarks or many signs of human habitation. Here, the bleached yellow walls of a Spanish colonial fort; there, a nomad's tent of patchwork blankets; and nothing else but endless sand and sky. There are no trees except for the tiny, thorny *ejdari* trees, the bark of which is good for curing goat hides, and the *atil*, which the nomads use to clean their teeth. And there are no roads except the tracks left by the guerrillas' jeeps. But even these are temporary; a wind comes and they are gone, like the dunes, which shift according to the seasons.

Sometimes the wind is gone and the desert is airless and terribly hot. At other times the wind blows hot and hard, changing the shape of the land. In the winter, when a wet fog from the Atlantic blankets the land and turns it green for the nomads' flocks of camels and goats, rain pools form. These aren't mirages but actual lakes, suddenly born in the desert's depressions; they fill up with sweet, pure rainwater to fill the goatskins. But a sirocco can blow away these lakes in hours; where the water rippled and danced is once again just hot desert. Then the mirage lakes return, winking on and off in the distance like quicksilver.

When the Spanish dictator Francisco Franco was in his deathbed delirium in late 1975, he signed over the phosphate-rich colony of Spanish Sahara to Morocco and Mauritania, thus betraying the nationalist Saharawis' hopes for an independent state. Spain's retreat coincided with a show of force by King Hassan II of Morocco, who marched 350,000 of his subjects into the colony in a massive public-relations exercise called the Green March. Presented as a spontaneous demonstration by the Moroccan people to recover a lost part of the 'greater Moroccan homeland,' the Green March was really a thin disguise for Hassan's simultaneous annexation of the territory, which he carried out by sending in Moroccan army troops to occupy key towns and crush local opposition.

As Hassan's troops moved in, they clashed with guerrillas belonging to the fledgling Saharawi independence movement, the Frente Popular para la Liberación de Saguia el-Hamra y Rió de Oro, or Polisario Front. Formed in 1973 to bring an end to Spanish colonial rule, the Polisario operated clandestinely within the territory while training its cadres in neighboring Algeria. It exercised little control over the native Saharawi population, which at the time numbered under 100,000 people, most of them semi-nomadic tribesmen or settled traders living in a handful of sunbaked towns. Now, however, the Polisario guerrillas rose up to counter Morocco's expansionist moves, seizing some settlements of their own from which to make a stand.

But it was no good. After several months of fighting, making a brave defense here and there, the Polisario finally retreated. Under heavy bombing from the air and sustained attack by Moroccan as well as Mauritanian ground troops, its guerrillas withdrew to safe bases across the Algerian border, taking with them large numbers of Saharawi civilians.

Moulay was a Saharawi boy of fifteen when his ambitious father added two years to his real age and enlisted him into the colonial police force. It was one of the few careers available to Saharawis that offered secure employment and steady wages. But Moulay's stint lasted barely three years because soon after he joined up the Spaniards announced their intention to withdraw from the colony. By the time they did leave, Moulay had become a nationalist, a secret member of the Polisario underground.

'I used to pass out the Polisario's leaflets when I was on my rounds,' says Moulay with a chuckle. He is now a burly man of thirty-three, with a boxer's broken nose, and curly blond hair. 'When the Spaniards left, I hired a car to take me into the desert so I could join them in their camps.'

For the rest of the 1970s, fighters like Moulay carried on the Polisario's war to regain the lost Saharawi homeland, raiding deep into the territory and even inside Mauritania and Morocco. In 1979, reeling from the Polisario's attacks and unable to pay its share of the war's cost, impoverished Mauritania swore off its own

claims to Western Sahara in an armistice with the Polisario. But
Morocco moved into the Mauritanian vacuum, and, with extensive
financial backing from the West, has poured enormous resources
into the war ever since.

The Moroccan monarch has been far from idle in finding ways
to thwart the Polisario Front. After years of hit-and-run raids, and
a few spectacularly embarrassing defeats dealt to his troops by the
guerrillas, King Hassan finally resorted to one of the most ancient
and primitive stratagems used in warfare: He built a wall. After all,
what else does one do with bothersome neighbors?

Hassan's Wall. It is, in its way, as historic as China's Great Wall
or Hadrian's Wall in Britain, for this is a defensive battlement many
hundreds of miles long, built and maintained at enormous cost and
enclosing much of Western Sahara to keep the Polisario out. This
berm of bulldozed sand and stone bristles with the accoutrements of
modern warfare, for Hassan has purchased the very latest in mines,
artillery, radar, and electronic sensors and installed them along its
entire length. And no fewer than 160,000 of the king's soldiers
guard it at all times, like medieval sentries on a castle parapet, forever scanning the wilderness beyond for enemies of the kingdom.

Few men can ever have reduced their enemies to a position of
such absurd futility. For, with such a simple gesture, Hassan has
not only imprisoned the Polisario in the desert, he has also walled
off the only parts of Western Sahara worth possessing: the Atlantic
seacoast with its fishing ports, the only inhabited settlements, and
the phosphate mines that are the Sahara's primary source of wealth.

Beyond the wall, only a barren strip of sand and rock stretching
to the unmarked Algerian and Mauritanian borders remains;
Hassan has relinquished it for the time being. Somewhat ludi-
crously, the Polisario trumpets this belt of land as its 'liberated
territory.' Like twentieth-century Quixotes, its turbaned fighters
charge across the abandoned scree in their olive-green Land Rovers

to engage the enemy in battle. But the enemy they confront is the inanimate and unbudgeable wall. Occasionally they breach it, engaging the Moroccan troops in bloody battles and inflicting heavy casualties, but these are meaningless victories in a war that to all intents and purposes has already been lost.

Still, the guerrillas fight on, claiming that theirs is a war of attrition. Their hopes rest on the assumption that King Hassan is incapable of paying the huge cost of defending the wall forever and will eventually negotiate with them, or even withdraw. Another optimistic scenario is that Hassan will be overthrown in a Moroccan 'people's revolt.' However it happens, the guerrillas say, when their day comes, they will be there, ready to move in across the wall and install themselves as Western Sahara's rightful rulers.

In the years since Moulay and tens of thousands of civilian Saharawis joined the Polisario in their Algerian camps, the refugees' number has grown to as many as 170,000. These Saharawis are no ordinary refugees, but believers in a dream fostered by the Polisario Front and nurtured in the chrysalis of their desert exile. The dream is to see their homeland become in reality what they have already declared it to be, the 'Saharan Arab Democratic Republic,' their own independent state. They have prepared for that day with their own state flag, national anthem, prime minister, Cabinet, and, most important of all, citizens: themselves, the Saharawi people.

The Saharawis are an amalgam of several Hassaniyah-speaking tribes of Berber origin who in the old colonial days were called Moors.* Many have a visible complement of black African blood, and the result is a handsome blend of Semitic and Negroid

---

*Hassaniyah combines Arabic and Berber vocabularies and uses a mostly Arabic grammar.

features. Saharawis have burnished brown or copper-colored skin and dark brown eyes and hair; some are quite tall and lithe. A small number are full-blooded blacks, former slaves who were freed by Polisario proclamation after the 1975 exodus. Today, the ex-slaves and their former owners live as equals, both having come to terms with their new common identity.

'It takes a lot to motivate people to leave their homes and their TVs and go into the desert to fight, but this is what we have done,' says Mahfoud Ali Beiba, a bearded and athletic guerrilla commander who is second only to the Polisario president, Mohamed Abdelaziz. 'But the Polisario didn't just fall from the sky. The anti-colonial struggle of our people goes back a hundred years, but it lacked clearly defined objectives. The Polisario has filled this internal vacuum by organizing a country. We began to 'conscienticize' the people so that the conflict wouldn't just remain a matter for discussion, but lead to action, and become a total conviction.'

As Ali Beiba holds forth in the salon of a house used for greeting visitors to Aoussert camp, near the Algerian garrison town of Tindouf, an ex-slave hovers in attendance. He serves coffee in porcelain demitasse cups embossed with the Saharawi emblem. A high-cheekboned, blue-black man with downcast eyes, he moves in and out of the room, placing the cups before each man in deferential silence. The guerrilla leader wears an unadorned military uniform: simple olive green with a slight sheen to it, like the kind worn by Cubans. Or perhaps it is that he looks Cuban himself, like a mulatto. He also looks careworn; he has the deep dark bags and alert eyes of someone with many responsibilities.

Although only thirty-seven years old, Ali Beiba sits on the Polisario Front's seven-member executive committee; he was one of the Front's founding members. In addition, he is the Saharan Arab Democratic Republic's prime minister, its justice minister, and its interior minister – all at the same time.

Ali Beiba was raised for this life. He spent his boyhood on the run, moving with his family from one part of the Spanish colony to the other as his fugitive father, a Saharawi nationalist, tried to evade the colonial authorities. 'My childhood memories are of being chased by soldiers and airplanes with my family, and that has obviously left its mark on me,' he says.

In the 1960s, as he grew up, Ali Beiba was influenced by the African national-liberation movements then fighting against Portuguese colonial rule in Guinea-Bissau, Angola, and Mozambique. Closer to home, the former French colonies of Algeria, Morocco, and Mauritania had each recently gained their independence; the hard-fought Algerian war of independence especially set a model for other anti-colonial struggles. Most important, newly independent Algeria offered arms, financial support, and sanctuary to the Saharawis.

In 1973, Ali Beiba and other young Saharawi nationalists founded the Polisario Front in an attempt to include Western Sahara in the roster of African liberation struggles. He was only twenty at the time. A year later, Ali Beiba left the colony because the Spanish authorities were after him. His destination was Syria, where he claims with intentional vagueness to have studied 'general administration.' These 'studies' were cut short by the Moroccan invasion of 1975; Ali Beiba returned to join the fight. Since then, his life has been taken over by the independence struggle. He has a wife, whom he met during the war, and two children, born in the desert camps where the Polisario reigns supreme.

In their desert exile, the guerrillas have made great efforts to consolidate their hold on their refugee constituents. One way they have done this is to tutor the Saharawis for nationhood. The tutelage begins with the way the Saharawis live. For instance, all four camps – strung in a north-south line along the Algerian border with Western Sahara – are named after the main towns of

Western Sahara itself: Dakhla, El Aaiún, Smara, and Aoussert; taking this premeditated similitude a step further, most of the refugees have been installed in camps whose names correspond with those of their original homes. In a rehearsed denial of their refugee status, the Saharawis claim only the name of the town they come from, never referring to where they live as 'camp.' This can be confusing: When Moulay introduces himself, he says his family was originally from Smara but moved, first to El Aaiún and finally to Dakhla.

'We have tried to create a framework of being in one's own country,' says Ali Beiba. He explains that the camps are deliberately isolated from any Algerian settlement – to prevent 'assimilation' – and that each camp's structure has been designed to 'echo' the administrative structure of the actual country of Western Sahara: The camps have been divided into *wilayat*, provinces, and the *wilayat* have been subdivided into *dairat*, districts, named for the geographic regions of Western Sahara. This was the first step taken by the Polisario.

The second step was to make all the people live in tents. 'We could obviously have built houses for the people if we had wanted,' says Ali Beiba. 'But this isn't our home; our home is the Western Sahara, and so we have stayed in tents to emphasize the temporary nature of our exile. And finally, from the very beginning it was laid down that only the women, children, and old people are refugees. The man isn't a refugee. He is a Saharawi soldier, fighting inside liberated territory.'

The Polisario case for national legitimacy obliges them to undertake this ritual exercise of denial. Official Polisario policy maintains that its Saharan Arab Democratic Republic represents a majority of the Saharawi people and governs from within liberated territory. This ignores the fact that, except for the unwalled 'Belt' with its smattering of nomads who tend the revolution's herds of camels and goats, the Polisario 'state' and its citizens are refugees living in tented camps on Algerian, not Saharawi, soil.

To bolster its claims to the land, and aware of the importance of traditions in asserting a distinct ethnic identity, the Polisario has encouraged a revival of traditional Saharawi folklore, artisanry, and song and dance among the refugees. The version of history packaged by the Polisario's 'Ministry of Culture' dates back to Neolithic times, with archaeological evidence of an ancient Saharawi civilization in the form of cave paintings, arrowheads, and stone tomb-monuments. Mahfoud Ali Beiba says the collectivized system the Polisario has imposed is a faithful reflection of indigenous Saharawi culture – proof that a strong national and ethnic identity fuels the insurgency.

Like utopian experimenters in communal socialism, the Polisario has erected a Brave New World in the Sahara Desert. Its control is unchallenged and nearly absolute; its revolution is all-wise and all-powerful, and it is the great provider, as well. Everything is channeled through the Polisario. Food, water, clothing, electricity, and housing are all provided free of charge by the Polisario; each camp has its day-care centers, primary schools, youth centers; there is a 'national' high school, and university scholarships abroad are available through the Polisario's contacts with friendly foreign regimes. Civilian committees and subcommittees called 'popular councils' govern most aspects of camp life, functioning as the eyes and ears of their respective Polisario-controlled ministries. After 'independence' they will become the Polisario government's civil bureaucracy.

Perhaps most important, there is no money in the camps. The people have no use for it. Living a thousand miles from anywhere, without passports, the Polisario's Saharawis are the most dependent of people. And that's how the Polisario wants it – now and for the foreseeable future.

'The Saharawi people still aren't sufficiently mature for a multi-party system,' says Ali Beiba. 'While I believe in a diversity of ideas, I don't believe in an immediate multiparty system because that would require a civic sense more advanced than that which now exists.'

Children, mothers, and old men are usually the only people in evidence in the camps. Young men and women are either off boarding at the 'national high school,' abroad at university, or, if not actually serving at the Front, then undergoing basic training at one of the Polisario's military training centers. When the young are not in school, they gather in centers named after Polisario martyrs and play Ping-Pong, paint and draw pictures, or rehearse amateur dramatics. Little children run around playing games and singing songs, chasing each other around tents.

In the late afternoon, when the sun is low, the white-bearded old men gather together outside the tents on the cooling sand. Dressed in their white or sky-blue *dra*, the Saharawi men's smock, with their heads wrapped in black turbans, they take off their leather sandals and sprawl or sit cross-legged to talk, wriggling their bare toes in the sand.

Swathed in iridescent saris and head scarves of lime-green, fuchsia, and Prussian-blue cotton, the women look like tropical birds. They walk in sandaled feet, with the gentle sway of browsing gazelles.

Life goes on inside the large rectangular campaign tents, each housing a separate family. The tents are laid out across the sand like orderly villages, in rows, their peaked roofs, straight sides, and once-white canvas carefully stretched taut by rope tethers. A small cookhouse of chocolate-colored earthen bricks squats to the rear of each tent. Water is brought in buckets from communal spigots.

During the worst heat of the day, when the air is still and hot inside the tents, the flaps are opened to allow air to move. All the people nap, or move very slowly about their tasks. Only in the cool air of dawn, or after sundown, do Saharawis get their work done.

The war is invisible, except for the uniformed fighters' jeeps, which roar in and out of the camps all the time, carrying guerrillas to and from the Front. No weapons are visible anywhere; they are kept out of sight while the men are at home.

The Saharawis consider themselves to be the citizens of a sovereign nation, and in many ways they are just that. After all, perceived reality is its own reality. So, like nouveaux riches anxious to acquire the appearance of old money, the Saharawis have adopted the trappings of national sovereignty in the form of an emblematic series of martyrs, slogans, and symbols that express their revolutionary and ethnic identity. The most potent of these symbols is the national flag, a red star and crescent moon superimposed on three horizontal bars of black, white, and green, running into a red triangle. The star and moon show the Islamic nature of their people, say the guerrillas, while the red symbolizes the blood of their martyrs. The green stands for hope, and the white for peace. The black, on top, represents the combined horrors of past colonialism and the present time of war and deprivation. After independence, the black will be moved to the bottom, because all that is bad will have been overcome, and the white of peace will replace it on the top.

The political iconography is everywhere: TODA LA PATRIA O EL MARTIRIO ('All the fatherland or martyrdom') is splashed in graffiti on walls throughout the camps. And carved into women's earrings, painted on cushions, stenciled onto porcelain tea services, is the Saharawi national emblem – crossed rifles over an anvil, the national flag sprouting out of each barrel, topped by the crescent moon and star and enclosed by two sheaves of wheat. Like a designer label, 'RASD,' the Spanish acronym for the Polisario state, is stamped on women's saris, written in large letters on walls, and even woven into woolen rugs.

In this atmosphere, conversations can be frustratingly one-sided, with the Saharawis chanting rehearsed, epigrammatic jingles, like mantras, in response to any question, as if to hasten the moment of their freedom from exile. And their speech is peppered with terms that are always pronounced totemistically.

Any talk of 'the Revolution' leads to announcements that 'the Saharawi People' are fighting 'the War for the Liberation and Independence of Our Homeland Against the Occupation Forces of Morocco.' In the same vein, 'the Front' is the preferred label for the never-mentioned wall; finally, death is never just that, but Martyrdom.

Abba is a child of this nation-in-waiting. He was barely ten years old when the hostilities began. His family were shopkeepers in the town of El Aaiún, the Spaniards' colonial capital located halfway between the coast and the phosphate mines of Bou Craa. Now El Aaiún flies the Moroccan flag and plays host to Moroccan soldiers.

And Abba's family are no longer shopkeepers, but refugees. When Abba was only thirteen, his father was killed fighting with the Polisario, becoming 'a martyr on the field of honor.' Abba was proud of the way his father died. As he grew up in the refugee camps, he wished for nothing more than to follow in his father's footsteps and become a Saharawi soldier himself. Like all Saharawi youths, he underwent military training after finishing high school, but then, instead of being dispatched to the Front, he was sent to university in Algiers. When he returned, the Polisario assigned him a job in its protocol wing.

Today, Abba is a trusted minder and guide for guests of the revolution. A slender man of twenty-three with hazel eyes and a serious demeanor, he shows visitors the Polisario's desert miracle, extolling its virtues in a hoarse, resonant voice. Still, he would prefer to be off with the fighters. 'Don't think I am complaining,' says Abba. 'No, no. I am happy to do whatever the revolution requires of me, as are the rest of the Saharawi people.'

There are, however, not a lot of other options. Raised in a community whose existence is based on the goal of national liberation, young Saharawis like Abba grow up with a unique sense of identity: They are Saharawis, but they are also Polisario – the two being virtually indistinguishable. Like youths who grow up in a company town, they have a destiny ready-made for them. The revolution is the only employer. And, like a religious cult that has reshaped its disciples' lives, the revolution not only possesses their past, it also holds the key to their future. People no longer speak willingly of the 'time before' their desert exile, when day one of the 'new life' began. In this life, the Polisario is their Creator.

'We don't want to remember the past,' Abba says during an audience with Wadha Ibrahim, a majestic Islamic judge living in Dakhla's *daira* of Argab. The most remote of the camps, Dakhla is also the biggest, housing sixty thousand Saharawis on a bleak desert plain surrounded by dunes that shine black and gold in the daylight.

The judge is giving a historical sketch of the Saharawi people, but falls silent on the question of which tribe he is from. He looks to Abba for help, but Abba only stares uncomfortably at the ceiling, then to the floor of the judge's tent. Nobody speaks. Finally, Abba says, 'We don't want to ask the people what tribes they were from. We want to forget the past.'

Visibly relieved, the old judge nods vigorously in agreement. 'Yes, the tribes were just dividing the people,' he says. 'Now; what we like to talk about is the Saharan Arab Democratic Republic.' Indeed, the Saharawis have little else. The Polisario has removed them from their homes, collectivized most private property, detribalized them by stripping the old sheikhs of their traditional authority, and educated the young to despise the old ways.

Reared on the Polisario's myths of their own creation, the new generation of Saharawis look to an idealized future as their means of escape from the desert that has been their entire life. A symbolic image of the hoped-for future dominates the interior of the Martyr Said Gaswani Baha Youth Club at Aoussert camp. A huge, black-fringed yellow banner covers an entire wall. Movie blockbuster-style lettering across the top spells out TODA LA PATRIA O EL MARTIRIO, and below, the map of Western Sahara looms above a huge setting sun, its beams arcing up toward the map and the slogan in the sky. In the foreground spreads a Saharan landscape of sand dunes. On the left, a line of camels, goats, and children advances toward the sun. On the right, a column of combat vehicles crammed with fighters is on the move, the spiky silhouettes of their weapons pointing upward, alert and ready for battle. Together, says the picture, the Saharawi people are advancing along paths that converge, in the dawn of a new day.

'Thank you for coming and welcome to the revolution!' shouts Muhammad Lamin Sidalli, a nomad living in the 'liberated' desert Belt with his family and his herds. 'Come in, come in, sit down, sit down!'

Gap-toothed, with a tangled gray beard and wearing a dirty black-and-white-striped shepherd's djellaba, the herdsman is obviously accustomed to visits from the guerrillas. As his wife rushes to prepare tea, Lamin continues to offer rhetorical pleasantries. When the tea is ready, his wife brings it on a tray, gives it to Moulay to pour – a gesture that honors him – and sits down among the men.

Lamin laughs when asked if he is a member of the Polisario Front. 'Of course! All Saharawis are – so how could I not be?' He laughs again at the strangeness of the query, and adds: 'The

Moroccans were wrong to invade; it was not the correct thing to do and it was against the Shari'a laws. It was not their land.'

Moulay is intrigued by Lamin's expressed commitment to the Revolution and asks him, 'If the Polisario Front needs anything, will you give it?'

Lamin bobs his head up and down emphatically: 'Yes, yes! Anything it wants is mine. And anything we need, we can ask from the Polisario. If it wants me to do any job, I will go!'

By continuing in the hard nomadic life, Lamin is unlike many Saharawis, who have opted for the easier life of the camps. 'I feel healthiest in the desert.' Lamin smiles. 'And I have the animals, so I have stayed. There are many families like ours along the Belt. We depend on rain, and so, since all the nomads depend on the rain, we are just like brothers. We travel alone with our own families, but, where it is green, we all meet and then we see each other again. And even with the wall, we still do the same things as before: We have camels and goats and go from place to place. There is still rain, and we still go freely in the liberated zone. There is still plenty of space to wander. In the spring, the time of green, we still find enough for our animals to eat.'

Nomads like Lamin are also valuable to the Polisario's roving units of fighters: Left to wander with their herds of camels and goats throughout the Belt, they are able to keep a permanent watch on Moroccan positions and troop movements along the wall, and can be relied upon to provide shelter, food, and water to the fighters. If they didn't serve this purpose for the Polisario, they wouldn't be there.

Another day, Moulay gives a lift to an ancient, buck-toothed crone in a black robe. She is out in the desert on her own gathering firewood; she has a small bundle under one arm. She seems little surprised to see Moulay's jeep, and once aboard, begins complaining loudly that her sons have gone off to the Polisario's camps and left her shorthanded to tend to the camels and goats.

'I have one son with me but he is almost useless because he is always ill,' she shrills. 'Now the land is green and the animals have multiplied. Some go in one direction and the rest in the other, and it is hard to keep track of all of them by myself. So tell one of them to come and help!'

Her nagging continues unabated until a nomad encampment looms out of the desert; it is the old woman's home, and Moulay leaves her there, amidst her gaggle of bleating goats and useless son, but not before she has extracted his promise to relay her complaints to her errant sons back in the camps.

Except for the nomads, the Belt has no human inhabitants; it has a luxuriant emptiness. Where the earth meets the sky there is a great clarity of color: The sky is very blue, the earth very yellow. The long and muscular land, with its mesas, wadis, and fleshy dunes of sand, also gives up strange mineral growths resembling people frozen into sleeping statues. Mostly, the desert is flat, and its surfaces of salt-crusted white or glistening black slate are puckered and strewn with fossils, rocks of salmon sandstone, pinkish quartzes, and stones whipped into rounded swirls of petrified sand like confectionery thunder eggs. Occasionally, there are gorse bushes with dry, gnarly boughs, and the larger, spiky thorn trees that camels like to eat. And everywhere, like raisins, goat droppings are sprinkled among the stones.

It is early spring, and in some places, nourished by a few rains and the wet Atlantic fogs of winter, small plants have sprouted. At a distance they appear as a uniform green tinge on the land, but this is an optical illusion. Close up, one can see that the plants are sparse, each one separated from the next by several feet of arid desert earth, while all around, armored black lizards with baleful orange eyes and great crenellated neck ruffs guard the entrances of their tunnels. Falcons wheel overhead in the wind currents, seeking prey.

Infrequently, military trucks appear out of the blowing sand to trundle past, jouncing steadily over the uneven ground. The men crammed in back wave as they pass: fighters headed to or from the Front. Only their eyes are visible through their wrap-around turbans. One afternoon, a truckload of them stops beside a rare stream. They are toughened and grimy from spending months in the desert. Now they are returning to the camps for a much-deserved rest with their families, and they want to look their best. Some squat at stream's edge to shave and wash their clothes; others polish boots and scrub dirty hair and feet.

One night, in a nomad family's tent not far from the wall, Moulay tells a story of going on a guerrilla raid deep inside Moroccan territory, and how he almost didn't return. As he speaks, he waves his big fists – one of them missing a thumb – in descriptive circles.

The nomad woman puts chunks of aromatic sap on a charcoal brazier, and, like an olfactory Turkish bath, the tent is clouded with perfumed smoke. Next, her plump daughter brings a battered pewter chalice and pours cologne into the men's cupped hands.

With Abba interpreting, Moulay speaks in Hassaniyah laced with a crude Spanish; he refers to himself and his comrades as *matadores*, killers, but what he really means to say is that they were warriors.

'It was in the month of April,' begins Moulay. 'We were two groups of *matadores* who entered Morocco. We continued on until we saw all kinds of Moroccans; they had horses, tanks, and helicopters, and then we started the war. It was at nine o'clock at night, in a place between two hills. But soon we were surrounded, and we said to ourselves, "We have to get out, dead or alive," so we made a run for it.

'We had four camels, and they were killed. They had carried our food and water. We continued on. Sometime later they caught us again; a guard called out "Halt!" We killed him and kept going. Again the Moroccans saw us as we drew water from a well and fired on us –'

Abba interrupts the story to laugh uproariously, rocking back and forth. Moulay grins with pleasure. Wiping the tears from his eyes, Abba explains what is so funny.

'When the shooting started Moulay jumped into the well to hide, but there were already some Moroccans there! They begged him not to kill them, and so he didn't, but he took their rifles. '

Moulay continues: 'We lost one man there, so at that point we decided to break up into twos and threes to improve our chances. We went on – no food, no drink. By this time we hadn't eaten for three days.' Moulay pauses to squirt fresh goat's milk into his mouth from a leather bladder, then passes it on. He pulls the collar of his gray wool greatcoat up over his ears – the night is cold – and resumes his story.

'We climbed the mountains. An old woman saw us and came to us on her knees lamenting: "First Moroccans from the south – now, ghosts from the north!" She thought we were ghosts!' Moulay cackles. 'After we had convinced her we weren't ghosts, she told us the Moroccan troops had killed her livestock, and she showed us how to cross their lines. But just as we were about to cross, on the top of a hill, we stumbled and fell all the way down the hill. The Moroccans heard us and attacked us with rifles, bombs – everything. We shouted to each other so we wouldn't lose one another in the darkness. Later we found each other and made a plan to ambush the Moroccans. My friend threw a grenade while I opened fire. We killed six and the others shouted for us to stop because they were wounded. We searched them and found some AK-47s and some canteens.

We took them and kept going. We continued until we heard a dog barking . . .'

On and on goes Moulay's story. Finally, he concludes, weak with hunger, the '*matadores*' arrived safely back in the camps. This adventure happened when Moulay was twenty. Thirteen years of war have gone by since then, and there are many more such stories in his repertoire. Retold in the time-honored oral tradition of desert folklore, Moulay's epic adventure is much more than a tall tale. As a warrior's story, it forms an integral part of the Polisario's creation myth.

In the end, like the desert's mirage lakes, the facts of the stories themselves aren't as important as the impression they create. Each story lends further weight and substance to the new history being woven and allows the insurgents to mark their own passage through time.

And the new history is that the Saharawi refugees have been reborn as the Polisario's people in their desert crucible. There, they have been endowed with new vision and have arisen from the ashes of the past, free, like so many desert phoenixes.

Because they are literally walled off from their birthplaces, the Saharawis actually have it easier than some other dispossessed peoples. This physical separation and their isolation from other communities allow them a greater fantasy life about their current predicament and what the future holds for them. The pain of their displacement, though very real, is somehow assuaged by the fact that they still feel themselves to be free: Their land may be occupied, but *they* are not an occupied people. The Saharawis look around at their desert; its horizons are endless. So too, it would seem, are their possibilities.

For the Palestinians living under Israeli occupation in the West Bank and Gaza Strip, there is no such imaginative freedom. The wounds caused by their displacement are not allowed to heal: Many Palestinians travel each day to and from menial jobs in Israel past the razed remains of their former villages and farms. For some of the young men, raised in the refugee camps and told stories of the former way of life, the idea of returning to these family lands has acquired an almost mystical imperative.

Unlike the Saharawis, who see the past as shameful, the Palestinians consciously revive it as proof, however sordid, of their suffering and as justification in their struggle for a homeland. And they also idealize the past. At least *then*, the young Palestinians say, their parents lived and roamed freely in a land called Palestine.

In the Gaza Strip, languid camels and little trotting donkeys pull wooden carts along streets almost overtaken by sand. Young children play in stagnant puddles at the roadside; a spider-webbing of electrical wires dangles from poles overhead. Here and there, minarets protrude above the maze of dirty cement houses, megaphones raucously blare out the muezzins' calls to prayer, and everywhere there are people and more people.

By Israeli highway only an hour south of the Western, Jewish city of Tel Aviv, the Gaza Strip is a sudden plunge from the world of modern Europe straight into the medieval Middle East. Past the heavily guarded Israeli military checkpoints at the border, the roads disintegrate and the people are no longer European, but Arab. The men wear robes and kaffiyehs, and the women are concealed behind veils and ankle-length robes. Everywhere are piles of uncollected refuse and the rusting hulks of wrecked vehicles.

Just twenty-six miles long and between four and five miles wide, Gaza is one of the most overpopulated places on earth. Over 750,000 Palestinians live here, many of them refugees from towns and villages that are now part of the state of Israel. With a touch of black humor, Gazans say that the Strip has become so crowded they no longer have anywhere to bury their dead.

Breij is one of seven refugee camps in the Gaza Strip. It is also one of the smallest, housing twenty thousand people. Almost everyone who lives here came in 1948, after losing their homes in the war that brought about the state of Israel.

After four and a half decades of existence, Breij has taken on the slummy permanence of a typical Gazan village. Originally a tented camp on the site of a former British military garrison, Breij today is a welter of mean, unfinished-looking cinder-block houses. It has a skyline of flat roofs littered with television aerials, water tanks, and jutting construction rods; someone is always building a second story to house a married son's new family. Between the houses spreads a labyrinth of narrow alleyways with open sewers running down them.

Breij has a couple of small makeshift mosques, a slaughterhouse, some crude automobile workshops, and a small market for meat and produce. Several shops sell cheap clothes and shoes made in Arab factories on the West Bank. There is a clinic run by the United Nations Relief and Works Agency, UNRWA, which administers all of Gaza's refugee camps; a Quaker-run kindergarten; a defunct tuberculosis hospital fringed by dusty eucalyptus trees; and a youth club, closed down by the authorities.

The camp's dirt roads are laid out in a rectangular grid that can be easily patrolled by the Israeli military; its houses are subdivided into several large blocks by these streets. Also for security reasons, only two of Breij's entrances remain open; the rest are blocked by bulldozed dikes of dirt. Outside the main entrance, an Israeli military camp has been built. Surrounded by earthworks topped by ugly looping razor wire, its squat prefab sentry towers overlook the edges of Breij.

The military camp sits between Breij and the main road running from Gaza city south to the Egyptian border at Rafah. Across the road are two large citrus-packing plants, closed, their yards filled with stacked crates and disused forklifts. Beyond, Nuseirat, another refugee camp, is built on the dunes right next to the azure Mediterranean Sea.

All around Breij grow rows of orange, olive, and almond trees. In the spring it is beautiful here. There is a sea breeze, the sun sparkles, and the scent of orange blossoms suffuses the air with heady perfume.

Sami is the eldest son of one of Breij's first refugee families. His family's home has a beautiful fig tree growing in the center of its courtyard. Around this open space are several small rooms where the family sleeps – girls in one, boys in another – and the kitchen. Straw covers the floor of another room full of large furry rabbits and warbling pigeons. In a tiny cubicle, Sami's father's cluttered sewing-machine repair shop is squeezed, with its secret spyhole that looks into the alleyway outside. Sami's father often comes here after curfew to peer out at the *shabbab*, the youths, writing their instructions for the next day's demonstrations on the walls.

In the family room, Sami's framed diploma from Yemen University hangs beside a gaudy orange and green prayer carpet depicting the Dome of the Rock and Al-Aqsa mosque in Jerusalem. Sami's father is proud of his son's examination papers and likes to show them off. The papers show that Sami was an average student: He got a 'satisfactory' in 'Fundamentals of Socialism' and 'History of the Yemen Revolution,' with a 'very good' in social psychology.

Sami is a tall young man of twenty-four with hunched shoulders and a scraggly beard. 'Don't get confused by the beard,' Sami says with a laugh. 'I'm no fundamentalist.' A member of the Democratic Front for the Liberation of Palestine, DFLP, a radical Marxist PLO group, Sami went through four years of university in the People's Democratic Republic of Yemen, where he earned a B.A. in English. Returning home, he had hoped to find work as a primary-school teacher, to 'sculpt the minds of children.'

But it was not a good time to be finding a job in Breij. All of Gaza was in turmoil as the intifada, the Palestinian uprising against Israeli rule that began in December 1987, came into full swing.

Instead of a teaching post, Sami quickly found a position in Gaza's underground movement. Together with other militants in their twenties and thirties, he helped organize the mostly teenage *shabbab* who led the daily round of rock-throwing and tire-burning confrontations with the Israeli military. He carries a clasp razor in his jeans pocket that he likes to show off, saying that if the Israelis try to catch *him*, he won't make it easy for them.

One night after curfew, the entire family gathers around while their handsome, crippled mother tells a story they have each heard many times. Dutifully rapt and full of restrained emotion, they listen to her in absolute stillness. Only Sami's adolescent sister, forbidden to be present in the company of strange men, is not in the room. But, brimming over with curiosity, she keeps peering out from behind the door of the women's room, flipping back her long dark hair to hide again each time she is spotted.

The town where Sami's mother was born is now part of Israel. During the war of 1948, she was just a little girl. One day a Jewish guerrilla appeared in the doorway of her family's home and tossed in a grenade. The explosion killed her mother and left her crippled. Somehow – she doesn't remember how it happened – she became separated from her father, who was away from home at the time. But after searching everywhere, he eventually found her in the Jerusalem hospital where she had been taken after the blast.

She and her father joined the exodus of Arab refugees fleeing Palestine, as her father looked for a place where he could find work and raise her decently. First he took her to Beirut, then back to Jerusalem, and finally to Hebron, which was occupied by Jordan at the time. With a smile of pride and in a hushed voice, she recalled how one night, in an act of real daring, her father took her on a donkey from the Hebron hills to Egyptian-occupied Gaza – all the way through Israeli territory.

She grew up in Gaza; there she met her husband and raised this family. For her sons, their mother's maimed body and dragging limp are physical proof of the nature of their enemy. Each time they hear her story their sense of duty to avenge her is dramatically revived. Such a family legacy makes it clear that Sami can never be just a schoolteacher.

Stories like the one told by Sami's mother have become cherished family heirlooms in the unfolding Palestinian oral history. In another family, the father has kept the keys to the home he fled in 1948. Today it is the comfortable residence of a Jewish family, but the keys still hang in a prominent place in the family's refugee home, lest any of the children forget the past.

Like history's handmaidens, these stories and artifacts ensure that Palestinian history is passed down from father and mother to son and daughter, and with it the inherited duty to avenge the past. Dispossessed of their land, the Palestinians have little else but their history with which to make an identity. As the conflict endures, they add to this history, seeking to give it more weight, as if by doing so they can somehow bring closer the day when they return to their land.

Without a physical environment of their own in which to chart their progress as a people, the Palestinian refugees instead take pride in their ability to suffer. Proud of their capacity to endure pain, they earn self-confidence in acts that arouse further retribution from their enemy. The adrenaline-filled battles of the intifada release the pent-up frustration, rage, and testosterone of the *shabbab* and fuel the paradoxical belief that, even if at the close of the day they are worse off than when it started, they are doing *something* to change the way things are. The Palestinians believe that in the end their suffering will be rewarded. Like hit-

and-run victims lying at the roadside, they hope that the humane instincts of a passerby will stop their hemorrhaging before it is too late. But in the meantime, they continue to dart in front of cars, competing with one another, daring the traffic to run them down.

In many homes portrait photographs of young men hang high on the walls, like icons. Usually, the photos are of a martyred or imprisoned son – something to be proud of because it proves that the family has done its bit for the Palestinian cause. They are also a reminder of the persistent nature of the struggle. Outside one home in Breij sits a derelict truck that belonged to a man killed years before by the Israelis. His parents refused to sell it or even move it; over the years, the truck has become a part of the street. Rusting and sprouting weeds, it is a Breij landmark, the monument to a community martyr. And inside the house, the dead man's aged parents have kept his room exactly as it was on the day he died.

Sami is full of the new folklore spawned by the intifada. He tells a story about Jabaliya, the largest of Gaza's camps, which, as the place where the uprising began, has acquired huge significance as a symbol of resistance. Although the story is probably apocryphal, it illustrates the Palestinians' need to elevate their struggle above the reality of tedium and misery in the camps.

'Some merchants from Gaza city sent a truck full of potatoes to hand out to the people of Jabaliya, and do you know what happened?' Sami asks rhetorically. 'So selfless were the people there that no one would accept the potatoes! At each house the lorry came to, the people said, "Give my share to my neighbor," and so on the lorry went, from house to house, unable to give its load of potatoes away. In the end, it left Jabaliya as full as it had come!' Sami's story glorifies the Palestinians' existence by highlighting their bravery, willingness to sacrifice, and sense of community: the idealized virtues aspired to by the youth of Gaza.

One of Sami's closest neighbors is Mahmoud, a member of Al-Fatah, the mainstream branch of the PLO that is headed by Yasir Arafat. Mahmoud is strong and fair-skinned with auburn hair and blue eyes. In Israel, he passes for a Jew. Ever since childhood, he and Sami have been rivals. When they were boys, each played on opposing soccer teams in the camp, and, according to Mahmoud, 'Sami's team always lost.' Now they belong to opposed factions of the PLO and are on speaking terms only because of the alliance forced on them by the intifada.

Despite their rivalry, the two have much in common. Like Sami, Mahmoud is also active in the uprising, but he participates as a member of Fatah's Al-Shabibeh youth organization. Wherever Fatah is strong, the Shabibeh is influential in planning and carrying out the dictates of the intifada's underground leadership.

Mahmoud has also learned some English, studying at Gaza's own Islamic University until the Israelis closed it down soon after the intifada began. He is jealous of Sami's years of study abroad, dismissing them with the claim that Sami's rival faction had offered such scholarships as a way of wooing youths away from Fatah. To Mahmoud, this proves that Sami's superior education – not to mention his political activism – owes more to opportunism than anything else. While Sami had a good time abroad, Mahmoud stayed behind and suffered with his people. Mahmoud measures his worth against Sami by determining who has suffered more, as if the winner will be shown to be the better Palestinian.

One day a tough-looking young man shows up at Mahmoud's house. Jaquer has just come from Jabaliya, where he lives, having skipped out while the camp is under curfew. Dirty and rank with sweat, he plunks himself down in Mahmoud's family room. Throughout the day, Mahmoud defers to Jaquer, allowing him to interrupt and make frequent loud and vehement comments. Soon enough, the reason for Mahmoud's unusual passivity, and for Jaquer's unruly behavior, becomes known.

'I am the father of three daughters,' he announces. 'And until the intifada, I would have had a fourth child, a son.'

According to Jaquer, his brother was the first martyr of the intifada, shot dead by the Israelis in the Jabaliya riots that sparked off the uprising. Jaquer's pregnant wife, who was present when it happened, ran forward to kiss her dead brother-in-law. From some distance away, helpless to do anything, Jaquer looked on in horror as an Israeli soldier hit his wife in the abdomen with his truncheon, causing her to miscarry.

Jaquer grabbed a knife and ran forward to kill the soldier, but the soldier escaped. 'If I ever see the soldier again I will kill him, wherever it is,' Jaquer says, his face twisting into a bitter smile. 'If I am driving a car and see him on the roadside, I will swerve the car to hit him; if I have a knife I will stab him . . . Now, the ninth of every month, which is the day it happened, is *my* day.'

Finished speaking, Jaquer folds both his hands on his chest and with an expression of deep feeling looks up at the ceiling. 'I can never forget.' Among sufferers, Jaquer is king.

The *shabbab* see themselves as the latest incarnation of the Palestinian fedayeen, the guerrilla fighters of their parents' generation. When Gaza was under Egyptian control, these fighters carried out numerous raids into Israel. But once Israel occupied the Strip, the fedayeen were hunted down and either killed or imprisoned; armed resistance from within Gaza was crushed.

The 1967 Six Day War added the West Bank, the whole of Jerusalem, and Gaza to the lands occupied by Israel. Under the aegis of the recently formed Palestine Liberation Organization and its leader, Yasir Arafat, the fedayeen now operated out of bases in Jordan – until that country's leader, King Hussein, fearing their growing strength, cracked down in 1970 and forced them to leave. Without ground to fight on, the focus of Palestinian resistance throughout the 1970s shifted to international terrorism, a bloody series of hijackings, murders, and bombings. Meanwhile, the guerrillas regrouped in Lebanon, and began launching rockets and raids into Israeli territory from bases there.

After Israel's 1982 invasion of Lebanon, the PLO was finally forced to withdraw from Beirut and relocate its headquarters fourteen hundred miles away in Tunis. The move made it clear that however well trained and armed they were, Palestinians operating *outside* the Occupied Territories could now do little to further the cause of an independent Palestine. For several years the situation festered, until the intifada began and abruptly shifted the battlefield yet again, this time to its inevitable, final arena within 'Palestine' itself.

The events that set off the uprising were themselves strangely mythical: First, like a Palestinian Icarus, a lone guerrilla flew on a hang glider into Israel from southern Lebanon. Upon landing, he took on an Israeli military camp, killing six soldiers before he was gunned down. The incident captured the imagination of Palestinians throughout the Occupied Territories; Israel's vaunted border security had been punctured, and the notion of Palestinian resistance was given new life by a singular act of heroism.

There were also confirmed reports that an Israeli sentry who could have stopped the attacker had instead run away in a cowardly panic. Along with the feeling of elation that the attack generated among Palestinians, this suggested that the Israelis' legendary bravery was only a myth, just as their supposedly impregnable defenses had been. Maybe they were really afraid of the Palestinians.

One event followed another. Next, in broad daylight, an Israeli Jew was stabbed to death by an Arab in the rabble of Palestine

Square, in downtown Gaza city. This sectarian murder was an act of deliberate provocation. Within days, retribution seemed to come, in the form of an accident: An Israeli military truck driving along Gaza's crowded roads careened out of control and killed four workers standing at the roadside. But, with Palestinians always ready to believe the worst, the rumor quickly spread that the crash was no accident but a premeditated Israeli reprisal for the stabbing. Rioting broke out in Jabaliya camp, where the four men had lived, and the intifada was born.

The unrest spread quickly. Within days, it established itself as ritual throughout the Occupied Territories and inside Israel itself. Each day, *shabbab*, wearing their checked kaffiyehs over their faces like masks, took to the streets to taunt the fully armed soldiers of the Israeli Defense Force. Invariably, someone was killed, as the soldiers fired on the youths with tear gas and live ammunition, or beat them senseless with wooden batons.

The Israelis tried to subdue the unrest by every possible means. Soldiers were ordered to break the bones of rioters they caught, and many did so. New prison camps were set up, where thousands of Palestinians were detained for months, without trial, in harsh conditions. Now it became a terrorist offense to throw a Molotov cocktail; offenders' homes were blown up by Israeli demolition experts.

Other collective-punishment tactics attempted to hurt the Palestinians economically, and included sealing off Gaza for days at a time. This prevented the tens of thousands of Gazans dependent upon menial jobs inside Israel from reaching their places of work. Another routine punishment was to impose domestic-confinement curfews on entire communities, forcing people to stay inside their cramped homes for prolonged periods, sometimes for days on end.

These Draconian measures did little to quell the disturbances, and seemed only to intensify the Palestinians' desire for confrontation.

With few exceptions, the *shabbab*'s weapons were not lethal; they soon saw that if they bore the brunt of the casualties, the ensuing publicity strengthened their cause. The list of 'martyrs' grew longer, and the Palestinians gained widespread public sympathy as the victims in an unequal David-and-Goliath struggle. For the first time in years, they shed the terrorist tag they had borne as a result of the PLO's armed activities.

While the *shabbab* exerted themselves on the front line of the intifada, the competing underground organizations to which many Palestinians give their loyalty tried to control and organize them. The main wing of the PLO, Al-Fatah, soon asserted its leadership over the uprising, but on the ground it was forced to cooperate with its traditional rivals. These ranged from PLO groups like the DFLP and the Popular Front for the Liberation of Palestine (PFLP) to the fundamentalist Muslim Brotherhood and its radical offshoot, Islamic Jihad, which are especially strong in Gaza. Also in Gaza, the new and violent Islamic Resistance Movement, Hamas, emerged to compete with Al-Fatah for the intifada leadership.

Cooperating with one another through a shadowy grouping of underground committees, these groups form a clandestine leadership, the Unified National Command of the Uprising, which sends out edicts to be implemented in the cities and camps of 'occupied Palestine.' At the grass-roots level, Sami, Mahmoud, and other politically organized men operate as underground cell leaders, transmitting the Unified Command's directives to the mostly teenage *shabbab*. To give a coherent focus to the violence, they also coordinate activities between camps, towns, and villages throughout the Occupied Territories and within Israel itself.

Ahmed is a Fatah leader in Breij. For terrorist offenses – 'Making explosions,' he says with a shy smile – he served five years of a life sentence in Israeli prisons; he was released in an exchange deal for Israeli hostages held in Lebanon.

Now, Ahmed is back in the camp, lying low. Through the Shabibeh organization, Ahmed used the Breij youth center as a place for recruiting, organizing, and indoctrinating *shabbab* for Al-Fatah. But ever since Gaza's schools and youth clubs were closed down, all this work has to be conducted clandestinely. Meetings are held in one another's homes or in unoccupied buildings around the camp, with lookouts posted to warn of approaching Israeli patrols.

Two of Ahmed's youngest acolytes are the sixteen-year-olds Yasir and Dasir. They are best friends. Yasir has a pleasant open face; he wears a gray scarf tied rakishly around his head like a turban. Dasir has curly brown hair, and an angelic child's face that contrasts with his mature eyes; he wears a black-and-white checked kaffiyeh to indicate his loyalty to Al-Fatah.

The two see their role as 'providing good examples to the younger boys, and lecturing them on the liberation struggle.' They have accepted the Unified Command's orders to limit their use of force to stone-throwing for now, but, with Ahmed's permission, they state their intention to escalate to knives and guns if stones aren't enough to win concessions from Israel. They hope the day will come soon.

'I want to be a commando, to fight for the return of the holy places, and die for my country,' says Yasir.

'If there is liberation, I'd like to be a doctor, and, if not, a commando,' says Dasir.

'These are our children,' interrupts a veteran Fatah man who, with Ahmed, supervises the *shabbab* at such meetings. He waves his hand to indicate Yasir and Dasir, who sit quietly listening as he speaks. 'They were born here, but they know where their fathers are from. They know where their real homes are. And they want to change their lives. But they finish high school and what can they do? Go out and work for the Israelis — hard work and low pay — that is all there is. Is this life?'

Dasir is one of seven children whose refugee father works in an Israeli factory. 'The uprising is a simple way for me to express my feelings,' says Dasir. 'I can't wait for others to solve my problems, so I must do it myself. And I'm not afraid of the soldiers, because, even if they kill me, it's for our land. I'll give whatever I have to get our land back.'

For the first ten years of Yasir's life, his father was in an Israeli prison – 'for Fatah,' Yasir says proudly. Since his release, he has been restricted to the Occupied Territories, where he is unable to find work to support his family; Yasir and his sister and brother are looked after by relatives instead.

'We are the soldiers of the PLO,' says the Fatah man. 'But we don't say so to the Israelis because they'll put us in prison. The difficulty is that they are right outside, and they have guns. We live under occupation and have only our stones. We know that the stone doesn't *do* anything. But we're looking beyond the stone to be able to say to the outside world what we want. For now, the stone speaks for us. When the Jews wrong us, such as the time I saw them poking an old man with sticks to make him sing, they give us the courage to do more back at them.

'What should I do? I have only stones. When I hear their politicians speak about us – about getting rid of the Arabs and so on – what should I do? Should I wait a hundred years for my rights? What would you do if *you* had lived under occupation for forty years?'

The intifada has never been a matter of stones, Molotov cocktails, and graffiti only. Early on, its leaders contemplated the incremental use of violence, but held it in abeyance. But boys like Dasir and Yasir passionately want to stab, shoot, and blow up Israel's soldiers, not merely throw rocks. 'We already know how to throw rocks and disappear,' says Yasir. 'So we can also shoot the soldiers and disappear.'

One compensation for the impatient youngsters is the authorization by the uprising's leaders to eliminate collaborators among their own people. Already, several have been secretly executed by the intifada's commandos in Breij. 'The commandos take suspected informers to an empty place and interrogate them,' explains Yasir. 'Then, when they confess, they are killed with knives.' With an imaginary knife Yasir grabs Dasir from behind, and holding his head in an armlock, demonstrates how the victims' throats are slit, the knives plunged repeatedly into their hearts and lungs.

One day, Dasir and Mahmoud show up without Yasir or Ahmed at a rendezvous on the outskirts of Breij. Ahmed is in hiding, because the Israeli authorities are hunting down former political prisoners like himself, correctly suspecting them of helping to organize the intifada. Yasir is under arrest. He was taken away by soldiers who came to his home last night. Collaborators in the camp have undoubtedly passed his name on to the Israelis as someone active in the rioting.

Mahmoud and Dasir don't seem worried about their friend. Unless the Israelis have something specific to pin on him, they say he will probably just be beaten and held for the usual eighteen-day detention period, then sent home. Mahmoud and Dasir are proud of Yasir, who will undoubtedly emerge from prison tougher and wiser; he will also be the envy of the younger boys because of his experience.

Meanwhile, the *shabbab* are preparing an important three-day general strike called by the intifada leadership. They are fasting to show their obedience. 'This is training for us to learn patience and how to go hungry like the Palestinian fighters have had to do in Lebanon,' says Dasir. Before fasting, they spent a day in the mosque, praying for help against their enemies and visiting the graves of martyrs.

Obviously, the intifada's leaders see the advantages of infusing the *shabbab* with a blend of Palestinian mythology and Islam to get results on the battlefield. In Breij, it is working well: Dasir's eyes are bright from hunger, sacrifice, and prayer, and he is looking forward to the coming battles.

On the first morning of the general strike, Dasir and Mahmoud are up and on the move early, organizing the *shabbab*. Already they are loitering in groups of two and three at street corners, and there is tension and anticipation in the air. Some boys have already hung the banned Palestinian flag in prominent places, and fresh graffiti is splashed on the walls. Black scudding smoke rises from hot orange flames where rubber tires are on fire. Mahmoud is taut and quiet with his sense of responsibility. He shoots meaningful glances to Dasir, who moves catlike among the waiting youths, murmuring instructions and tactical advice.

Small boys approach the high dirt barrier separating Breij from the Israeli military camp. They begin throwing stones. Older boys join them, hurling volleys of stones with their cloth slings, called *mugla*. Then some chant, 'P-L-O! Is-ra-el no!' Soon the soldiers appear, dressed in their riot gear. Some begin to take aim and fire tear gas, while the rest, only momentarily pausing on the dirt parapet, come running down. They charge, batons out and guns drawn. The *shabbab* shout 'Allahu akbar!' – 'God is great!' – in a single roar of defiance, and also fear, as they turn and run, vanishing down side alleys to their homes, rushing to grab onions, halved lemons, or cologne, all antidotes to the tear gas billowing everywhere. Afterward, as sections of the camp are cordoned off and searched, the hush is broken only by a few gunshots and the high whine of racing Israeli jeeps, their gears grinding, and distant shouts in Hebrew.

After an hour, the Israelis have mostly gone, and it is safe to dodge from house to house and inspect the damage done. The Israelis have vandalized the home of Nasser, a husky man in his early twenties. He holds up his baby nephew to show the bruises on his foot where a soldier has stepped on it. Nasser's fat mother leads the way into her small kitchen, where garbage has been emptied onto the floor. 'What have I done to deserve this?' she asks.

A neighbor, an old woman, comes in crying. 'We are weeping and laughing at the same time!' she says, and then begins to laugh hysterically. Nasser's brother, a bearded man the others jokingly call 'the Sheikh' because of his devout nature, stands in the middle of the room, waving a large butcher knife and yelling. 'I want all of my children to be commandos! I want to kill the Jews with this knife!'

'I don't think Hitler was as evil as these people are to us,' Nasser says. 'Believe me, I know.' He pulls up a trouser leg to show the spot where, on an earlier occasion, the soldiers shot him, and to a mark on his hairline where a second bullet grazed his brow. 'I have a B.A. in world history.'

At a friend's house, the damage is much worse. Usama is a dark, handsome young man in his twenties who chain-smokes cigarettes endlessly. He recently returned to Breij after two years studying engineering in Italy. Like Sami, he was swallowed up by the intifada as soon as he came back. Now, tragedy has struck his family, and soldiers are looking for him and his brothers. Usama doesn't say why, except that the information to arrest them must have come from 'collaborators.' On the Israelis' last raid a few days ago, he and his brothers were elsewhere, but his sixty-year-old mother was here.

'They came here looking for us, and told my family to come out of the house. A soldier hit my mother on the head and stomach. Blood came from her mouth, and she died within five minutes,' Usama says.

With a tone of wonderment, Usama describes how the soldiers returned later and broke the locks on all the doors and windows in his home; they even tore the arms off the chairs. He leads the way to a room where a large bird cage sits empty – breeding songbirds is a favorite hobby of Gazans – and points to the cage's open door. 'They came in here and let our canaries go. There were eighteen of them.'

Knowing that the soldiers are still looking for them, Usama and his brothers no longer sleep at home, but are hidden in the houses of friends. He has only come home today briefly, like a fugitive, to see if the rest of his family is all right. Another setback: Usama was to be married this week, but now the wedding has been indefinitely postponed.

Back outside, a burnt-rubber stench and the blackened cinders on the dirt alleys of Breij mark where the day's battle raged. Round black rubber tear-gas canisters litter the ground like overripe fruit, and brass shell casings lie scattered around like cigarette butts. From the electrical wires overhead, dozens of entangled flags hang like children's kites – the banned green, black, and red Palestinian flag, and Islamic Jihad's signature all-black banners – tied with string to stones and flung there by the *shabbab*. The beautiful calligraphy of Arabic graffiti is everywhere, on all the walls, mutely calling the people to action.

Dasir, who had vanished along with everyone else when the soldiers charged, now reemerges. Smiling broadly, he asks, 'Well, what did you think? It was a good demonstration, wasn't it?'

Just as they have mythologized their own lives, the Palestinians have also granted larger-than-life status to their enemies. One morning, as Sami is drinking tea at a house on the main road near Breij, a convoy of Israeli military jeeps escorting a yellow Land Rover races by. 'That was Rafi in the yellow jeep,' Sami says. Rafi is the hated commander of the Israeli forces in the area. All the *shabbab* refer to him by his first name, with the kind of familiarity reserved for true enemies. Some of them speculate that he isn't an Israeli at all, but a Druse, a member of the Arab tribal sect that has been largely coopted by Israel and whose men are renowned for their brutality. Sami calls Rafi a fascist, a sadist who likes to beat Palestinians 'with his own hands.'

Whatever the truth, Rafi is much on the minds of the *shabbab*, though he is only one of Breij's demons. Much more frightening are the Jewish settlers, the paramilitary civilians who have moved provocatively into large areas of Gaza and the West Bank under the protection of the Israeli military. The presence of the settlers in Gaza fuels Palestinian fears that Israel eventually plans to take all their land and kick them out of even the Occupied Territories. The settlers, meanwhile, make little effort to alter their terrifying image: When they drive through Gaza, they brandish automatic weapons, and their homes are in fortified reserves, surrounded by sentries and razor wire.

Understandably, the Palestinians believe the settlers to be little more than soldiers in civilian disguise, and as such, legitimate targets for their rocks and Molotov cocktails. Not surprisingly, there are hostile encounters between the two communities, each one adding volatile material to the demonology already rooted in the Palestinians' minds.

In Breij there is a little boy of nine, Riad, who was 'kidnapped' by the settlers and has survived to tell about it. As the son of a famous PLO commando doing seventeen years in an Israeli prison for terrorist offenses, Riad was already a camp celebrity, but now he is truly famous in his own right. He has even grown accustomed to being brought out by his family like a prize show dog to be viewed by curious visitors.

Like so many others, Riad's tale has become woven into the popular folklore of Breij, part of the unfolding creation myth of Palestine. As the boy stands expressionless and obediently still in the center of the circle of staring adults, his grandfather tells what happened on the fateful day.

'I was sitting and eating lunch outside, at the front of the house, and the child was playing nearby,' begins the man, who wears a hajji's white headdress to show he has made the pilgrimage to Mecca. 'I was looking after him, because his father was away at his work. Three settlers wearing civilian clothes came running up from the main road. They stood at the gate. I said to them "Welcome," thinking at first that they were another kind of people. But two had pistols and one had a rifle and they began pointing them around and yelling in Hebrew. They grabbed Riad and I asked, "What are you doing? If the child did anything wrong, I will punish him!" and I tried to take him back. They pointed their guns at me then and said, "Let go or we'll shoot you," and they went back to the road, carrying the child.'

At this point the grandfather stops, overcome by emotion, and says pleadingly, as if begging his listeners to believe him, 'I tried to get him back, but couldn't.'

He ran to telephone the police. Then, by chance, another of his sons, who was working near the main road, saw the settlers carrying the boy, and he and other people began yelling and running after them. But they weren't able to catch up. As the settlers drove away with Riad, this son memorized their car's license number. The authorities quickly arrived on the scene and they were told of the abduction and given the license number.

Soon, word came back from one of Gaza's border exits that soldiers had stopped the car, and that Riad was safe and sound. Within two hours, he was home. 'We never expected to see the child again,' says one of Riad's uncles. 'We thought they would kill him if they weren't caught.'

The family's belief that the boy would be killed for throwing stones at the Israelis' car – which is apparently what the settlers had accused him of – shows just how far the negative mythology has taken over rational perceptions in the Palestinians' minds. But the demonization of their enemies is also an important source of self-confidence for the boys fighting the Israelis. Believing the worst about the Israelis makes it easier to take drastic action against them; when the day comes that the *shabbab* are asked to kill instead of throwing stones, they will do so without any qualms.

In Breij, and in the Polisario's camps in Western Sahara, young warriors awaken each day with a growing sense of portent and the weight of their responsibilities, for they are the makers of history for people who seek a future as well as a past. They also live with the knowledge that with each new action taken, substance is added to their myths of creation – that of new states, struggling to be born.

This process of self-invention is vital, providing the guerrillas with a bonding ethos, a powerful impetus to persevere in their struggles. Without a past – or, like the displaced Palestinians and Saharawis, even a home – there is no future either, and so the guerrillas must at least possess their own histories. Accurate or mythified, these histories are the repositories of their cultural identities, as essential to their struggles as the weapons with which they fight.

TWO

A Parallel Reality

At first Las Flores seems like any other village in El Salvador. Old men wearing straw hats play cards on the stoop of a rambling house at a corner of the plaza. In the parching sunlight outside, families of chickens, ducks, and pigs trundle across the rough cobblestones, rooting for food.

Several boys peer into the open shutters of the rudimentary dental clinic where a young woman lies on a cot, her mouth yawning open for the dentist. A courting couple strolls hand-in-hand toward a bench in the center of the plaza, to sit in an illusion of privacy, out of earshot, yet in full view of the village at the same time.

San José de las Flores is wedged against a couple of green hills planted with corn; about fifty houses surround a large cobbled plaza. At one end there is a wedding-cake church, white, with old arched wooden doors and a bell tower. A royal palm rises from the cobblestones by the church steps. Nearby, standing at about the height of a man, is a cement pyramid erected by the Rotary Club, its base buttressed by an encircling bench.

At the heart of the plaza is a concrete basketball court. A single shade tree overhangs one end; the rest of the court is crowded with uprooted bean bushes laid out to dry in the sun. Opposite, a rough, red-tiled gazebo on wooden pillars shelters a hand-cranked corn mill and domed clay oven. Here, every morning, the wives and mothers of Las Flores line up. Each has her blue or red plastic bowl filled with kernels of bright yellow maize, to be ground into *masa* for tortillas.

The adobe houses around the plaza have deep front porches with wooden pillars supporting red-tiled roofs. If painted at all, the houses are white and streaked with brown dust or clad in the hideous institutional-green paint that seems to have found a final resting place in Latin America. Lanes lead off from the plaza's four corners, weeds sprouting between their stones, and soon give way to dirt footpaths that vanish into the forest and fields beyond.

A winding jeep track of purple volcanic dust leads from the provincial capital, Chalatenango, and ends here. Behind Las Flores, the land climbs up into broken hills and then drops down to the Sumpul River. On the other side is Honduras. Las Flores is the end of the line.

Despite appearances, something is different about Las Flores. When an outsider arrives, the little children *don't* immediately run up asking questions or begging for sweets. No one approaches. People raise their heads briefly and then turn away, as if uninterested. And they don't look again.

Strangers aren't immediately welcomed in Las Flores. The villagers don't introduce themselves, nor do they ask outsiders who they are, where they come from, or where they are going. The atmosphere is not unfriendly, exactly. There is a cautiousness; voices are hushed, and even when the plaza hums with conversation, an outsider cannot hear what is being said.

Even when carrying out the most innocuous of everyday tasks — fetching firewood, drawing water, grinding corn — the people in

Las Flores seem to exude a special sense of purpose. The way they carry themselves says that everything they are doing is vitally important. It is as if somewhere along the empty dirt road leading here an invisible frontier has been crossed.

And it has. The journey to Las Flores has led into another, parallel reality, a place altogether different from the world just left behind, yet existing alongside it. The inhabitants here live according to their own laws and ideology, in a state of rebellion against the world beyond.

Whenever Giovanni visits Las Flores, he comes on foot, emerging silently onto the plaza from the lane that runs next to the Comedor Popular. His carefully groomed mustache and tinted spectacles give him an air of intellectual sophistication. He is a mestizo, but his thick black hair and dark skin show his predominantly Indian blood.

Melida, a shy teenage girl, is at Giovanni's side wherever he goes, keeping a few feet away, like his shadow. She is short and pudgy with long, wavy auburn hair; she carries a walkie-talkie. Occasionally she listens to it or talks into it and adjusts its long antenna.

Giovanni always has something to do. He strides busily back and forth across the plaza to speak with someone here or confer with someone else there. People often approach Giovanni, and some discreetly hand him small pieces of paper, neatly folded into little squares. He always stops, carefully unfolds the paper, and reads the message inside. The messengers wait patiently, silently watching his face, which is always deadpan. When he finishes reading, he folds the papers into squares again and places them in a clear plastic bag he keeps in his top shirt pocket. Then, after brief words to the messengers, off he goes again.

It is hard to tell exactly what Giovanni is doing or who he is. No one in Las Flores seems to know his full name; only 'Giovanni,' no surname. They can't tell you about his family or his background, either, because Giovanni isn't from Las Flores. He doesn't even live here, but comes when he wants to – quick, unannounced visits with Melida trotting by his side.

There is a good reason for all the mystery: Las Flores is a nerve center of one of the oldest revolutionary fronts in El Salvador's civil war. Here in Chalatenango province, two hours by car from the capital of San Salvador, the guerrillas of the Frente Farabundo Martí para la Liberación Nacional (FMLN) have found sanctuary and endured for more than a decade of warfare against the country's U.S.-backed armed forces. Government writ ends about eight miles away, at the military roadblock on the edge of the town of Chalatenango.

The hills around Las Flores belong to the Fuerzas Populares de Liberación (FPL), the most hard-line of the five Marxist guerrilla factions that make up the FMLN coalition. Although the guerrillas are active throughout the country, the 'Chalate' backwoods, with its smattering of peasant communities and their hardscrabble corn patches and pig farms, is the group's real home ground, and Las Flores has always been its *'capital.'* In one heady period, the guerrillas proclaimed Chalate 'liberated territory' and half-jokingly dubbed it the People's Republic of Chalatenango.

More mature now, tempered by years spent in the bush, the guerrillas have graduated beyond such triumphalist rhetoric, but they still consider the area one of their 'zones under control.' This is a fair claim. Except for the army's periodic sweeps, when the guerrillas melt into the underbrush, the FPL is the de facto authority in the region.

The guerrillas' authority is wielded by people like Giovanni; Giovanni is a senior officer whose duties include the supervision of workshops producing the FPL's own 'popular armaments.' Melida is his *radista*, communications aide. Their faces may be familiar to the people of Las Flores, but their true identities remain a secret. 'Giovanni' is a nom de guerre, as is 'Melida.' False identities abound in Las Flores, because this is a community whose survival demands the concealment of real names and past lives. Like San José de las Flores and its façade of 'civilian village,' the people who come here also maintain a diplomatic fiction concerning what they are really all about. And the note-passing is the guerrillas' own secret *correo*, an underground mail system used by field commanders to relay news to one another.

The guerrillas have scattered their camps throughout the woods behind Las Flores. Within minutes they can be packed up and gone, hiding or taking with them the accoutrements of an entirely clandestine society: field clinics, radio transmitters, an underground press, munitions and explosives workshops, arms caches.

Over the years, the guerrillas have gone forth from their hiding places and dealt devastating blows to the army. In turn, the Salvadoran army has responded with massive brutality, trying to neutralize the FMLN's pool of civilian support by 'draining the sea of fish.' With places like Las Flores serving as windows through which the guerrillas view the civilian world, the partisan villagers have been prime targets of the government forces. After all, El Salvador's war is not really about winning territory, but the hearts and minds of ordinary citizens – and ordinary citizens make up the majority of its casualties.

The government's counterinsurgency tactics have ranged from wholesale massacres, beginning at the start of the conflict in 1980, to a routine of indiscriminate aerial bombardment and army sweeps toward the end of the decade. More than eighty thousand people have died in the war, many of them unarmed civilians. Guerrilla sympathizers – politicians, peasants, priests, trade unionists, students, and teachers – have typically been picked up, tortured and then killed by the government 'death squads,' their bodies either left in public view or 'disappeared' altogether. Of El Salvador's 5 million people, at least 500,000 have fled the country, while a million more are internal refugees, displaced from their homes by the fighting.

About two miles outside Las Flores is the spot beside the Sumpul River where, on a single day in 1981, the army massacred about six hundred local civilians. After El Sumpul, as the locals now refer to the atrocity, the people living around Las Flores fled into Honduras, abandoning their villages to the crickets, the snakes, and the skirmishes between the army and the guerrillas. For most of the 1980s, Las Flores was a ghost town.

In the eyes of the government forces, a civilian living in a guerrilla zone is expressing solidarity with the enemy, a 'crime' punishable by death. At least that was once the case. More recently, as a result of the cold scrutiny of human-rights investigators, church officials, and journalists – and U.S. congressional legislation requiring evidence of its good conduct in exchange for the continued flow of vital military aid – the army has eased up. Murders and even mass killings of civilians still occur, but not as often or as gratuitously as before.

This more flexible atmosphere allowed just enough of a safety margin for the refugees to begin trickling back. In 1987 the government reluctantly permitted larger numbers to return, one way of improving its abysmal human-rights image. Now several hundred people live openly in Las Flores and a few nearby hamlets, having obtained an extremely tenuous legitimacy for their presence with the support of the Catholic church, international charities, and, of course, the FMLN.

These are no ordinary people, but peasants whose lives were drastically transformed in the first decade of the war. Most have endured personal tragedies of the most horrific kind. Some are survivors of massacres like El Sumpul, who found safety in squalid

Honduran refugee camps. Others spent years on the run inside El Salvador, hiding from the army while trying to survive, foraging in the bush for food and living in caves. Most are ardent supporters of the FMLN, the people known as *las masas*, 'the masses.'

If the army could, it would extinguish these 'popular communities,' as it did before the FMLN was strong and could defend its civilian followers. But, while Las Flores's people are marginalized and often harassed, they are no longer hunted down like dogs. In El Salvador, this is a significant change for the better; it is why the people in Las Flores carry themselves so proudly and speak triumphantly of having 'reconquered their homes.'

The ties binding the inhabitants of Las Flores to the FMLN are deep, and if at first glance the village seems normal enough, a closer look around the plaza proves otherwise. Revolutionary graffiti is splashed everywhere in black and red paint: ORGANIZATION FOR THE STRUGGLE; STRUGGLE FOR THE VICTORY-FMLN. Many of the walls are bullet-pocked from machine-gun fire, or cratered and shot through where a rocket or mortar struck. On one corner house, an exploding shell has left a sunburst design, shrapnel marks shooting away from its center like dancing flames.

On either side of the church's arched door looms the stenciled black-and-white face of the martyred archbishop Oscar Arnulfo Romero, an icon of the Salvadoran left. This prominent display of his image places the church squarely on the side of 'the people': In life, Romero was a proponent of the Catholic doctrine of liberation theology, which advocates revolutionary social change on behalf of the poor.

Another sign of the *compas*, as everyone calls the guerrillas – slang for *compañeros* – is their imposition of a dry law. This is a measure aimed at underscoring their authority while keeping people's minds clear to concentrate on the revolution. The only liquor store is boarded shut, its façade still colorful with a wildeyed painted rooster, symbol of the national *aguardiente* (cane liquor), Tic Táck. This explains the absence of drunks in Las Flores's plaza. In any other village, at least several of the stinking and swollen, purple-faced *bolos*, *aguardiente* drinkers, would be curled in their stupors on the church steps day and night. In Las Flores, several young men barely in their twenties, each missing an arm or leg, have taken over the church steps. Most mornings they can be found there, leaning their backs against its great studded door. As the dawn freshness burns off in the morning sun, they survey the plaza.

Even the name of the Comedor Popular Nuevo Amanecer ('New Dawn Popular Eatery') lacks innocence. The rustic diner is a guerrilla-sponsored soup kitchen for the *compas*. They get their meals here when they are in town, and can run a tab if they want. The revolution is a good customer and always pays its bills. Two doors down, the community day-care center looks after the guerrillas' infants. Several teenage girls care for two dozen children during the daylight hours – rocking the littlest ones to sleep in rainbow-striped hammocks – and in the evenings they hand them back, not to their mothers, but to their grandmothers.

These old women really run Las Flores, holding down the home fort for their daughters and sons who are off at 'the front,' an ill-defined label for the shifting theater of war, which can be halfway across the country or somewhere in the trees right outside of town. Only occasionally, when things are quiet and the army isn't around, can their grown offspring come here themselves, to meet one another, make love, and bounce their babies.

Just as the 'mothers' of Las Flores are mostly old women, the only males are either very young boys – ten and under – or men over fifty. The young men, when you see them, are all wearing the uniform of the FMLN. Las Flores can be empty one moment and then, a sweat-soaked column of *los muchachos*, the boys, trudges silently through before vanishing again.

While the youths fight, the old men farm, spending most of their days tending to the corn patches and bean fields that blanket the knolls around the village. Here the FMLN's social revolution is already under way. When the collective work is done the old men work on their own plots for an hour or two, then trudge back to the plaza. Tired and dirty, most of them go immediately home to wash and eat and fall asleep in their hammocks. Those with enough energy left play cards with their friends at dusk on the front porch of the Comedor Popular.

The life is communal, socialist. This is what makes the atmosphere in and around Las Flores unique. The people here are living out an ideal sustained only by the protective guns of the FMLN. Through war, the *compas* and their people have wrested a place for themselves to live as they see fit, even if this was not all that they had dreamed of when they set about making revolution – when they believed that the whole country would soon be theirs. Even so, it is what they have ended up with.

'Haroldo' has overseen the guerrillas' clandestine Radio Farabundo Martí broadcasts for the past ten years. A balding and bespectacled intellectual in his mid-thirties, Haroldo was a young poet of considerable repute before the war; during his years in the hills, he has continued to write and to publish as well – but under his real identity, not his nom de guerre.

Despite his deep commitment to the revolution, Haroldo is openly wistful about the world beyond '*la montaña*.' In El Salvador, *la montaña* is much more than just 'the mountain' – it is where the guerrillas are, where the revolution harbors its strength; it is the country's 'other reality.' But Haroldo laments the divide between his clandestine rural home and the government-held city where he grew up, two worlds that are, in his words, 'as different as water and air.'

'They have different viscosities. The communal life we lead here is more in keeping with the way we'd like to see the world, but it's not better in every way. We need one another, because we want to build a new society, and it's going to take a lot of *this* life, and also a lot of *that* one. We're trying to open roads between both worlds, not to make a separate bucolic kingdom. We want to get the whole country out of its misery, for there to be no frontiers within the country.'

While the war lasts, though, Haroldo's 'new society' is only possible in places where the *compas* can operate openly, like Las Flores. For all his wishful thinking about an undivided future for his country, many things will have to happen before that fusion can take place. The people who have spent the war living with the *compas* or as refugees are very different from those who have remained in the cities. Whether Haroldo likes it or not, internal frontiers do exist within the country, and they are psychological as well as physical.

In Chalatenango, the physical boundary between the worlds lies at the army roadblock down the dirt road from Las Flores. When the war is over, this obstacle will be removed, but the distance between the people living on either side will still be there. What concerns Haroldo is how to extend the *compas'* way of life beyond the confines of Chalate and make it a part of everyone's reality in a reunified, postwar El Salvador. Meanwhile, the war continues, and for the *compas*, having a place apart is the only way to survive.

All day long, the sun beats down on the plaza. In the heat, the village appears deserted, but life goes on in the cool interiors of Las Flores's homes. By mid-afternoon, the air is hot and thick, and the plaza is dead quiet as the village slumbers.

But it is late July, the onset of the rainy season, and thunder-clouds soon appear overhead. Each day they grow larger, until the sky becomes the color of gunmetal and then, amid explosive thunderclaps, comes the rain to wash down the plaza. The ducks and hens emerge to splash and peck in the puddles, and the village is quiet except for the trickle of water, the fading claps of thunder, and the breeze. Then the fresh, cool air is suffused again with the mingled aromas of wood smoke, sweet corn, and strong coffee beans roasting on open fires.

In the coolness of dusk, the village returns to life. People appear in their doorways, squatting on the stoops to exchange gossip. Soon the plaza is thronged with people talking loudly together, like a theater audience buzzing with excitement before the show begins. But on center stage here, the only actors are an unkempt, delightedly screaming gaggle of kids playing on a sand pile at a corner of the basketball court. One boy, repeatedly leaping into the air, shows the others his kung fu kicks, complemented by high-pitched martial roars.

One evening, as a long sunset fills the plaza with pink light, everyone plays a crazy kind of basketball – the kids against the grown-ups – and the whole place is filled with the frantic delighted pants and shouts and stampeding feet of people at play. On other nights someone starts the town's single generator, and the few naked light bulbs dangling from wires around the plaza begin to glow. A large television set is placed on a table of the verandah of the Comedor Popular, and then, like moths drawn to a lantern, everyone gathers to watch its static-filled images. First is always the evening news from the capital, followed by a soap opera, one of the flamboyant Mexican or Brazilian *telenovelas*, melodramatic family sagas featuring the extremes of good and evil, the characters either fantastically rich or desperately poor. The villagers watch uncritically, completely entranced, their faces unconsciously aping the actors' exaggerated sobs, jeers, and scowls.

And one night there is a dance. The music booms out from a portable boom box, everyone rocking and shuffling to Creedence Clearwater Revival, the current favorite. Teenage lovers stumble and grope on the basketball court, and their younger siblings, dancing at the edges, mimic their movements. Guerrilla boys and girls in ill-fitting uniforms dance awkwardly in their boots, weapons slung over one shoulder. Groups of shy adolescent girls watch from doorways around the plaza, hugging themselves and whispering to each other, giggling hysterically whenever a boy dares one of them out onto the court.

One afternoon, a new sound can be heard over the murmur of the plaza: a distant mechanical growl like a jackhammer that starts and sputters for long intervals. At first, people just go about their business as the sound continues. It is merely a backdrop to the other noises in the plaza, unremarkable.

Then someone notices a plume of smoke in the distance. People begin to gather and stare. The cardplayers leave their game, still clutching the cards in their gnarled hands. The children become quiet and get up from the sand pile. The women from the Comedor Popular stop patting their tortillas and come outside, wet flour stuck to their hands like paste. Together they gather in a silent knot at the edge of the porch. They stare beyond the red-tiled roofs of the plaza, toward the hills ringing the next valley about two miles away.

There in the green bowl of land below the flanks of the shorn hills, a helicopter gunship is flying around and around in a circle, like a dragonfly. It is shooting long and continuous bursts with heavy-caliber machine guns.

The smoke billows and the dark gray cloud grows. One of the old cardplayers stirs and says it is only a smoke bomb. He can tell because of the type of smoke. The army is trying to use the helicopter to evacuate its soldiers from the spot where the *muchachos* have ambushed them and pinned them down.

Meanwhile, the gunship hovers in its dark circle ever closer to earth, shooting and shooting. And the smoke is rising implacably up and over the silhouette of the ridges. Then, abruptly, the growling noise stops and the mechanical dragonfly is gone. The smoke lingers momentarily and then begins to drift and thin, vanishing against the last blue of the day.

The cardplayers sit back down, the boys return to their sand pile, and the women disappear into the house to pat out more tortillas for the evening meal. The incident has only barely chilled the plaza; moments later, it is warm again; the kids are yelling, the men chuckling and cursing one another fondly, and from inside the Comedor Popular comes the pat-pat-pat of the women making tortillas.

The people of Las Flores take the war in stride, but they are quite conscious of the peculiarities of their way of life. One morning, several young guerrillas show up carrying shovels and, with a wheelbarrow, begin carting off sand from the pile on the basketball court. An old woman watches this flurry of activity impassively. She doesn't know what they are doing and because they haven't announced their intentions, she isn't about to ask them. For a long time she remains staring blankly at the working *compas*. Finally, with a mischievous look and cupping a hand over her mouth to hide her missing teeth, she whispers in a low, conspiratorial voice, 'Maybe it's something *clandestine*!' Then she doubles up with laughter at her own joke.

The revolutionaries have their own brand of humor, often black and full of innuendo. It seems to be part of the ethos they share, a way of coping with lives that are filled with loss and tragedy. One of the funniest *compas* is Jacínto, a lanky character in his thirties with a ragged beard. He doesn't make it into town very often. When he does come, he circles the plaza like a whirling dervish of good humor, cracking jokes, bear-hugging people, and asking how they and their families are.

'*Vergón, vergón!*' Jacínto cries happily whenever he hears some good news. '*Vergón*' comes from '*verga*,' meaning 'prick' or 'cock,' but in Salvadoran slang it is an exclamation of delight, akin to the Americanisms 'all right' and 'cool.'

'Hey, *compa*! Tell your wife I send her a big hug from me,' he calls out one evening with a friendly leer to a stolid-looking peasant farmer who is walking by. 'But don't you go getting jealous, now.'

The peasant grins good-naturedly and responds in kind: 'Don't worry, I won't, *compa*. I'll give her the hug.'

Back in the late 1970s Jacínto was a protest singer; he played his guitar and sang at many of the antigovernment demonstrations that led up to the civil war. Then, when the military repression became too great, he made his way into the mountains. That was nine years ago. Now he works with Haroldo and the rest of the Radio Farabundo Martí team as a technician.

'I'd like to sing and play the guitar again,' says Jacínto soulfully. 'But with my other duties there's little opportunity to practice, and my fingers are already forgetting the chords.'

Jacínto has come to Las Flores for a three-day rest break that his comrades have urged on him; he's been in the bush without letup for three months and is a little run-down. He laughs at the irony of his coming to Las Flores 'for a vacation.' As he laughs, the nostalgia that has overtaken him is forgotten.

At night Jacínto slings his hammock in the day-care center. Rats scurry back and forth on the roof tiles, and rain pours through the gaping holes where mortars have struck. He repeats aloud a bittersweet, consoling proverb the Salvadoran guerrillas use to remind themselves of *why* they are *where* they are. "'We're like priests: celibate, if not because we want to be; poor, if not because of vows; and we've taken orders of obedience . . . because of the war, we have to.'"

The next morning at breakfast in the Comedor Popular, a grizzled fighter sits down to share the single table and bench, and announces, as if offering a sacrament: 'The best food is hunger.' Jacínto grunts his acknowledgment like a gruff amen, and both of them dig into their meals.

This is another thing that makes Las Flores different, what sets its inhabitants apart from those in other communities: They are there to make a political statement. Everything they do has a purpose, for they are a people at war. And the *compas* may joke and become momentarily lighthearted, but then they bring themselves abruptly back to earth with a sobering reminder of their reason for being: to make revolution.

The most senior guerrilla around Las Flores, the *jefe político-militar*, is Sebastián, or Sébas. Like Giovanni, with whom he coordinates guerrilla operations in the area, Sébas makes frequent lightning appearances in the plaza before vanishing again. Usually he comes through, walking at a half-trot, sweating heavily and carrying an AK-47 slung on his shoulder. He never smiles and always looks worried. He wears a little green Mao cap, a black T-shirt and matching fatigues with big side-pockets on them, and boots. Sébas has the white skin of a *chele*, the Salvadoran slang term for a fair-skinned person. Fair skin is synonymous with the upper classes, most of whom are of European descent.

Sandra and Sabina, Sébas's plump, walkie-talkie-carrying *radistas*, both in their early twenties, always precede him into the village. Moments later, Sébas comes through the plaza, sweating. He waves and calls out to onlookers, and he is gone again. He invariably leaves behind him a certain alertness that wasn't there before. It is as if the people are able to read on his preoccupied face a battlefield status report.

But no one can ever really relax, not completely, because the enemy can attack at any moment, and it is always possible that someone from the community will die. So Las Flores's people live in anticipation of violence, creating a quiet tension that is an integral part of the village's atmosphere. Everyone has a stake in whatever happens here: Every family has a son or daughter in the revolution; it is only because of them that Las Flores can live in relative peace and go through the motions of being a normal village.

The fighters are mostly teenagers, some as young as thirteen. Clearly proud of their roles in the revolution, they wear VIVA FMLN kerchiefs around their necks and begin to puff and swagger when they know they are being observed.

'You know,' Jacínto remarks as a group of adolescent guerrillas saunters by one day, 'sometimes I think to myself that on the one hand it is a special feeling to see one of these *cipotes*, these youngsters, grow up into a good man, a guerrilla. You know? But it's also sad that it has to be this way . . .'

One morning at the Comedor, Sandra and Sabina have a recent issue of *Time* magazine, which has a cover story about the international phenomenon of 'child warriors.' They leaf through the magazine eagerly, but when they cannot find any pictures of El Salvador, they express genuine disappointment that the FMLN's youngsters have not been included.

'They went all over the world, didn't they?' Sandra says disgustedly. 'So why didn't they come to El Salvador?'

Sandra isn't from Chalatenango, but from a province bordering the Pacific Ocean. She joined up three years ago, when she was eighteen, but has been 'involved' since she was thirteen. 'My parents were always with the *compas*,' she explains without further detail. 'So it was natural for me.'

When she came of age, her parents supported her in her decision to become a *compa* herself. Now she maintains contact with them via hand-carried letters. Her father's letters reach her in the mountains through the guerrillas' underground communications network. In them, he often urges her to try and be faithful to the 'moral values' set by Ernesto Che Guevara, whose self-sacrifice for his ideals is a model for all revolutionaries to follow.

'I haven't been able to read as much about Che as I'd like,' says Sandra. 'The government system here in El Salvador makes it difficult.' Then, with a laugh: 'After the revolution, that'll change.'

'After the revolution.' The young *compas* of Chalate utter such phrases often, usually in the context of a humorous boast like Sandra's. But these are more than mere slogans; they imply a kind of epigrammatic resolution about the future their efforts will bring. Sandra says 'After the revolution' with the casual determination of a girl living in a nation at peace, a nation with regular, fair elections and a stable political system. It is as if she has said 'After the next elections.' For Sandra, the phrase captures the meaning of her entire existence.

As much as any shared political philosophy, however, it is the war's collective tragedy that gives these guerrilla survivors a sense of common destiny, and helps them adhere to their revolutionary course. Prevented from participating in mainstream society because of their political beliefs, the *compas* and their followers have forged a parallel reality through their own sacrifice and the blood of their loved ones. After all their years in the hills, the revolution is the only life known to most of the *compas*, and their commitment to it transcends ideology.

Sébas is from the capital. He studied sociology at the National University of El Salvador there but left his education unfinished when he went underground. Except for two years as a political prisoner, he has been 'in the mountains' ever since. Now, his student days seem as if they were part of another lifetime. He has been in the revolution for so long, he says, that he no longer has any personal goals.

When the war is over, Sébas wants to return to these Chalatenango hills to do practical development work – 'things like roads, running water, and electricity' – on behalf of communities like Las Flores. 'It would be a way to repay them for their support for the FMLN, and for having suffered so many of the consequences of the war,' Sébas says. But of course, whatever he does depends upon 'the will of the revolution.'

Aside from his undiminished sense of revolutionary obligation, Sébas admits to another, more personal reason for his remaining in the hills after all these years: The government forces 'disappeared' one of his sisters, the youngest child in his family.

Sébas isn't alone in his grief. Many of the other *compas* have also suffered great personal tragedies. Giovanni's family has been decimated by the war, nine of its twelve members killed. 'Mother. Father. Brothers . . . sisters. There are just three of us left,' Giovanni says one afternoon in a flat voice, and then laughs gently. 'It's a whole story, about the dead ones.'

Haroldo has lost family, too. The woman he loved, the mother of his son, was 'disappeared'; the euphemistic epitaph means she was almost certainly raped and tortured before being murdered. A similar horrible fate befell his next *compañera*. Haroldo's son, now seven years old, is living with relatives in the capital. For his own safety, the fate of his mother and the true identity of his father are well-kept family secrets.

A couple of years ago, Haroldo wrote a poem entitled 'All Kinds of Reasons,' which seemed to say it all:

Here you find me:
Just completed my thirty-second year
a widower twice over.

I have fungus
and dandruff
and a rotting molar;
in my left ear
I am deaf,
but no bullet has touched me yet.

I've swallowed dust,
mud, fog,
I've chewed stone
with my teeth,
but I've fought at the side
of the struggling multitudes
at their barricades.

Embraced by the fire of the revolution
in this canyon,
uphill,
downhill;
loving as I love this life, poetry,
and the people,
how can I not offer up my bones?

Giovanni's camp basks in the shadows of its own pantheon of revolutionary martyrs. It sprawls along a hilltop in the tangled
overgrowth of an abandoned coffee *finca*, about two hours from Las
Flores. The valley below is dotted with similarly deserted farms.

To prevent detection from the air, the camp is scattered under
the trees around a peasant's adobe house. Hammocks are strung
under the eaves in front, and the *compas'* canteens, web belts, and
rifles hang from the rafters. Surrounding the house, a half-dozen
one-person *champas*, makeshift tents of plastic spread over crude

wooden frames, have been set up by most of the *compas* to sleep in
at night. Melons grow wild on a yellow-leafed vine in the rubble of
a collapsed side wall.

A bulletin board has been tacked up on a large tree that rises up
in the center of the camp. Attached to it is a hand-lettered 'Poem
to Oscar,' penned by the camp poet, Jaime.

> Oscar, protagonist of history,
> brave man of tenderness and love –
> of smiles and caresses for youngsters,
> of humility and sincerity;
> man loyal to the party,
> who loved his people and dear ones,
> now your flesh and bones have disappeared –
> but your smile, your jokes, and your stories
> live on in each of us who knew you.
>
> Brother Oscar, I remember, brother
> when we went out on duty
> sharing a cigarette
> or a coffee – a little milk . . .
> and once in a while a piece of bread.
>
> You, *compañero*,
> knew how to break the wall of the oppressor –
> with your enthusiasm,
> with your love of duty, of study –
> all to give more to the revolution . . .
>
> Today, dear brother
> you are gone from us,
> leaving your story on the path behind you –

a hard man who has left us
your example to follow;
we'll carry on defeating the enemies of the people,
in the way you thought and think –
because you haven't died
YOU LIVE ON in each combat,
and in every story.

REVOLUTION OR DEATH!!!
WE SHALL OVERCOME!!!

Jaime 16.24.90

Next to the ode to Oscar is a stenciled portrait of the fierce-looking Comandante Dimas, killed in battle a few months ago. Underneath it is written his immortalized challenge, '*Compañero*! Are you totally ready to pulverize the enemies of the people?'

A hundred yards away through the trees is the cookhouse. A fresh stream runs beside it. Inside, two girls stoke the smoky wood fire; it is kept going permanently for the guerrillas' meals of beans, tortillas, and coffee. The cooks are wearing old, worn dresses and combat boots. Santiago, a spindly peasant in his forties with a fox-like face, helps them by fetching water and chopping kindling for the fire.

Farther down the hill and well hidden from view, several rudimentary workshops churn out 'popular armaments.' A mixed group of amputees and young fighters whose limbs are still intact spend their days cutting and hammering sheets of tin into rocket casings and packing nitroglycerin into antipersonnel mines intended to blow off the government soldiers' feet.

But making explosives is only one of the responsibilities that Giovanni oversees. His camp is also the headquarters for the local propaganda team. Their work is extremely important, for apart from responding to the enemy's propaganda with counterblasts of their own, the unit's task is also to inculcate the *compas* with revolutionary folklore. The poster of Comandante Dimas, by now sent all over the front, is one of their more successful recent creations: Among the young fighters, Dimas now holds the status of a legendary hero.

The propaganda workshop is run by Olga, an ungainly Basque woman with large hips and cropped, prematurely gray hair. She is a former factory worker from Bilbao, Spain, who joined the revolution three years ago out of a spirit of international solidarity.

Olga is assisted by Carlos and Adriano. Carlos used to be a schoolteacher. He has a Ho Chi Minh beard and wears a cloth cap, which he seems never to remove. Like Olga, Carlos is prematurely gray, yet neither of them is past their early forties. Adriano, a good-looking young man of twenty and a talented caricaturist, has only been in the front for a year, since returning from exile in Nicaragua, where he grew up.

The trio works at a table under the spreading boughs of a huge old *amate* tree that shields it from the army's observation planes. Every morning, after doing their exercises and singing the FMLN anthem with the rest of the *compas*, they meet at the cookhouse with their aluminum canteens to beg some coffee from the cookhouse girls. Then they retire to the table under the *amate*, where they spend their mornings inventing slogans, making decals, and writing leaflets, all the while listening to Radio Havana crackle and hiss on their little shortwave radio.

Except for Olga, Carlos, and Adriano, most of the other *compas* are backup personnel – sentinels and runners who carry messages between the guerrilla commanders. There is a constant flow of people from all over the front, many of whom carry messages for Giovanni. Every morning he holds court on a fallen tree trunk, just out of earshot of the camp. Here he meets with people, dispenses orders, and writes out messages. His *radista*, Melida, always hovers in the near distance, conferring frequently with him and sending and receiving coded messages on her walkie-talkie.

The camp is designed to be evacuated within minutes if an army attack comes. Every morning the propagandists retrieve their materials – a stenciling kit, a silk screen, paints, brushes, Magic Markers, an old manual typewriter, paper, and pencils – from plastic bags buried in the ground, and each afternoon replace them. Also in the mornings the *compas* strip and pack away their *champas*, leaving nothing standing but the frames.

The younger *compas* spend most of their days hanging around until Giovanni sends them on a mission somewhere. They are keenly aware of their own isolation and desperate for knowledge of the outside world, about which they are as innocent as young children. They ask about the Middle East – 'Is it in Africa?' – about wildlife – 'What do giraffes look like?' – and about life in North America and Europe – 'What is snow like?'

One of them, Cornelio, called Conejo ('Rabbit'), is twenty-six years old and struggling to teach himself to read from a first-grade primer that is so well-thumbed some of its pages are crumbling away. Conejo is from a peasant family in Chalatenango, but he has been with the *compas* for ten years and doesn't even think of himself by his real name any longer; he is his pseudonym. When, after several years in the hills, he finally saw members of his family again, they called him by his real name, and he received a shock. 'At first I didn't understand at all, and then after a minute, I realized it was me they were talking to,' he says.

The rest of Conejo's family is politically aware and, like himself, conscienticized' about the revolution – they know what's what – except for one sister, who isn't at all. He hasn't seen this sister since the family split up in the early days of the conflict, but he knows that she has lived a life separate from the rest of the family, and is so politically ignorant that she is actually afraid of the guerrillas. Amazed that the war has divided even his own family, Conejo gives a short, resigned laugh, shaking his head.

In Chalatenango, the experiences of individuals are continuously grafted onto the larger revolutionary history that is evolving. The result is a hybrid of popular folklore and grim oral testimony, loosely structured by Marxist philosophy and Catholic faith. This synthesis of what people think and believe makes up the *compas'* unique reality.

At the age of eighteen, Sandra immigrated into the mountains, where she could become a revolutionary fighter. Yet long before that moment, as the child of parents who were themselves *compas*, she had been a secret inhabitant of the guerrillas' world, merely waiting for the day when she could pick up a weapon.

Haroldo seeks to break down the frontiers between El Salvador's separate worlds and make them one. His comrades do this work with their guns, but he mostly tries to do it with his thoughts, speaking across the divide by publishing revolutionary poetry under his real name, while giving propaganda broadcasts from the mountains on Radio Farabundo Martí as 'Haroldo.'

Across the world, in the tropical jungles of Burma, another group of people inhabits a parallel reality as palpable as that of the *compas* in El Salvador. For their vision of life, these guerrillas look not so much to a fresh, untested future as to an idealized past, comfortable and snug with nostalgia. Ethnically distinct from their enemies, in their war they exalt their own cultural identity in an attempt to stave off assimilation. Here, there are no 'hearts and minds' to be won. The Karen's war is the oldest kind of war: over territory, between tribes.

In the Burmese jungle, the monsoon season is about to begin.

The wind blows, and the huge green-and-black bamboo stalks move together to make a rushing, pattering sound like an oncoming shower. An explosion tails off into a high shimmying sound while overhead a large piece of shrapnel rotates audibly, landing somewhere beyond in the great bamboo.

The commander arrives, walkie-talkie in hand, just in from the trenches at the killing ground. Major Than Maung is a youthful-looking man of fifty-four with a broad nose and large sensuous mouth. On his beret, he has sewn an insignia patch from *Soldier of Fortune* magazine showing two crossed daggers thrust through a beret. The betel nut he chews constantly has colored his lips a deep scarlet. Than Maung's face is a mask of stress, all straining nerves and muscles. He works his jaw incessantly, and his eyes are vague and unfocused. This is disquieting, because otherwise his athletic body, well-pressed uniform, and rakishly tilted black beret make him the perfect model of a professional military man.

Standing in his concrete bunker, open to the forest on the side facing away from the shelling, and crowded with crude wooden beds, the major listens, head cocked. With each boom of the afternoon's mortar barrage, he stiffens and barks orders into his walkie-talkie. Waiting for a reply, he stands poised, alert to the radio crackle and the noises beyond, his gaze on the forest wall; he is here and not here at the same time. Once, after a triple volley of enemy shells comes whirring in, he murmurs aloud: 'They are pinpointing our position.'

The sun falls behind the tall bamboo, and darkness takes over from the shadows. Soon, the bamboo stops rustling, and with it the shelling stops, too. Then the rain comes. As the drops fall heavy and thick, Than Maung uncoils, his hooded eyes sharpening in their focus, shifting away from their relentless probing of the jungle. Then too, his jaw stops working against itself, and his face becomes calm and unlined, his voice more fluid. His body slumps, at ease. The offensive isn't coming today. Tonight, Kawmura is safe from assault. After the rain, the crickets start up, making their shrill wall of sound that is like another kind of silence.

Poised on Burma's southeastern frontier with Thailand, Kawmura is one of the last bases still held by the ethnic Karen guerrillas. They have been fighting a secessionist war against the central Burmese government for almost half a century. Occupying an oxbow bend on the Moei River, the little peninsula of Kawmura clings like a tiny leech to the Burmese body, surrounded on three sides by Thailand.

Before it became a battleground, Kawmura was a thriving black market for smuggled Burmese goods. It was also a populous village where the Karen lived with their families. Many Karen still recall the good times, when Thais crossed the river in search of shopping bargains. Those days ended in 1984, when a government assault destroyed the village. Since then, the area has been overtaken by jungle, and the few buildings that are still standing have gradually been torn to bits by the daily bombardment of shells.

Now, a heavily mined and booby-trapped piece of ground at the peninsula's neck divides the warring parties. Barely fifty yards deep and three hundred wide, this stretch is called 'the killing ground.' Because the devastated village is exposed to constant enemy fire, the guerrillas have abandoned it and now inhabit only the farthest fringe of the peninsula, where they are dug into bunkers along the riverbank. Across the river and a couple of miles down the road inside Thailand, their families live in a refugee camp. From there, many of the fighters' women visit regularly, crossing the river in dugout canoes to bring homecooked meals to their men at the front.

Major Than Maung is Kawmura's commander. Before he joined the guerrillas of the Karen National Union (KNU), at age twenty-five, he was a Seventh-Day Adventist mission schoolteacher and had intended to become a preacher. Nearly thirty years later, he is still devout and listens to nightly sermons on his shortwave radio. His family also lives across the river in Thailand, and he sees them whenever he has time off – usually on Sundays – but in recent weeks he hasn't left Kawmura at all. Six weeks ago, his men pushed back one bloody onslaught, and he expects another before the rains begin again in earnest.

The night is quiet except for a couple of explosions in the hours before dawn. Then men begin to cough, and soon it is day. Long after sunrise, the camp basks in cool shade from the bamboo that arches and sways above, blocking out the direct rays of the sun.

In the early morning, the major's bunker seems peaceful and domestic. Squatting outside, a walnut-skinned boy in a green sarong washes bamboo shoots in a large tin dish the color of old silver coins. Older men sit around chewing betel nut in silent pleasure, red lips pursing over their grinding teeth. As the boy works, he wiggles his bare toes in the clean black earth. A family of geese waddles slowly on mustard-yellow feet, looking for food beneath the stilted cookhouse. In the sunlight outside, some ducks move toward them, intent on the same quest.

Dangling from the split-bamboo rafters around the major's bed are small plastic bags containing various personal items. To protect them from the damp and the insects, they hang from pieces of wire twisted into hooks. One bag is full of shaving gear, soap, and other toiletries; another holds an album of family snapshots. Propped against the bunk next to the major's is an artificial leg with its metal hinging; the leg is a loud, plastic-doll pink. Temporarily ownerless, it leans against the bed like a bicycle between rides, a reminder that this is the front line in a war.

Across the river in Thailand there is peace, but here, because this is Burma, Kawmura has come to be a place where men kill one another. They do so for a purpose that has nothing to do with this particular oxbow bend in the narrow, muddy Moei River, but a larger idea, an abstraction. And the front line, a couple of hundred feet away from Major Than Maung's bunker, is a mess of fortified, zigzagging trenches and underground dugouts where guerrilla boys live like half-subterranean creatures, alert for the enemy beyond.

An old man sits in a canvas reclining chair, taking it easy in the shade of a wooden hut. One of the founding members of the guerrilla movement, he says he has seen action every year since 1948. As he speaks, the first enemy mortars of the day begin; with each explosion, the old man squints his eyes in the kindly way some elderly people have, cocking his head forward a little and nodding in pleasure, as if each bang reaffirms his existence.

Under the shade of a giant gray kapok tree, a woman tends a rudimentary teahouse. Her face is whitened with tamarind-bark powder for health and beauty. She smokes a large cheroot and serves a group of young Burmese student guerrillas who are fighting alongside the KNU. They are also smoking cheroots. One of them wears a T-shirt that reads: THE OFFICIAL I HATE CATS BOOK.

Farther along the riverbank is a longhouse on stilts, where a tattooed man with a broad face and one leg lies in a hammock, surrounded by young boys. The man's tattoos spread in a luxuriant and exotic pattern from the inside of his sarong all the way down to the knee of his remaining leg. All of the boys have tattoos. On one boy's arm is a kung fu fighter flying through the air in mid-kick. Another boy has what looks like a cockroach on his forearm; it seems to have been copied straight from a similar insect depicted on a nearby spray can of Bayer insecticide.

These boys are underaged volunteers. Tired of their schoolwork and the routine of life in the refugee camp, they have come here asking to become fighters. The amputee looks after them until the

Karen leadership decides whether they are to become soldiers or will be returned to their parents.

Like boys of their age anywhere, they aren't deterred from trying to have a good time: They tease, joke, and wrestle with each other. But because of the expected new offensive – and the mortars that come crashing in all around them – everyone has been ordered to stay close to the bunkers. If the boys were living across the river, they would expend their energies playing soccer, but this is Kawmura, and they have only a few square feet in which to stray, and so, standing near the mouths of their dugouts on the path, they play a game like pitching pennies, using large jungle seeds.

Kawmura forms a front line of defense for Kawthoolei, the name used by the Karen for their rebel state. In the Karen language 'Kawthoolei' means 'Promised Land.' The *thoolei* is a beautiful, long-stemmed white flower, like a giant wild tulip, that grows in abundance in the Karen's traditional territory along the Burma-Thailand border.

The Karen homeland is a long, thin sliver of land that extends for several hundred miles along Burma's border with Thailand. Most of the Karen's stronghold lies over the long, jungle-covered Dawna Range, where Kawthoolei abuts the Thai border, in the north by the Salween River, and farther south by its tributary, the Moei.

Ever since Burma gained its independence from Great Britain in 1948, the Karen and more than a dozen other ethnic minorities have fought wars for autonomy against the Burmese government in Rangoon. Because of these perennial insurgencies, Burma has actually been a true nation-state in name only. It is, rather, a fractious amalgam of warring ethnic groups, each seeking autonomy within arbitrary boundaries created by past wars and the colonial cartographers of the British Empire.

The Karen people's feud with the country's ruling ethnic Burman majority goes back centuries, and was useful to the British when Burma was a colony. Of all the ethnic groups, the Karen were especially faithful and loyal to their British colonial masters, who favored them during the years of empire. When Burma was invaded and occupied by Japan in World War II, the 'loyal Karen' fought as guerrillas alongside the British, while Burmese nationalists made their pacts with the new imperial warlord, Japan. After the war, Britain resumed control of Burma only to oversee its early transition to independence. Amidst the jockeying for a larger share of power in the new independent Burmese government, the Karen National Union attempted to secede from the state.

Just as the KNU was an orthodox political party that simply went underground, its military wing, the Karen National Liberation Army (KNLA), likewise had an extraordinarily conventional origin. This fighting force arose out of the embattled remnants of the First Karen Rifles, one of the ethnic battalions created during British colonial rule.

After negotiations broke down between the KNU and the Burmese government, the Karen Rifles mutinied, beginning a three-month battle from around their garrison at Insein. The Karen fell back, dispersing to fight a guerrilla war from the wilderness of the swampy Irrawaddy Delta southwest of Rangoon. But the guerrillas made little headway, and in the end, the delta was virtually conquered by the government. Beginning in the 1960s, the KNU shifted its headquarters and theater of war to the Karen heartland along the Thai frontier. And from there the Karen have continued fighting ever since.

In Kawthoolei, the Karen have devised a remarkably workable 'guerrilla state,' lacking only international legitimacy to make its status official. They have not attempted some socialist experiment, breeding a Karen version of the New Man in the jungle; instead they pursue a disarmingly mundane emulation of the British colonial administration that governed Burma before independence.

Still, the Karen steadfastly call their adopted way of life 'the revolution.' The revolution is unquestionably totalitarian. Every aspect of life is codified either by the KNU's all-encompassing bureaucracy or by tribal custom. The latter lends an exotic flavoring to the Karen: When not in the green uniform of the KNLA army, the men wear sarongs, or on special days don a traditional red tunic with vertical white stripes and hanging fringe.

Despite their formal adherence to religions imported by missionaries, the Karen are by tradition animists, and the omnipresence of tattoos among Karen youths attests to the enduring power of underlying tribal customs. Most of the tattoos are intended to offer protection from the dangers posed by wild beasts and illness; others nowadays are more politically emblematic – for example, KAWTHOOLEI, spelled out on the knuckles of both hands; or a silhouette' of Kawthoolei; or brave slogans such as GIVE ME LIBERTY OR GIVE ME DEATH – KNLA.

Meanwhile, the Karen's mimicry of the British is a conscious and faithful effort; Kawthoolei comes complete with a civil bureaucracy and posts for district officers. The Karen National Union has a cabinetful of ministers for everything from war to sports. There is a judiciary, an educational system, and a taxation system, and the KNLA, like the British army, has a rigid military hierarchy, with ranks from sergeants all the way to brigadiers. Each Karen army brigade has a corresponding 'military district.' Even Karen religions, if not strictly British, are mostly of the imported, conservative variety – Baptist, Seventh-Day Adventist, and Catholic – and many of the Karen are regular churchgoers.

Sunday is an official day of rest. At the KNU headquarters of Manerplaw, the day begins with a service in the Baptist church under the trees on the square. When it is over and the hymn

singing stops, the devout guerrillas and their wives file out dressed
in their best clothes, the women holding aloft beautifully colored
parasols. Afterward, it is customary for the young fighters to come
to the prime minister's office to puff cheroots and watch videos.
Sprawled barefoot and bare-chested on its cool split-bamboo floor,
they watch raptly whatever is shown them. One of their favorites
is *Rambo III*.

An orderly ramble of bamboo and teak houses on stilts under
huge shade trees, Manerplaw sits on a bluff above the Moei River
a day's journey north of Kawmura, not far from where the Moei
flows into the Salween.

On the grassy square at the heart of Manerplaw, a white picket
fence and well-tended flower bed surround the president's two-
story, pale blue residence. In the square, soldiers practice their
marching. At the beginning and end of each day, they gather here
to raise and lower the Kawthoolei flag, a red rising sun on a field
of white.

Under the old shade trees around the square are the ministries,
large open-air houses on stilts. The offices of the defense minister,
prime minister, and the education and justice ministers are all here.
This is Kawthoolei's government; each morning, six days a week,
its civil servants arrive for work, and after a little while, the thunk-
thunking of old manual typewriters and the buzz of voices begin to
fill the morning quiet.

Paths lead into the trees away from the square. One curls away
past some barracks and the prison – two large teak cages guarded
by ten-year-old boys with guns – to a drill ground and soccer pitch,
its grass clipped and edged with carefully placed lime-washed
stones.

It is deceptively peaceful; the only sounds at Manerplaw are the
cicadas, birds, the slapping sound of people walking by in rubber
flip-flops, and, always in the background, the whooshing rush of

the river. The rain, which comes every afternoon, comes hard and falls like liquid silver, drawing a heavy curtain across the unremitting green of the land.

The occasional roar of motor canoes is the only reminder that a faster-paced world exists beyond Kawthoolei. The wooden dugouts powered with belching car engines come and go throughout the day on missions of war and commerce. But these noises are only momentary, and Manerplaw soon lapses into its tropical somnolence. Somehow it is easy to imagine forty years slipping by here.

Unlike Kawmura, where the enemy is faced across a few dozen yards of jungle, Manerplaw is still beyond Rangoon's reach, across a dense range of mountains. Even so, people speak about the day a few years ago when a lone warplane from Rangoon appeared abruptly overhead, discharged several bombs, and vanished again. The bombs didn't kill anyone, but the incident was alarming for its portent. But no more planes ever came, and gradually Manerplaw's civil servants and military planners, perhaps a little more vigilant than they were before, settled back down to the bureaucracy of war.

While the Karen entrench themselves in Kawthoolei, the nation of Burma has been caught in a time warp. Its military government has ruled in a parody of state socialism since the 1960s, with the result that Burma has become poorer and poorer. While trumpeting the country's independence, the xenophobic regime sealed this potentially wealthy nation off from the outside world, so today Burma is mostly untouched by the usual trappings of the global consumer monoculture. Levi's, Coca-Cola, Marlboros, and Big Macs have not yet arrived. Most Burmese still wear their traditional sarongs, ride bicycles rather than cars, eat rice and fish paste, and smoke hand-rolled conical cheroots rather than factory-made cigarettes.

Since the official currency, the kyat, is almost worthless, a huge black market for smuggled foreign goods has flourished, especially along the Thai border, where commerce has traditionally been dominated by the Karen. The Karen operate their own customs gates, taxing all goods bought or sold; the revenues earned help fund their insurgency against the state.

The trade is conducted as it has been for centuries: Merchants in towns throughout Burma employ professional smugglers to get their goods to and from the border. In place of roads, smuggling trails snake throughout the Burmese wilderness, and in a system unchanged since medieval times, teams of barefoot porters take the place of mules, carrying huge loads on their backs for arduous treks lasting several weeks. They drive herds of cattle and water buffalo, carry out precious gems and rare antiquities – anything that can be sold or traded on the Thai border in exchange for consumer goods unavailable in Burma. These trails lead to the well-defended KNU customs gates on the Kawthoolei border with Thailand.

Teak logging is the other main source of income for the Karen. On the Moei and Salween rivers, Karen sawmills cut teak and other hardwoods into planks to fill sales contracts with Thai timber companies, and in the dry season, a select number of Thai logging firms are allowed to cut their paid-for quota of teak.

For decades, the government in Rangoon was unable to do much to unseat the Karen. Its own forces were spread thin fighting insurgencies elsewhere; but even without other distractions, Rangoon had neither the aircraft it needed to bomb Kawthoolei, nor the all-weather road access necessary in order to launch a sustained offensive. But by the mid-1980s, Rangoon was in such need of Kawthoolei's resources that conquering Kawthoolei became a priority. The regime launched a series of military campaigns against the Karen's positions in what has become a bloody annual dry-season offensive.

In each offensive the Burmese army has gained some new position. It bought field artillery from Sweden and, by forcibly

conscripting Karen civilians to work as porters, dragged the
weapons up into the Dawna mountains to positions overlooking
the Karen bases. From there, the army could bombard the Karen
with impunity throughout the year.

Gradually, the KNU's territory was whittled down to a few
well-entrenched bases like Kawmura, and it looked as though the
Karen might soon be defeated.

Then, several things happened that transformed the dynamics of
the war. First, in August 1988, the army brutally crushed
prodemocracy demonstrations by students and teachers in Rangoon
and other cities across Burma. This spurred an exodus of thousands
of students to seek sanctuary in Kawthoolei. There, many of them
joined the KNU with the intention of carrying on their struggle,
with guns. This increased threat of insurgency from Kawthoolei
made its eradication as a rebel base all the more urgent for the military regime in Rangoon.

Coincidentally, a disastrous mud slide caused by overlogging in
Thailand brought into harsh focus that country's rampant destruction of its own hardwood forests. The Thai government called a
halt to all logging within its borders and immediately obtained a
series of Burmese timber concessions for its logging companies
from the cash-hungry Rangoon regime. The deal left the Thais free
to begin clearcutting Kawthooli's trees in open disregard for the
Karen's longstanding status as the de facto trustees of the forests in
question.

For Burma's military rulers, the deal brought enough quick cash
to buy new, modern weapons with which to attack the Karen.
Rangoon didn't waste any time: in the next offensive, the Burmese
army pushed hard, and five Karen bases fell in the first six months
of 1989. Burma was even confident enough to send troops across
the border at Kawmura, using Thai territory to attack the KNU
from behind. Although they managed to repulse that raid, the

Karen realized that things had changed, and that they now had to watch their backs as well as their fronts.

There is a bitter irony to the situation. For decades the Karen fought in obscurity, yet enjoyed relative peace and prosperity within Kawthoolei. But just as their political currency and their ranks were boosted by the Burmese students, they found themselves under renewed attack from Rangoon, and apparently sold out by Thailand at the same time. Now, with their economic resources drastically reduced, they have less reason than ever to be confident about their future.

Than Maung coordinates his defense of Kawmura with the KNU's regional headquarters in the nearby Thai city of Ban Mae Sot. A border boomtown roughly three hundred miles northwest of Bangkok, Ban Mae Sot is set in a fertile valley of stilted villages, iridescent green rice paddies, and muddy gray water buffalo. The jungle hills that rise up in the near distance mark the Burmese frontier. At their base, the Moei River forms the boundary between the two countries. Kawmura and another KNU frontline base, Palu, are both within a half-hour drive of Ban Mae Sot. Whenever fighting occurs at either base, the explosions reverberate throughout the town.

Major Soe Soe is the KNU's regional commander. He has a severely pockmarked face and wears thick spectacles over rheumy eyes. On one arm he has a large green tattoo that says, in English, FOR KAWTHOOLEI. He lives in an unpretentious two-story suburban house outside Ban Mae Sot. On the ground floor is a terrazzo verandah with a teak table where visitors wait to be summoned to his upstairs office. Above the doorway hangs a shiny, fringed banner made of gold paper with red letters wishing all a Merry Christmas, whatever the time of year.

Soe Soe married a Thai woman; they have several children, who attend school in Ban Mae Sot. Though Soe Soe lives an outwardly normal suburban life, no different from that of any of his neighbors, the business he attends to is war. A regular stream of visitors – Karen guerrillas and refugees – comes and goes from his house. Careful to keep a low profile, always dressed in civilian clothes, Soe Soe gives no visible indication of his real activities, although everyone in Ban Mae Sot knows what they are.

From his home, Soe Soe helps oversee the defensive operations at the border bases and monitors enemy movements through his own spy network. But he complains that his duties force him to keep such odd hours that he is turning into a night creature, which is having adverse effects on his health. Indeed, Soe Soe can rarely be roused before noon, and during most of the day he moves around in a daze. Whenever he can, he escapes from his house and the routine of Ban Mae Sot to commute to the war itself, fighting alongside his 'boys' at the front line. This is when he is happiest; when he doesn't come home, the women in his house fret after him as though he were a businessman who has stayed too late at the office.

Lately, Soe Soe's responsibilities have increased significantly with the influx of Burmese students. Like many Karen, Soe Soe is suspicious of the students, because most are ethnic Burmans and because he fears that Rangoon has infiltrated their ranks with its own intelligence agents. At the same time, he recognizes the students as a potentially valuable resource that the KNU can't afford to ignore. With this in mind, Soe Soe has begun a program to train selected students for special missions to be carried out deep inside Burma. The training is being conducted by Major Robert Zan, Palu's commander and one of the KNU's most seasoned fighters.

One day, Robert Zan comes to Soe Soe's house. He is wearing a green sarong and his torso is covered in white bandages: He is recovering from gunshot wounds suffered in battle a month or so ago. With a sick man's pallid thinness and gleaming, intense eyes, Robert Zan looks a little crazy. But he is extremely lucid and speaks in a loud, emphatic tone.

Some of the Burmese students who have joined them might be enemy spies, he shouts, but this is a risk worth taking. For forty years, the Karen have fought in the jungle without any positive result. Now, with the students as their allies, they can penetrate Burma's cities and perhaps alter the course of the war. This will mean a change of tactics. No more set-piece battles in the jungle: Now they will carry out car bombings, sabotage, and assassinations. These are things the Karen have always been loath to do, but now it is time to try them – and the students offer a perfect opportunity to do so.

Robert Zan is training the students in these things and sending them back to their cities, to take the battle to the Burmans on their home ground. He knows there will have to be many sacrifices, but that is what he is here for. And the students have to know this as well – that is, if they really want to free Burma from tyranny. Robert Zan's eyes dance and sparkle as he speaks, and he smiles at the sound of his own words.

War always creates odd bedfellows, and if it is strange for the fleeing students, many of them fiercely nationalistic Burmans, to seek refuge among the separatist Karen, it is also understandable. The Karen offer them the relative sanctuary of Kawthoolei as well as the opportunity to learn how to fight in a real guerrilla war. No longer will they be mere schoolboys wielding sharpened bicycle spokes against fully armed government troops shooting live ammunition. The students and the Karen still have considerable mutual distrust and ethnic prejudice to overcome but, for the moment at least, they fight a common enemy. And the alliance has already brought about some alterations: In the new, pragmatic spirit of coalition, the Karen have agreed to set aside their independence claims in favor of a degree of autonomy within a future federal Burmese democracy.

The students, meanwhile, still confront the most basic obstacles in their new life as revolutionaries. Unused to the hard life in the jungle, many gave up in the first few months and returned home. But a hard core of two or three thousand remain, learning how to become guerrillas. The lessons have been tough. Not only have the new revolutionaries buried their first battle martyrs, but over thirty students died from malaria in the first year alone.

Apart from those involved in Zan's special guerrilla program, other students have received their basic training in live combat, rotating in and out of frontline bases like Kawmura. Most, though, are still unschooled in warfare, living rough in jungle camps like Thay Baw Boe, located a distance away from the Karen's own camps.

Thay Baw Boe is an hour's walk through a teak forest from one of the KNU's customs gates on the Moei River, and near enough to Palu to hear the fighting there. The erratic booms of artillery echo distantly; they sound like trees being felled.

Life in the camp is tedious and predictable. The daily routine begins at daybreak, with the appearance of wrinkled gray elephants. They lumber through the camp's parade ground on their way to the teak forests, urged on by Karen mahouts. Above, the slopes of the Dawna Range are shrouded in mist.

The students emerge sleepily from their huts and muster under the red flag emblazoned with their emblem, the orange 'fighting peacock.' There they sing their anthem and do calisthenics; then they eat their breakfast of hot, sweet tea and bread. At eight A.M., one group runs off at a half-trot into the surrounding forest for military training. Their instructor, cradling a small submachine gun and wearing a black headband and fatigues, runs beside them, melodically barking orders. The rest gather on the rude wooden benches of the dirt-floored structure that dominates the center of the camp. Like the other huts set around the parade ground where the flagpole stands, this building is made of split bamboo, its roof of large brown *talaraw* leaves woven together. A carefully painted sign in front of the building reads, JUNGLE UNIVERSITY: THAY BAW BOE CAMP.

It is Jungle University's inaugural day of classes, and an intense Aung Htoo is giving the first lecture. Today's subject, politics, concerns the 'feudal' crop-taxation system imposed on farmers by the military government. Aung Htoo tells the students that this system is unfair and will be done away with 'after the revolution.'

Until a year ago, Aung Htoo was a lawyer, who lived with his wife and three young children in the town of Tanguii. Now, at the age of thirty-eight, he has given all of that up. He has even reconciled himself to the possibility that he will never see his family again. Their place in his heart has been taken by the burning desire to overthrow the Burmese dictatorship. Like the students sitting raptly before him, Aung Htoo has become a revolutionary.

Every bit as intense as Aung Htoo is Aung Lwin, leader of the students at Thay Baw Boe. A former high school physics teacher and activist for a liberal branch of the Baptist church, he is born to his present role – a hybrid of Rotary Club booster, Boy Scout troop leader, and guerrilla commander. Unlike Aung Htoo, Aung Lwin has always had impersonal priorities; he has left no wife and children for the cause, just books, 'lots of books on politics . . . and about three hundred students who are organizing an underground right now.'

A tireless and inspiring orator, when he is in camp Aung Lwin spends much of his time trying to bolster the students' confidence, reminding them that their goal is nothing less than the liberation of Burma. Frequently he exhorts them with catchy slogans and proverbs: 'We are like candles. To give light we must endure burning.'

Outside camp, he talks up his 'fighting peacocks' to whoever will listen, hoping to get something, anything – a bag of rice, a cash donation, or a couple of guns – to take back to them. He lives at Thay Baw Boe but spends much of his time traveling to and from Thailand, meeting with Karen commanders like Major Soe Soe, upon whom he and his comrades still depend for most of their food, clothing, and medicine.

The students' political leaders are based in nearby Ban Mae Sot, but Aung Lwin is growing increasingly critical of them, saying they seem unwilling to leave the comforts of Thailand and share, even temporarily, the living conditions he and his 250 students are enduring at Thay Baw Boe. As life in the jungle becomes familiar, the students have begun to form a factional sense of identity as guerrillas, separating them from their leaders on the 'outside.' A new crop of leaders is emerging from the student camps in Kawthoolei, charismatic men like Aung Lwin who have proven their willingness to suffer in the camps along with everyone else.

Aung Lwin has been preparing for this way of life for years, since he was a student at Rangoon University. He boasts proudly of his participation in all the students' significant antigovernment demonstrations, reciting their dates almost liturgically: 'Seventy-three, seventy-four, and seventy-five.'

After graduation Aung Lwin worked as a Baptist community organizer for three years in remote Chin state, and then back in Rangoon for another four years. But the years of social work brought him little reward: The government blocked his efforts. Eventually, he came to believe that the only way to improve the lives of his fellow citizens was to 'get rid' of the government. How to do it was the problem.

An opportunity to learn some answers came in 1979 when Aung Lwin was chosen to attend a six-month training seminar for Christian activists; the seminar, held in the Philippines, was organized by the Catholic church there. It amounted to an intensive political education, as Aung Lwin was taken to see for himself the inequities of life under the Marcos dictatorship, and what was being done by the church to build up Filipino civic resistance to it. He also met with the communist New People's Army guerrillas, an encounter that he says inspired him to devote his life to bring democracy to his own homeland.

Arriving home, Aung Lwin immediately put what he had learned into practice, embarking on what he called 'grass-roots-level cell training: giving the people an analysis of the social and economic system of Burma.' The goal then was to build a nation-wide network of social activists, 'working peacefully at the community level to bring about democratic change.' Since then, the political situation has deteriorated; peaceful change is probably no longer possible in Burma. But Aung Lwin doesn't feel his efforts were in vain: He believes the cells he helped build can now be activated as guerrilla cells.

Aung Lwin's role models are Mahatma Gandhi, Che Guevara, and Jesus Christ. 'I would like to say first of all that I hate war and love peace. Gandhi is my hero, but in Burma, our government is special, they *kill*, and so we can't fight them through nonviolent means. Che Guevara worked not only for his own country and people, but for oppressed people everywhere. But my great revolutionary teacher is Jesus Christ. And it is also time in Burma to act like Christ when he used violence in the profaned temple, so we can change things.'

Aung Lwin believes that the time to use violence finally came in August 1988, when the Burmese army ruthlessly quelled the wave of student protests that had paralyzed Rangoon and other Burmese cities. At least three thousand students and other civilians were killed when the troops attacked, shooting, bayoneting, and even beheading protestors.

On the day the army opened fire, Aung Lwin and his class of students were demonstrating in front of the American Embassy. It was an experience he cannot erase from his memory: Dozens of his students were gunned down in front of his eyes. 'The rest of us had no choice but to flee and seek a way from the jungle to destroy this evil regime.'

As the bloody crackdown gathered force, Aung Lwin and his surviving followers joined the growing exodus of students fleeing Burma's cities for the Thai border. 'We were like Abraham in the Holy Land, lost . . . and then the Karen helped us along the way. We were on foot; it took seven days through the jungle, along the Dawna Range. We had no money, nothing, but the Karen helped us – fed us, clothed us, and gave us shelter. They were like fathers with us.'

And here they are, almost a year later. The mosquitoes, meals of rice and fish paste, bouts with malaria, and the day-in, day-out routine of life in muddy jungle encampments have only added fuel to Aung Lwin's revolutionary fervor. 'For us, it is like a dream. We want to build a new Burma. So we've joined hands with the Karen and other underground revolutionary groups. And I firmly believe that the new Burma we dream of will surely come true.'

Aung Lwin's student cadres still have some learning to do before they can call themselves true guerrillas. For now, they train with wooden guns in the teak forest, read well-thumbed copies of Orwell's *Animal Farm*, Machiavelli's *The Prince*, and even the U.S. Constitution. In Jungle University, they have begun learning two other essentials for their lives as border revolutionaries: the Thai and Karen languages. They have built a clinic, planted a vegetable garden, and started up other 'self-reliance projects' to raise funds for themselves. They want to be self-sufficient, like the Karen.

But the students are homesick and lonely. Unlike the Karen, they aren't living in their own homeland with their families nearby.

The students' homes are back in Burma, beyond the mountains over which they fled, in what already seems like another country. They know many of the older Karen also began this way, leaving homes and families behind in Rangoon or the Delta. But this is small comfort, because over four decades later the Karen are still here, fighting. The idea that they too might have to live out the rest of their lives in the jungle haunts the students, and they try hard not to think about it.

At the age of sixty-two, KNU vice president Than Aung considers his own life in the past tense. In his own thoughts, he can't separate his life from the insurgency that has taken up the better part of it. If he was once wistful about lost opportunities, he has long since reconciled himself to his fate, saying, 'I was quite happy with my revolution, although I had wanted to be an engineer.'

It seems appropriate, somehow, that this venerable denizen of the Karen war should also be the man in charge of student affairs for the new national opposition umbrella group, which operates from KNU territory. When they see this tiny, wizened man, the students must wonder if, forty years on, they will be like him, their lives mostly behind them, still fighting for a future that hasn't yet been won.

Than Aung is cancer-ridden and has chronic bronchitis. He is also almost totally deaf, the result of a lifetime of quinine treatment for malaria. His voice whistles because of missing teeth. Despite all of this, he seems strangely unworried at his state of disrepair, and attributes the fact that he is still alive simply to 'the grace of God.'

The aging fighter is equally at ease about the state of the Karen revolution, which now appears as ready as his own decrepit body for an imminent demise. Perhaps it is just that he is old, used to the ebb and flow of life, and knows that wars, too, follow the same pattern. During his years at war, Than Aung met and married his wife, raised seven children with her, and buried her. Still the war continues, life goes on.

Now, Than Aung is stoic and even a little amused at the way his life has turned out. In the end, he doesn't see how he could have lived his life any differently. 'This was the first and last chance for the survival and freedom of our people. Burma is not a democracy, and without a democracy, our people can never survive. When there is a democracy in Burma, then all this revolutionary business can end.'

This sense of duty to one's people is also something the students express, even if they are just beginning to learn what it means to make sacrifices. With their commitment to revolution still in such a fragile state, it sometimes seems that they repeat their affirmative dogma for themselves as much as for their listeners, as if repetition will fill them with the same certainty of their own destiny that men like Aung Lwin appear to have been born with. In the end, if they have done nothing else, they have restated their sense of purpose.

Yet how out of touch with the modern world their idealistic volunteerism seems, how 'nineteenth-century.' In the developed, modern world, few people are willing to die for their ideals, much less for notions like the common good. It is as though Burma's isolation from the twentieth century has allowed philosophies that already seem worn and hollow to the outside world to remain untested, even pure.

The purity of vision possessed by its people gives Burma a Shangri-La quality. It contrasts starkly with the degraded political culture immediately across the border in Thailand, with its rampantly consumerist society in which everything is for sale at the right price. Little idealism is in evidence in Thailand; that country's own Communist insurgency dried up a few years ago when the few remaining fighters were amnestied and bought off with bank loans and farmland.

The driving force behind the Burmese guerrillas' special identity is their unstinting idealism. In their sarongs, T-shirts, and rubber flip-flops, the Burmese – both the Karen and the students – are indistinguishable from the Thais on the bustling streets of Ban Mae Sot. What truly sets these people apart is in their minds.

Although culturally, ethnically, and ideologically distinct, the Burmese are linked with the Salvadoran guerrillas through a shared revolutionary ethos. Aung Htoo, the former lawyer, has chosen the path of revolution because of the injustices he sees in Burma; Sebastián, the onetime sociology student in El Salvador, has the same reasons – and a murdered sister. All of them – Than Aung, Haroldo, Jacínto, Aung Lwin, Giovanni, Sandra, Sébas, and Aung Htoo – *could* have been something else, but instead have opted for a much harder life, in which little is certain except a prolonged familiarity with loneliness, hunger, sickness, and death. Each has committed himself or herself to an armed struggle in order to achieve the combined ideals of social justice and new political and economic systems for their countries. This willingness to sacrifice themselves for a larger ideal is what being a guerrilla is all about.

As in Jacínto's proverb, the guerrillas are 'like priests,' having taken vows of self-sacrifice in order to carry forward their revolutions. Since they are unable for the time being to overthrow the governments they fight against, their lives have become rehearsals for the power they hope to exercise one day on a national scale. In the refugee camps of Gaza, the desert of Western Sahara, the hills of Chalatenango, and the teak forests of Kawthoolei, revolutions are under way, and the guerrillas already dwell in separate realities, parallel to those they are rebelling against.

THREE

Earning a Living

The *shabbab* of Gaza speak longingly of escalating the intifada's level of violence to include the use of guns. They brag that whenever they need to, they will be able to obtain weapons without any problems. They know a number of ways.

'Close by, there is the border with Egypt,' says Mahmoud, explaining that weapons could be thrown over the security fence by allies on the Egyptian side.

'We can buy the guns from the Israelis themselves,' interrupts Ahmed, 'by selling them drugs.' He tells of the time he sold an Israeli soldier hashish in return for an Uzi submachine gun. He refuses to say what he did with the gun, or whether he still has it; he merely gives a mysterious smile. 'No, my friend, weapons are not a problem for us. If we want them, we can get them . . .'

For all their bombast, the *shabbab* have little chance of ever becoming a fully armed guerrilla force. Quite apart from the difficulty of acquiring arms within Israel's well-policed territory, there is little outside financial support available to them, either, except for limited clandestine funds trickling into the territories from the PLO and Islamic fundamentalist organizations abroad.

In the end, all wars are about economics, in terms both of why they are fought and how they are waged. Having adequate material support is the key to survival for most insurgencies, if not their ultimate political success or failure. There is real truth in the old Maoist dictum that to survive, guerrillas must be like fish and swim in the sea of the people. But, though the people can provide guerrillas with food, shelter, intelligence, and recruits, they usually can't provide guns and ammunition – all the military equipment necessary to carry on the struggle. And so most guerrillas have foreign patrons as well, powerful benefactors who for their own purposes wish to see a change in the systems opposed by the guerrillas. The challenge for the guerrillas is to maintain the integrity of their struggle in spite of their foreign sponsorship.

The 1960s, 1970s, and 1980s were boom years for the Third World's guerrillas. The collapse of Europe's colonial empires in the aftermath of World War II brought much of the developing world up for grabs, and it was there the new superpowers sought out proxies to fight one another. During the cold war, guerrilla groups could obtain aid from Washington, Moscow, or Beijing, as the rivals discovered new strategic interests to exploit in the other's territorial backyard. Only in areas deemed nonstrategic have guerrillas found their causes ignored.

Among insurgencies, the Palestinian intifada is unique because it does not require the logistical support essential to most. And yet, although its 'fighters' use mostly rocks and knives instead of guns and bombs, the intifada is no less an insurgency for all that. It represents the latest genesis of Palestinian resistance after all other forms of violent struggle have been tried and have failed. But the *shabbab* seek nothing less than what was sought by the fedayeen

commandos and airline hijackers before them: a Palestinian homeland.

The end has remained the same; only the means have changed.
Where once it required a regular supply of cash or guns and
ammunition, the Palestinians' struggle today depends upon their
continued ability to mold international public opinion in ways
favorable to their cause. In this sense, the very poverty of the
intifada has been a weapon in the campaign to preserve its image,
that of a David-versus-Goliath revolt by unarmed boys against
gun-wielding soldiers. The fact is the Palestinians have little
choice.

One of the more humiliating facts of life for Palestinians living
under Israeli occupation is that so many of them must work for
their enemies in order to survive. But there is no other work available, especially not in Gaza. So, every day of the week except
Friday, the Muslim holy day, more than seventy thousand Gazans
journey into Israel to menial jobs. They make up Israel's pool of so-
called black labor, its equivalent of South Africa's township
migrant workers, or the Mexican 'wetbacks' in the United States.

In the mornings, a stream of lumpy, light-blue Peugeot taxis
and old-model Mercedes crammed with Palestinian men and boys
flows north toward Tel Aviv, passing under the scrutiny of the
Israeli army checkpoints at the territory's northern border. Every
evening, prohibited from staying overnight in Israel, they return to
Gaza.

The days are exhaustingly long and the work often dishearten-
ing. Although, with the connivance of their employers, some of the
workers are able to stay overnight in Israel illegally, sleeping on
factory floors or in restaurant stockrooms, most have to return
home, only to rise again long before dawn the next day to begin the
journey back to their workplaces.

Whatever their academic qualifications, the Palestinians invariably end up doing menial jobs, working long hours as poorly paid cooks and dishwashers in Israel's restaurant kitchens, as factory workers, and as laborers on construction sites. Massoud, one of Mahmoud's friends, is a Cairo University graduate with an Arabic-language degree he has never been able to use. Most weekday evenings he can be found at home, covered in plaster dust and numb with exhaustion at the end of a day's labor.

Construction work is the most cruelly ironic of all, because the Palestinians are physically helping to house their enemies in the land of their own forefathers. With each new apartment block raised for the growing influx of European Jewish immigrants to Israel, or Israeli settlers upon occupied land, the laborers erect a new obstacle to their own future on the land they call Palestine. But, for now, with families to feed and children to clothe, they have no choice but to find work where they can.

Mahmoud might carry some weight in the *shabbab*'s militant underground in Breij, but he still has to work for a living, and so he puts in six eighteen-hour days a week as a waiter at a roadside shashlik-kabob restaurant in Rishon le Zion, a Jewish city near the coast between Gaza and Tel Aviv. Mahmoud was lucky to find his job; he says he was hired only because he looks Jewish. 'The customers won't go into a restaurant where the waiters look like Arabs.'

Although he has learned to speak Hebrew well, Mahmoud still spends most of his days in fear of discovery by the soldiers from a nearby barracks who regularly come there to eat. 'If one of them knows I am a Palestinian, he can say to the owner to fire me, and the owner *will*, because he wants to keep his customers – but he can always find another waiter.'

The experience of working in such close proximity to Israelis hasn't diminished the tendency of the Palestinians to demonize them, or vice versa. Rather, familiarity has bred increased contempt. Perhaps this has more to do with the almost total lack of communication between the two peoples than with any new-found insights about one another.

One of the most demeaning aspects for Palestinians about work-ing in Israel is the way the Israelis habitually ignore them. It is as if the Palestinians simply aren't there. This treatment makes the Palestinians, who already resent being reduced to menial work, feel even more humiliated and insecure. They realize that it isn't that they aren't *seen* by the Israelis, but rather that they have been made invisible because of who they are. What does this say about the Israelis' attitude toward their claim to be a separate people? If the Israelis don't even see Palestinians as individuals, how likely is it that they will ever see them as a community, much less grant them a homeland?

In the absence of all but the most negative or perfunctory kind of human contact – 'Hey you, bring me a coffee'; 'Fetch that tool'; 'Clean the floor' – the Palestinians' experiences in Israel only con-firm their worst suspicions about Israelis, while heightening their own alienation and rage.

Hisham is a neighbor of Mahmoud's in Breij, a member of the fundamentalist Muslim Brotherhood. While awaiting the results of a scholarship application to study chemistry at an American uni-versity, he works as the foreman on a work gang at an apartment complex being built north of Tel Aviv. What he sees during his workdays has fueled his hatred of Jews, and he shows it with a devout man's moral revulsion. On a spot in the road near where he and his men are erecting the new apartment blocks, he says, newly arrived Russian emigré women are openly prostituting themselves.

'They come here to sell themselves for fucking,' spits Hisham. 'And we hear that the Israeli whores are angry because they sell themselves so cheaply. Only a few shekels and they will fuck! The Russians think they will have a good life in Israel, but this is what they have come to do! They should have stayed in Russia – life would have been better for them. For everyone!'

The 'black labor' system benefits Israel, of course, by providing it with a cheap labor pool, and by effectively neutralizing a large, potentially troublesome group of mostly younger men within the Palestinian population. At the end of each working day, most of these men are too exhausted to do anything but sleep, much less think about subversive activities.

Not surprisingly, at the onset of the intifada, the PLO perceived an opportunity to scale back the Palestinians' economic dependency on Israel. At first, the Unified National Command tried to get the workers to stay home, to boycott their jobs, but this edict was highly unpopular and widely ignored. How were the workers to support their families if they stayed at home, they asked. Would the PLO pay their salaries?

Before long, the policy was abandoned, and the underground leadership compromised by ordering stay-at-home 'strike days' and the early closure of all Palestinian businesses during working days. These measures were more successful; they sent the Israelis a message about the intifada's popularity and organizational ability, but didn't cripple the Palestinians economically.

Attention also turned to another, more corrosive symptom of the long years of occupation: the network of Israeli collaborators within the Palestinian community. But at the beginning, it was difficult to determine what was collaboration with the enemy, and what was merely employment. An element of fear crept into daily life as the intifada's enforcers began setting down the new definition.

As with the system of black labor, the collaborator network reveals another paradoxical side to the intimate relationship that has evolved between the Israelis and the occupied Palestinian population. Although the Palestinians' poverty has provided Israel with a means of penetrating their community by bribing people to become its spies, the Palestinians have learned how to use Israel's vaunted 'benign occupation' to their own advantage. From early on, the leaders of the uprising have utilized their access to Israel to help coordinate strikes and demonstrations between Gaza, the West Bank, and Israel's volatile 'Israeli-Arab' community.

Sami is one of the Palestinians who have managed to exploit the system. Since he was abroad for so many years and therefore managed to avoid trouble with the Israelis, he found he was not on their security registers. So in the early days of the intifada he was able to travel freely in and out of Israel without problem. Unlike his rival Mahmoud, Sami didn't work; he was unemployed and lived at home with his family. His several working brothers supported him while he devoted himself more or less full-time to the intifada. At one point, Sami was traveling between Gaza and Nazareth, the large Palestinian town inside Israel, to 'organize' Palestinians there. He was also looking ahead to organizing in Haifa and in Tel Aviv, where the Arab workers form a potentially subversive presence to be cultivated by agitators like himself.

Allowing so many Palestinians to work within their midst has made the Israelis vulnerable to attack within their country, not just when they go into the Occupied Territories as armed soldiers or settlers. Stabbing attacks against Israeli civilians have become increasingly commonplace and are openly endorsed by Hamas, the militant Muslim organization supported by Hisham and his friends. In response, Israel has tightened its controls on the flow of workers coming to and from the territories.

Now, in addition to the increasingly frequent curfews and travel bans that seal off Gaza for days at a time, a new, computerized security system has come into effect. Only Palestinians cleared by the security forces have been given special identity cards that allow them into Israel to work. Anyone who has been detained for secu-

rity offenses – even minor ones – is now prohibited from entering
Israel.

The new measures have presumably brought the Israelis a rich
harvest of new collaborators. Fearful of the consequences of being
permanently prohibited from working in Israel, many young
men – often their families' sole breadwinners – will agree to pass
on information in exchange for a clean identity card. For those who
have been banned, the outlook is bleak. But, with the Palestinians'
ability to convert their suffering into something that ennobles the
struggle, being a 'banned' person can be of use in the intifada.

Muhammad, Mahmoud's brother-in-law, is banned from working in Israel. Muhammad is thin, with a sunken-in, ex-con's look
about him. Recently released after spending two years in Ansar
Three, an Israeli prison camp in the Negev desert, Muhammad is
now back in Breij, living in his father's home. He is one of Breij's
'ninjas,' a label used for the *shabbab*'s masked enforcers. Since he
can't work in Israel, he has been given a job by the Breij intifada
committee: to surveil the camp's collaborators.

Muhammad's father is a cherubic-looking, pink-cheeked man in
a red-and-white-checked kaffiyeh. Wearing a distraught expression, he sits in a chair next to his son. The intifada has devastated
him: Of his five sons, three are in Israeli prisons doing long sentences for political offenses, and the other two – one of whom
is Muhammad – have only just completed stints in prison as well.
And that is not all. Muhammad's former bedroom in the
house has been sealed, bricked up, by the Israelis. In the Occupied
Territories, if your son is arrested for a security offense, the Israelis
can blow up your house, or else, as in Muhammad's case, they just
wall off the bedroom of the responsible family member.

The house is dark in the unlit mugginess of mid-afternoon.
How strange it is that Muhammad, sitting there in the downstairs
parlor of his parents' home, has a room all his own that he can't go

into. He has to sleep in the parlor. Now, one can't look at Muhammad without imagining his room, which he carries with him everywhere, like an invisible ball and chain.

How medieval it is somehow, that here in Breij, in the other refugee camps – all such crowded places – and throughout the Occupied Territories, there are dozens, hundreds of such rooms sealed off, forbidden to their owners. What stories does their prohibition tell? What kinds of dreams are harbored in their stagnant air? If you put all the rooms together, one on top of the other, like an architectural fantasy, how high would the forbidden building reach?

Having come so recently from that same punished household, Mahmoud's young bride is adamantly opposed to his continued involvement in the intifada. Like many young women of Breij, she cares little for politics. She wants only to build a new life, one with none of the despair and hopelessness endured by her own family. And so, for the sake of his wife and new family, Mahmoud is cutting back his activities with the *shabbab* so as to keep his identity card. Instead, he works hard and long at his job in Rishon le Zion. Meanwhile his banned brother-in-law Muhammad, with nothing to lose, has become a full-time 'ninja' in the intifada.

Anis, a close friend of Hisham's, was arrested on suspicion of belonging to Hamas. He was beaten – his jaw was broken – and after two months' detention he was released back to Breij. Now he can no longer enter Israel. Confined to Gaza, he has had no recourse but to create employment for himself. In a move that may ultimately cause the Israelis to regret having helped steer his destiny, Anis opened an Islamic bookstore in Breij. Today he sells Islamic texts, Korans, and cassette tapes of violent, 'jihad' music, which makes the young men and boys who listen to it glassy-eyed and willing to die. Business is good, and Anis no longer complains about his restricted life.

As the cases of Muhammad and Anis make clear, the *shabbab* have many ways of evading and undermining Israel's security apparatus without ever leaving Gaza. And, for that matter, there are also men who appear on no security-risk registers but are potentially dangerous nevertheless. The fact is that as long as the occupation continues, Israeli society will never be risk-free.

'Joe' is a nurse in Jewish Jerusalem's large Hadassah Hospital. Every night of the week except Friday, he rents a room in Ramallah, a city near Jerusalem on the West Bank. Each Friday morning he travels to his home in Rafah, Gaza's southernmost refugee camp, and returns to Jerusalem the next day.

Like most of his countrymen, Joe is usually too tired after his long workweek to do much more than sleep when he gets home to Gaza. But he comes because he is married, and his wife lives in Rafah. They have only been married a few months; theirs was a traditional arranged marriage, and because of all the time they spend apart, Joe still feels like a stranger to his bride. 'I have one day every week with her. What is that to get to know someone? And, when I get home, I want to take her out, to show her things, but there is nothing to do. Where can we go? There are no cafés or restaurants to go to in Gaza! We can't go out. So we stay at home, in our little room.'

Next, Joe begins to wonder aloud if he has made a mistake in getting married. As he speaks, he becomes more and more vehement about his situation and how much he hates his life. Abruptly, he says in a strange, smiling voice: 'You know, two patients die on my shift every night. I work on the cardiac ward. I'm the night nurse, and a lot of these people are old and they can die very easily. And two of them die every night. I just hope nobody thinks I'm killing them!' The insinuation in Joe's voice is obvious. After this outburst, he says no more, and suddenly he walks away.

Whether mere hyperbole or a confession of the truth, Joe's

words are a signal of his capacity to strike back at Israel. During the uprising, the Palestinians have learned that their poverty is both a weakness and a strength; as a weapon available to both sides, it is something they have learned to assess constantly, seeking always to keep the strategic balance in their favor.

Although they are vastly different in most obvious ways, the Palestinians share certain characteristics with the Karen of Burma. Both are ethnic groups seeking self-rule over their national homelands, and both have managed to keep their struggles going despite ever-increasing economic hardships. Just as adverse circumstances have forced the Palestinians to look inward, so have the Karen's shrinking territory and dwindling revenues shaken them from their lethargy, forcing them to reassess their policies in order to hold on to what is left and to survive in the future.

The two communities also share a colonial legacy: Until the late 1940s both were strategic pawns of the British Empire. But while Palestine has retained its geopolitical value, Burma has not. Once a territorial buffer in Great Britain's colonial domination of India, Burma ceased to be of importance once India gained independence. The new international tension lines in Asia ran through Indochina and beyond, and Burma soon fell into complete and total obscurity. This backwater status was compounded by the Burmese regime's long-term policy of nonalignment; as long as Rangoon sought little help from the Communist bloc, neither did the Karen's secessionist war garner much Western interest. As a result, uniquely for such a long-lasting insurgency, the Karen have always fended for themselves.

On Sundays the Karen mahouts along the Salween River take their elephants down to the river to give them their weekly baths. The green jungle banks are dotted with the pink-and-gray-mottled

beasts, and the mahouts stand like acrobats on the elephants' big
knobbly heads, scrubbing them with coarse brushes as large as
brooms. The elephants loll half-submerged in the water, playfully
curling their trunks and blowing water high into the air, like ani-
mated teapots letting off steam.

For the rest of the week, the elephants are at work in
Kawthoolei's primary industry, teak logging. Along the Moei and
Salween rivers, the activity has left its marks. Where there are
sawmills, the green riverbanks are scarred by red gashes, wood off-
cuts, and sawdust forming towering heaps. In the bleaching sun of
the timber yards, elephants move logs to and from the cutting
sheds. In their grayness, they stand out against the vivid oranges,
yellows, and reds of the sawn-open, mutilated trees.

On the Thai roads leading away from the Burmese border,
timber trucks loaded up with Kawthoolei's hardwoods move in a
steady flow, like soldier ants carrying away the amputated sections
of a great, fallen enemy. For miles along the dirt road leading to the
Karen base of Walli, the forest has been flattened into an immense
timber yard; thousands upon thousands of trees lie in cut and numbered stacks, ready for shipment.

Here and there the riverbanks also bear the scars of the Karen
guerrillas' other chief source of revenue: its customs gates, the
shanty markets where Burmese and Thai merchants meet to buy
and sell smuggled goods, under the eyes of the KNU's 'customs
agents,' who levy taxes on all goods traded.

The Student camp of Thay Baw Boe is located near one of the
Moei River customs gates. A constant stream of foot traffic goes by,
to and from the market. One afternoon a group of barefoot drovers
passes by the camp with a group of large, pink pigs. The pigs are
tired at the end of their long journey; they limp like fat ladies with
sore feet. As the drovers prod them with long sticks, the pigs balk
and squeal in protest. Another day, a Thai antiques dealer has

driven his pickup truck right up to the riverbank. He looks on as a dozen porters, stripped down to loincloths, their heads bent forward under heavy loads, pick their way toward him across the bouncing wooden suspension bridge, each carrying a different part of a giant antique Burmese ornamental drum. It is a museum-quality piece destined for Hong Kong's thriving antiquities market.

At Mae Le Ta, a small customs gate on the Salween River near Manerplaw, a Burmese cattle smuggler counts out the tax he owes the KNU. He leafs through a huge stack of paper money, proceeds from the sale of seventy head of cattle. He and two friends have hiked for a week to reach this spot from deep inside Burma. The man makes the trek every month, bringing livestock to sell. If the roving Burmese army patrols catch him, he says, he faces a beating and imprisonment, plus confiscation of the livestock. So far, he has been lucky.

A village has sprouted amidst the slashed-and-burned jungle around the customs shed. The few dozen shops along its single-lane street are run by ethnic Indian Burmese as well as by Karen. Their customers are the Burmese porters, who buy things here with their wages before making the return trek home through the jungle. Goods of every description hang in the open-fronted shanties: gaudy radios, watches, umbrellas, detergent, kids' toys, camouflage shirts, rubber sandals and fishing nets. Also: rolls of sarong cloth, flat, coolie-style *komau* hats, Wellington boots, Russian sardine tins, bundles of hand-rolled cheroots, white-and-red-striped shoulder bags called *tur*, the fringed Karen tunics, betel nut – even some electric guitars.

Ironically, the Karen's lucrative border trade is probably one of the reasons why their war has remained so obscure to the world at large. With their income from teak and tax, the KNU has never had to beg for alms abroad, but neither have its leaders ever learned the kinds of routine techniques employed by most modern insurgent groups in order to publicize their causes. Instead, as the KNU efficiently set about organizing its tropical bureaucracy, the Karen struggle didn't advance over the years as much as it became a settled, almost comfortable way of life.

To help them break the pattern set by their own inertia, the Karen have hired some foreign mercenaries to make their struggle more dynamic. Motosada Mori is a Japanese mercenary who often fights for the KNU. Mori has just come off a month's duty as a sniper at Kawmura's 'killing ground,' and now he is taking a much-needed break by going to Phuket, the Thai beach resort in the Gulf of Thailand. Afterward, he is going home to Japan for a while. One of the tasks awaiting him there is to review the publisher's proofs of a mercenary manual he has written.

Mori looks more like a bank clerk than a mercenary. He is gangly and buck-toothed and he wears glasses. But he has spent five years in the French Foreign Legion, learning his trade in the dismal Legionnaire posts of Chad and Djibouti. He emerged qualified in many aspects of warcraft, but his specialty is sniping. He has also taken a special course in explosives at a mercenary school in the Alabama backwoods, the same place where Sikh terrorists are suspected of training before blowing up an Air India passenger jet as it flew over the Atlantic in 1985 killing all 231 people on board.

Mori's trips to Kawthoolei are paid for by a wealthy Japanese businessman, for whom he works as a 'security guard.' The Karen are one of his employer's favorite causes, and he pays for Mori to come and help them. The KNU doesn't pay him anything, he says, it just provides him room and board and the weapons he needs to carry out his job. On this most recent job, he used a Remington Model 700 sniper rifle to kill Burmese officers. Mori only kills officers, and during his recent stint at Kawmura he has 'gotten two.' 'I got one with a head shot,' says Mori proudly. 'The other one was a heart shot.'

At the moment, Mori is considering an offer to stay on in Kawthoolei. He reveals that a Paris-based mercenary syndicate has a team of French mercenaries in Kawthoolei on semipermanent contract with the KNU, and it has offered him a job to join their team. It is a good offer, well-paid and on six-month renewable contracts, but Mori doesn't know if he wants to be tied down for so long in one place.

The Karen seem to have few moral qualms regarding the use of foreign mercenaries; they are loath to admit to it only because of the negative publicity such reports earn them in the media, and the ammunition this gives Rangoon for its own nationalistic anti-Karen propaganda. Major Than Maung is still jittery over the recent deaths of an American and a Frenchman at Kawmura, and publicly he denies they were fighting for the KNU.

Showing none of Than Maung's reticence, and with his trademark penchant for candor, Major Robert Zan sees little harm in soliciting help wherever he can find it, asking opinions on everything from car bombings to assassination, and requesting copies of a British explosives manual, *The Black Book*, of *Guerrilla Warfare* by Che Guevara, and of another he calls 'Memories of a Terrorist.' In return, he offers the post of London representative for the special guerrilla unit – the 'Supreme Special Command' – he and Major Soe Soe are training. The job is to include duties such as hostage-taking and hijacking on the Karen's behalf. Far from being opposed to foreign aid, the Karen find help from any quarter acceptable if it helps them achieve their end.

Following Robert Zan's cue, the novice students also speak unabashedly of the outside help they have received: Thay Baw Boe's students show off snapshots of themselves posing with a bearded Westerner they call 'Bob, a Canadian ex-SAS commando,' who trained some of them in specialized military techniques.

Aung Lwin lobbies anyone within earshot for help, he doesn't care who. Whenever an outsider visits Thay Baw Boe, Aung Lwin uses the opportunity to launch one of his flamboyant appeals for help. 'America *must* help us,' he beseeches dramatically on one occasion. 'Only your country can save us. At least, send us an American *flag* and we'll fly it alongside our own fighting peacock!'

However innocent they may still seem, the students have come a long way in their comprehension of how things work; they know now that wanting foreign aid doesn't always mean it will be forthcoming. In the beginning, some were so naïve they actually believed teams of masked, black-clad 'American ninjas' – as depicted in Hollywood-produced martial-arts movies – were going to swoop in on helicopter gunships and assist them in the 'battle for Burma.'

The guerrillas of Burma may look to outsiders for certain kinds of military expertise and even for their political inspiration, but they have never had to go far for arms. Since the Vietnam War, Southeast Asia has been awash in weaponry of every sort from both East and West. Obtaining weapons in Thailand is not a problem as long as there is money to buy them with: The KNU has sometimes bought weapons from the Cambodian guerrillas based along Thailand's eastern border, while Thailand's own powerful and corrupt armed forces offer another source of supply.

To avoid paying inflated black-market prices for everything, however, the KNU produces some of its own munitions. With pride, Karen guerrilla officers boast of the KNU's ability to independently manufacture their own mortar rounds, right down to the metal shell casings and gunpowder.

The Karen's program of self-sufficiency extends beyond munitions. Hidden in a bucolic jungle clearing on a fast-moving tributary of the Moei River near Manerplaw is the guerrillas' own prosthetic-limb factory. It is run by a handsome man of thirty-eight; he has a dragon tattooed all over his torso and has lost a leg in a land-mine explosion. In his riverine workshop, festooned with wooden hands, feet, legs, and arms, he and several amputee helpers work constantly to fill the KNU's orders; they currently have a backlog of four patients needing limbs.

The KNU Agricultural Department runs its own rice-paddy farms, called *taungyo*s. All the KNU's departments are supposed to be self-sufficient in food, and each employs men to farm its *taungyo*s full-time. In addition, the KNU encourages private enterprise among its cadres so as to free up its own budget for the war effort. Private *taungyo*s are cultivated to provide incomes for guerrilla families. One old general has a large rice *taungyo* of his own, farmed by underlings, while Ganemy, the prime minister's top aide, has a flourishing orchard surrounding his house. A little stream runs through his garden, where he has planted banana, pineapple, durian, litchi, mango, lemon, coconut, papaya, and avocado, grown to be sold in one of the KNU's border markets.

Elsewhere at Manerplaw, a rustic teahouse and general store perches among shade trees on the steep slope of the riverbank. On its porch, guerrillas and visitors come to catch the breeze off the river while watching the motor canoes come and go. The teahouse proprietor is the wife of a top KNU official. On the side, she also sells contraband Burmese gems.

One morning, she brings a small woven basket from behind her sales counter and sits it on the rough wooden table where customers sit to drink their tea. She then lays a clean white cloth on the table, and, removing several plastic bags from the basket, pours their contents onto it. Hundreds of gems tumble sparkling onto the cloth: star sapphires: dove-gray, blue, and pearly white stones; rubies ranging in color from blood-red to mauve; a single, chlorophyll-green emerald; and some mottled chunks of milky-green jade.

With the money she makes from selling the gems, the teahouse lady pays for the education of her nine-year-old son, who is attending a private school in Ban Mae Sot. But she claims to give half of all her profits to the KNU, and to support some indigent KNU fighters and their families with food, clothing, and medicine.

In Kawthoolei, there is a gray area where economic self-sufficiency leaves off and self-enrichment begins; the teahouse lady's charitable causes are her way of showing she knows what amount of profit is seemly and what isn't.

The students, meanwhile, are far from such profit-making ventures. They are still trying to make ends meet with handouts from the KNU and some international charities, and their own small-scale efforts to become self-supporting. At the end of their first year in exile and in recognition of their sacrifices on the battlefield, the KNU's president, General Bo Mya, presented Thay Baw Boe's students with a symbolic gift of some AK-47s, a few RPG-7 antitank rockets, and a mortar or two. These were a big boost to the students' armory; until then, all they had were seven antiquated carbines bought from Thai border guards with money raised by singing carols during their first Christmas in exile. When they serve at the battlefront in Kawmura or Palu, most of their weapons are loaned to them by the KNU.

To reduce their dependency, the students do whatever they can to raise money. Early on, some tried burning trees to make charcoal for sale in Thailand, but this led to problems with the Karen, who consider the forests theirs, and the students had to stop. In the fields around Thay Baw Boe, they have planted soybeans, corn, and chilies, and they raise some chickens, pigs, and goats. A few rudimentary teashops in camp and some 'self-reliance' projects provide a trickle of funds: Tin fighting-peacock brooches, pro-democracy T-shirts, and postcards that say 'Support the struggle for democracy in Burma' are sold through front groups in Thailand.

For the students, the struggle for democracy in Burma has become a struggle to survive in Kawthoolei's jungle. They have made some headway, at least. Their clinic, which they urgently needed because of the area's endemic malaria, was built entirely with funds they raised themselves. It is a crude but functional dwelling with eleven cots, run under the supervision of a former veterinary student. Now, only the most severe malaria cases need to go to Thailand for treatment, while students convalescing from illness or wounds can return to camp and be cared for among their friends.

The students know that their own survival depends on knowing how to take care of themselves. They cannot expect the Karen to hold out forever. If the day comes when Kawthoolei falls, they must be prepared to fight on alone and move into the countryside as mobile guerrillas. They also know they will only be able to do that with the support of the civilian population; if they want to win people over in the future, they must be able to do so here and now. Toward this end, the students have welcomed the local farmers living around Thay Baw Boe to come in for treatment at their clinic, free of charge. It is a wise public-relations move.

One morning, soon after the clinic opened, a couple of Karen peasants came into camp, swinging their stubby *daw* machetes and herding a couple of doe-eyed water buffalo before them. Having heard the head 'doctor' was a vet, they were on their way to the clinic – not for themselves, but to have their water buffalo inspected.

Its future may now be precarious, but for years, Kawthoolei's stability as a sanctuary for the Karen guerrillas gave them preeminent status among Burma's insurgent groups. Most of the other groups are smaller or come from remote areas with little access to the outside world. So near to Thailand, Kawthoolei is a logical and convenient place for the Burmese guerrillas to gather in their ongoing attempts to forge greater unity between their armies. For this reason leaders and delegations from other guerrilla groups are always visiting Manerplaw to confer with the Karen leadership.

One week, it is a Shan guerrilla chieftain. Smooth-cheeked and with very small black eyes, he is an impeccable dresser, wearing a well-tailored light gray Burmese formal shirt with cloth buttons and matching slacks. On one finger gleams a gold-and-ruby ring; he also wears an expensive gold wristwatch. His teeth shine with silver plating, and his face and forearms are covered with tattoos. The tattoo on his forehead shows up blue-green on his smooth yellow skin.

The Shan leader used to receive support for his army from Communist China, but that ended in the late 1970s. Now, he says, the bulk of his revenues comes from taxes levied on the traders, tea planters, and silver and ruby miners operating in his area. He may be telling the truth, but the fact is that his territory, in the Shan hills, lies at the heart of the Golden Triangle, the remote opium-growing region, including parts of Burma, Laos, China, and Thailand, where half of the world's supply of opium is grown. (Most of the rest comes from Pakistan and Afghanistan.)

Virtually all the Burmese guerrillas are involved in the opium trade, and some even operate their own heroin refineries. The Karen stand out almost alone as being clean of the taint of opium. The KNU has had a clean record in the past and has long maintained a highly moralistic official posture condemning the drug trade, even upholding the death penalty for traffickers in Kawthoolei. But many of its guerrilla allies *do* traffic in opium, and naturally this puts the Karen in a real quandary.

One evening in Major Soe Soe's house, the drug issue becomes the subject of anxious discussion. It seems that the KNU is suspected by the U.S. Drug Enforcement Agency of involvement in the opium trade. This is untrue, Soe Soe says, but the KNU is in a difficult position in attempting to prove it. Since most of its guerrilla allies *are* involved, he says, it is awkward for the KNU to publicize its own antitrafficking policy too much. It is also dangerous, because any individuals speaking out against the traffic might find themselves assassinated. For these reasons, the KNU's policy against the drug trade has never been as unambiguous as it could be, but still, the Karen guerrillas thought everyone understood their true position.

Then, on several occasions beginning in late 1987, the KNU sent high-level delegations to meet with the notorious Shan drug lord, Khun Sa, in his territory. But the DEA, which monitors the Golden Triangle out of Thailand, became suspicious. The problem is, says Soe Soe, the real purpose of these meetings has been misinterpreted. The Karen's intention wasn't to cement an unholy alliance with Khun Sa, but rather to propose an opium-eradication program.

Soe Soe knows this because he participated in the meetings with Khun Sa. But despite some early hopes for success – the two guerrilla armies had initialed a document expressing their commitment to future cooperation – the initiative eventually failed. And today, Khun Sa is still trafficking in opium, while all the Karen have gained for their efforts is the suspicion of U.S. narcotics officials.

Now the KNU wants to set the record straight. It knows Khun Sa will never stop trafficking. There is only one way to curb him, and that is to kill him. If the Americans will provide covert aid for the KNU's guerrilla war, the Karen will arrange for Khun Sa's assassination, then wipe out his guerrilla army. Once they are gone, the problem of opium cultivation can be tackled realistically.

Soe Soe's argument is logical enough. After all, the United States has in the past backed guerrillas in Angola, Afghanistan, Nicaragua, and even in nearby Cambodia in the name of anticommunism. The Karen can argue that their credentials make them prime recipients for such aid: They are both staunchly anticom-

munist and ready to assist Washington in its much-publicized 'war
on drugs.'

At another level, the plea for American aid demonstrates a
growing anxiety within the KNU leadership about what the
organization is going to do for resources if the battlefield situation
continues to worsen. In recent years the Burmese government's suc-
cesses have reduced the KNU's tax and teak revenues by more than
half. The Karen are hurting economically, and they either need to
regain control of some of the lucrative border crossings they have
lost, or else find an alternative source of income. 'We have turned
down the mafias,' says Soe Soe pointedly. 'They approached us and
asked us to be involved, at least to turn a blind eye to their ship-
ments through KNU territory. They knew we needed money, and
they offered us a lot, but we turned them down.'

This is a genuine dilemma for the Karen, because unless things
improve for them soon, the fact is that they probably will not be
able to turn the 'mafias' down for much longer. In order to become
like the Palestinians – on whose behalf the international community brings intense political pressure to bear – the Karen somehow
must make themselves valuable to the West.

That may or may not happen. In the meantime, the Karen will
do whatever is necessary in order to survive. Ideology, idealism,
moral values, and religion – all of these can be modified, altered, or
even cast aside if life itself is threatened.

In El Salvador, a country dubbed strategic in the heightened cold
war rhetoric of the Reagan administration, the anticommunist
regime found itself on Washington's payroll because its guerrilla
opponents were Marxists. The guerrillas, meanwhile, looked to
Cuba and the Soviet bloc for protection and assistance.

The Soviets' backing did not mean the *compas* mortgaged their
autonomy, however. One reason is that the FMLN has never lacked

cash of its own. In the 1970s it built up a cash reserve of as much as $100 million through bank robberies and by kidnapping local oligarchs, diplomats, and foreign executives for ransom. Yet while the FMLN has always had money for arms, getting the weapons to its fighters has never been easy.

During its decade in power, the fraternally minded Sandinista regime in neighboring Nicaragua allowed the FMLN to use Nicaraguan territory as a rear command base and arms transshipment point. But from early on, because of intensive American-backed efforts aimed at interdicting this supply route, the *compas* tried hard to become locally self-sufficient.

The 'popular armaments workshops' in Chalatenango are part of that effort. One morning, in a field of sawgrass near Las Flores, Giovanni and some of his boys proudly shoot off a dozen home-made rockets, mortars, and grenades. Half of them are duds, and some fly wildly off course, but the *compas* are excited and the adrenaline is flowing; they clamor to take turns shoving the rockets into their firing tubes. As they do, everyone else cups their ears and runs for cover. After each successful explosion, they exclaim, '*Que buen cachimbazo!*' – 'What a good bang!'

Afterward, in the forest below Giovanni's camp, the guerrillas show off the top-secret workshops where the lethal pyrotechnics are made. In one, a teenage girl and two boys, one of them missing a hand, work with files on the tin casings of rocket-propelled grenades. Surrounded by flying sparks, a man solders rocket noses with an acetylene torch. A gas-powered generator nearby gives off a loud din. In another, a girl has laid out the casings for several dozen grenades and is filling each with gunpowder and nitroglycerin. Outside in the sun, a boy is preparing some large round antipersonnel mines called *minas africanas* ('African mines') or *quitapies* ('foot-takers').

Like the Palestinians, the *compas* are proud of their reputation for making do in adverse circumstances. The willingness to sacrifice is part of their revolutionary ethos. They point to the locally manufactured boots they wear, which last no more than three months in the field; their uniforms, which are a hodgepodge of civilian and captured military clothing; and their peasant diet of tortillas, rice, and beans, supplemented when possible with eggs or a little meat. Wounded guerrillas are tended by the FMLN's own experienced medical staff and by internationalist volunteers, often under appalling conditions; medicines are always in short supply. Still, no one complains. 'See what we have done,' they say. 'It may not be much, but it is ours, of our own making. '

The *compas* have looked to their allies more for political orientation than for material support. One evening in Chalatenango, the conversation of a guerrilla squad turns to the collapse of communism. It is a subject about which the guerrillas are noticeably sensitive: There is obvious confusion among them as to exactly what the FMLN's policy is on the issue, and how the changes affect its own officially Marxist-Leninist ideology. The *compas'* squad leaders brush the topic aside, telling the younger fighters that for the FMLN nothing has changed.

'One sees in the enemy propaganda that the Berlin Wall has come down, that the world has changed,' says a veteran *compa* in his thirties. 'But here in El Salvador, nothing has changed. The poverty and the repression haven't changed. Democracy here is still just an act of theater.'

Afterward, out of earshot of the rest of the squad, a political officer says, 'These things are debated at the higher levels, among the *jefes guerrilleros*, but not at squad level. It's over their heads. I'll bet you I can find at least two *compas* here who don't know the world is round . . . Anyway, what they don't see doesn't affect them. Here, what matters is that the price of fertilizer has doubled in the past year. Why should we throw more kindling on the fire by telling the *compas* about the problems in the Soviet Union?'

In El Salvador, the revolutionary New Man is still evolving, the clay of his form still fresh in his makers' hands. Here, in the cradle of the revolution, most of the guerrillas are ignorant about the imported political ideology espoused by their organization. But even without an ideological framework for their war, they know this much: Their enemies are the oppressors of the poor. With or without aid and inspiration from abroad, that will not change.

Of all guerrilla armies, the Polisario Front is perhaps the most dependent on external support. Existing as it does in an otherwise uninhabited desert, with virtually its entire civilian constituency living in refugee camps, it has never had much alternative. At the same time, this condition of dependency is also a primary source of its power base among the Saharawi refugees. The Polisario is the middleman between the Saharawis and the outside world; it brokers any incoming supplies of foreign aid. Possessing, as it does, virtually all authority as to the disposition of material wealth, the Polisario has assumed total control of the refugees' economic lives. It provides everything. There is no money, no land ownership; there are no houses, no banks, no mortgages, no electricity bills, no water bills – there aren't *any* bills to pay. Education is free – at any one time up to seven thousand Saharawi students are studying abroad – health care and clothing are free; everything is free. All the Polisario requires in return is the people's unswerving loyalty.

Having cast itself as an anticolonial national-liberation movement, the Polisario easily gained the support of the radical anti-Western states in the Third World. From the start, its most important ally was Algeria's socialist FLN government; others have included Libya, Yemen, Syria, Cuba, and Iran. Because the leftist Third World nations back the Polisario and because he has long made himself out to be a friend of the West, King Hassan II has been able to buy vast quantities of arms from the United States and France for his own war effort.

The Polisario has no illusions about winning the war militarily; the presence of its fighters in the disputed territory has been a means of exerting pressure for an internationally mediated referendum and a political settlement with Morocco. But first, the Saharawis need the interest and goodwill of the international community, commodities they have expended great energies in cultivating.

To this end, one of the Polisario's most remarkable achievements is the diplomatic recognition it has gained: More than seventy countries recognize the 'Saharan Arab Democratic Republic.' Its most important 'embassy' is the one in Algiers. A once-elegant French colonial villa high on the city's bluffs, it overlooks the Mediterranean and a seaside promenade: Boulevard Ernesto Che Guevara.

The closeness of the links between the Algerian regime and the Saharawi guerrillas is underscored by the proximity of Polisario headquarters to the Algerian air force base at Tindouf. Here, amid the dunes, the Polisario's administrative complex is spread out. Roads lead off in several directions to the guerrillas' refugee camps, military bases, and POW camps. Somewhere not too far away are batteries of Soviet surface-to-air missiles. Together with the nearby air base, these explain the absence of attacks by King Hassan II's modern air force.

So as not to be completely dependent on its allies, the Polisario has also built up an impressive international solidarity network, particularly among Western European leftists, which raises funds, publicizes the Polisario cause, and channels material aid directly to the desert camps. There, the Polisario's civilian relief wing, the Saharawi Red Crescent, distributes all aid received to the refugees through the Polisario's popular councils.

The Polisario's' reception center near Tindouf is always abuzz with foreign delegations: earnest young Basque nationalists; Spaniards from Zaragoza; Swiss parliamentarians in well-pressed safari suits; a well-meaning English couple from Kent who have driven down a fully equipped 'dental van.' (After donating several months of their time to fixing Saharawi teeth, the dental couple are to return home to their joint practice in Kent, leaving the van behind as a gift.) Some others see the Polisario as a suitably stalwart Third World revolutionary movement to assist in the Marxist tradition of internationalism. Wolf and Isabel, a German couple in their late thirties, previously worked building a primary school in Sandinista Nicaragua. Now, in their hometown of Bremen, they devote themselves full-time to the Saharawi cause, and have come to Tindouf to see where their efforts can help the most.

Well-trained young Saharawi men and women are dispatched as guides and interpreters for visitors of various nationalities. Abba is assigned to English-speakers, while a guerrilla called Bashir handles the Germans. Bashir returned to Western Sahara only recently, after eight years as the Polisario's representative in Bremen. Now, the Germans have come, and Bashir struts around the reception center like a stud horse. Wearing tinted aviator sunglasses, with his turban draped around his neck like a cravat, Bashir seems altogether more European than Saharawi.

During the day, the visitors are taken on identical tours of the refugee camps and their self-help projects. They are shown not only what the Polisario has done with the donations it has received, but how much more is needed. Then they are told what they can do for the Saharawis upon their return home: One group should raise money for a summer youth trip; the next should gather up hospital supplies; another ought to raise funds for a fleet of ambulances . . .

The Martyr José Indam Experimental Farm is one of the

Saharawis' model self-help projects. In the late afternoon, a breeze gently moves the greenery. The water sparkling in the irrigation ditch makes liquid warbling sounds. All around, plants bloom in uneven geometry, the waxy husks of vegetables gleaming from underneath a green mantle of dusty leaves: bright yellow peppers, red tomatoes, and dark purple eggplants. Beyond, pale desert spreads as far as the horizon, like a bleached carcass. A young guerrilla standing in the shade of a date palm explains that he and his comrades have planted twelve hectares and plan to extend these to sixteen – but only vegetables, not fruit trees or anything else that is long-term, because, he says half-jokingly, 'We don't plan to be here that long!'

The Polisario Front has always been caught in a peculiar bind: how to care for its people's needs, yet not make them so comfortable that they forsake the dream of returning to their own land. Everything it does is carefully calculated for political value and for its utility in maintaining the faith and loyalty of the refugees. These priorities are balanced against the dual images the Polisario seeks to project to the outside world: that of a refugee people, displaced from their rightful homeland and in need of the world's support; and that of an organized and resolute people doing as much as they can to help themselves, showing they have what it takes to run a country. And so, nearly two decades into their exile, the Saharawis still live in tents, not houses, and plant vegetable gardens, but not fruit trees.

As a place synonymous with the practice of warfare, Afghanistan is less a nation than a battlefield of history. The war here is waged without much lip service to higher ideals. It is an uninhibited contest for territory and men's loyalties, in which whoever gets more of both will be the winner. It is the old Afghan game of war as politics, but fueled and made bloodier by outside interests.

The Afghans are no rustic innocents; they have been fighting foreign invaders and one another since before the time of Alexander the Great. During the 1980s, Afghanistan may have appeared to be an ideological battleground between East and West, as the Soviet intervention was countered by massive support for the mujahedin from the United States, Saudi Arabia, and Pakistan, but for the Afghans, the war was only a higher-stakes version of their time-worn game of political rivalry between clan leaders and tribal strongmen, in which ideology counts for very little.

Early on in the war, the mujahedin parties set up their headquarters in the old British colonial garrison town of Peshawar in Pakistan, just across the Khyber Pass from the Afghan border city of Jalalabad. Eventually, the entire length of the rugged border-lands was dotted with Afghan refugee camps, secret military training bases, prisoner-of-war compounds, and supply depots. In return for the use of Pakistani territory, the United States and Saudi Arabia allowed Pakistan's military intelligence agency, Inter-Service Intelligence (ISI), to disburse the aid to the mujahedin. As quartermaster, ISI wields considerable power over the mujahedin, to the extent of telling them what to do on the battlefield.

Now, in advance of the Soviet withdrawal, the mujahedin have come under pressure to seize a city. If they do so, some of their backers believe, the Afghan army will melt like a sculpture made of ice, and Kabul, the ultimate prize, will be theirs. Much attention is focused on Kandahar, Afghanistan's second city and the traditional home of its kings. Kandahar, in the southern deserts, is cut off from the rest of the country; only its city center and airport remain in government hands, and its garrison can be resupplied only by air. But as the mujahedin attempt to tighten their noose, Moscow's jets bomb them incessantly in a final attempt to weaken their resolve.

The Jamiat-i-Islami ('Society of Islam') mujahedin party has a leading role in the siege of Kandahar through a well-positioned local mullah named Naquibullah, or Naquib. His mujahedin have recently overrun the last government position in the strategic Arghandab River valley, just north of the city. Jamiat-i-Islami coordinates the battle and resupplies its fighters out of Quetta, an ancient trading crossroads and the windswept capital of Pakistan's remote province of Baluchistan, adjacent to Kandahar.

Between Quetta and the Afghan frontier, there are a number of secret supply bases. Dug into a treeless hillside high in the Toba and Kakar mountains of Baluchistan, Toba is the last depot before the unmarked Afghan border, and except for the small Pakistani military post opposite, it is run by the mujahedin themselves.

Here at Toba, Jamiat-i-Islami has stored some heavy machine guns. Locked in caves behind heavy iron doors with padlocks, the guns are badly needed by Mullah Naquib's guerrillas, who now hold exposed positions and must have bigger weapons to fend off the escalating aerial and rocket bombardments. To remedy the situation, Mullah Naquib has sent one of his top aides, Mazen Agha, to collect some of the guns and bring them back, before Arghandab is pounded completely into the ground.

The days are bright and crisp. Snow lies in white patches on the ground. In the canyon, which funnels the winter winds, the cold is especially bitter. Dusk falls early because of the surrounding hills. By mid-afternoon, the canyon is bathed in deep cold shadow, while the knolls above stand out in honeyed, golden light.

From the air, Toba must be indistinguishable as a place inhabited by men. But the Soviets know it is there, and have bombed it once; three men died in the charred truck that lies crushed in the riverbed below, and five more in the rubble of the houses on the hill. The munitions caves are hidden there among the walled-in mud houses grafted onto the brown slopes of the hill. Here, each mujahedin group has its own little compound. The ocher-colored huddle climbs from the river right up the steep hillside. Sentry positions lie toward the tops of the hills, with footpaths zigzagging to and from them like goat tracks.

Jamiat-i-Islami's compound lies at the bottom of this curious community. The houses of Hizb-i-Islami ('Party of Islam'), Jamiat's archrival, sit above all the others, at the top. These two groups, whose fighters frequently engage one another in combat inside Afghanistan, maintain little contact here. Although they live within rock-throwing distance of one another, they have separate access roads to their own compounds, so little communication is necessary.

A Pakistani military post across the riverbed monitors all activity at Toba. Its presence also undoubtedly helps reduce the risk of fighting breaking out among the rivals. The Pakistanis take a look at whatever supplies leave Toba for the front; boxes of weapons are always being unloaded from trucks and inspected in the post's dusty yard as mujahedin mill around.

There is no road to Toba; the trucks ferrying men and weaponry to and from the front use the dry riverbeds that wind between the high, brown, scree-covered hills. Ravens play with the wind currents in these barren canyons. Alighting on the summits like sentinels, they watch the trucks creak by below. Occasionally, family groups of camels with long swatches of matted amber hair slope lethargically by, their Kutchi nomad owners following at a distance.

Mazen Agha is in charge of transport and logistics for Naquibullah. He arrived in Quetta from the front a few days ago. Now he is returning, via Toba, with a requisition order for some Soviet-made Zigoyak and Dashaka machine guns. He is all in black: He wears a black turban with gold stripes, black zip-up rubber Arabian Nights style boots with swooping pointy tips, a black full-length robe, a black vest with many pockets, and even a black beard. He constantly sucks on a wad of *naswar*, the Afghan's addictive tobacco-and-spices snuff, and has an incongruous, high-pitched giggle, like an adolescent girl's.

Mazen Agha has two bodyguards. Like him, they wear distinctive black robes and vests. Both eighteen, they spend all their time listening to love songs on a portable tape recorder and mooning into each other's eyes. Varidad is slim, dark, and handsome, and not very bright; the more alert Wazir is chubby, homely, with a shaved head. They are inseparable. The three ride together in a decoratively painted Pakistani truck shaped like a galleon, with ornate, built-up bulwarks for its cargo, and intricately carved wooden doors.

Their overnight stop in Toba has stretched into eight days, because a few miles back, on an ice-covered plateau littered with abandoned vehicles, the driver broke an axle trying to drive straight through a lake of mud and ice. For the Kandaharis, the delay has meant living in a kind of limbo. Toba is a peripheral place neither in the war zone nor entirely outside of it, with an atmosphere of tense anticipation derived from the eddies of excitement brought by the fighters traveling to and from the front.

Inside Jamiat-i-Islami's trash- and bullet-strewn compound, daily life focuses on keeping warm. There is a small mud hut with plastic sheeting stretched over the single window. Inside, a couple of beds with straw mattresses have been fashioned out of ammunition boxes. In the middle of the hut, a wood-burning stove made of scrap iron is kept burning all the time. Using chopped-up ammunition boxes for kindling, an adolescent boy with huge feet feeds the stove. His name is Rahmat Gul. He also makes the tea and serves the meals, but he is extremely clumsy, constantly tripping and dropping things, and the mujahedin ridicule him openly, calling him Mule's Ass. Terribly anxious to please, he usually laughs along with them, but one day they go too far, calling him Progeny of a Mule's Ass, and Rahmat Gul bursts into tears. This causes even more hilarity, and the others only stop hooting when Mazen Agha orders them to. But the point is made: Rahmat Gul is just a tea boy, a servant, and they are mujahedin, holy warriors.

On the wall above the beds is a poster honoring the Pakistani ruler General Zia ul-Haq, who was recently 'martyred.' It is carefully framed with wood strips from the packing cases of RPG-7 antitank rockets. A powerful ally while alive, the dictator has in his present condition become something of a patron saint to the mujahedin. In the picture, his peaked general's cap lies on a bed of flowers in the foreground while Zia is depicted floating in blue skies and perfect white clouds. 'Zia, Martyr of the Afghan Jihad,' says the Urdu lettering emblazoned across the top. Sphinxlike, Zia stares down permanently into the room, and, with his hooded eyes and hint of a smile, gives the unsettling impression that somehow he has cheated his assassins.

Rahmat Gul brings the mujahedin an unending succession of *nan*, the flat, round unleavened Afghan bread, and cups of hot, sweet mint tea, *chai*. This is accompanied, when possible, by hot gobs of glistening white sheep's fat, or by *shurwa*, a kind of sheep-fat porridge mixed with *nan*. Sometimes there are onions, which Mazen Agha opens by smashing them dramatically with one fist and then dividing the contents. He presides over the meals, spreading the food out on the same dirty cloth that he produces each day. Everyone eats with his fingers. At the end of each meal, Mazen Agha bundles the remains back into the cloth, and the leftovers provide the core of the next meal.

The days drag by. Mazen Agha hopes the Jamiat office in Quetta will dispatch a new truck to replace the abandoned one with the broken axle. He sent word back on the first day, but no reply has yet come. He wants to fulfill his mission and get back to Kandahar as quickly as possible, but he needs a truck.

Trucks loaded with weaponry and mujahedin come and go from Toba at all hours of the day and night, but none show up for Mazen Agha. Despairing, he returns to Quetta to plead for a new truck. Two days later he is back again, exhausted from the journey. He carries a bagful of fresh oranges and a box of honey cakes, but he still doesn't have a truck. He has been told there are none to spare; he has no choice but to wait for a replacement part so that his truck can be fixed.

Mazen Agha does not know what to do. He wants to leave, but he does not want to go home empty-handed. In between deep snoring sleeps, he awakens, throws his hands in the air and sighs loudly. Wazir and Varidad are getting restless as well. They have been reduced to tickle fights, and the batteries in their tape recorder are getting low.

Every day, the guerrillas religiously tune into the BBC World Service's Pashto-language Afghan news broadcasts. One morning, word comes of heavy fighting around Kandahar's airport at Mahalajat. This news makes Mazen Agha more agitated than ever, but still he can't make up his mind what to do.

In the end, Mazen Agha's dilemma is resolved fortuitously, when Ghulam Azrat, 'the Engineer,' shows up. He has been sent to teach Mullah Naquib's men to use the Soviet-made SPG-9 recoilless rifle, a quantity of which Jamiat recently acquired. Ghulam is very excited about it, in the way engineers often are about some new piece of machinery, and says the weapon will be extremely useful in shelling Kandahar from the outskirts where Mullah Naquib is based. He has brought one of the guns with him, still in its packing case, to use as a demonstration model.

Mazen Agha quickly realizes that Ghulam's arrival is a stroke of fortune. If he returns now with Ghulam and his SPG-9 in tow, the

blow of his arriving without the heavy machine-guns will be less-
ened. The matter is soon decided. The group, including Ghulam,
will return to Arghandab on the next truck coming through Toba.
Meanwhile, Ghulam is a welcome addition to the cast of characters
in the cold little hut. First of all, he is not a Kandahari, but from
Wardak in the north. While the others are dark, he is fair, with
curly blond hair and blue eyes. He also speaks fluent Russian.
Before the Soviet invasion in 1979, he attended the Soviet-run
engineering school in Kabul.

As a Russian-speaker and a trained engineer, Ghulam is
extremely valuable to the resistance forces. His job is to instruct
selected fighters how to use Soviet weaponry such as the SPG-9. To
keep him, Jamiat pays him a salary of a thousand Pakistani rupees
a month, just enough to feed his wife and two small children who
remain behind in Wardak, in territory controlled by the mujahedin. He gets to see them only every few months. As everywhere
in Afghanistan, the journey home is often long, invariably arduous,
and frequently dangerous.

As the group waits for transport to appear, Ghulam spends
hours poring over a little copybook with his engineer's notes on the
SPG-9. The others watch him in mystified stupefaction. One afternoon, he entertains Wazir and Varidad by reading aloud to them
from the Koran in a highly dramatic voice. They lie on their stom-
achs, chins rested on their fists like children at a bedtime
storytelling, completely absorbed.

One evening, Mazen Agha tells everyone to collect his things. A
truck has come; it is going to Arghandab and has standing space in
the back for a few men.

The journey is short and dramatic. Wazir and Varidad cling
together in the open back, singing songs about the war and martyrdom. The riverbed winds on deeper into the mountains and
then, suddenly, the canyon walls disappear as the track falls steeply

downward. The Baluchi driver pumps his brakes and downshifts for the descent, and for a moment, the truck is poised at the top of the plunging gulch, creaking and straining like a boat at the crest of a wave. Below, like the columns of a giant Roman ruin, huge, sheer stone buttes rise from the desert plain. Beyond stretches a vast brown carpet of land that vanishes into a horizon smudged by sand and dust – Afghanistan.

At first there are no people at all. Then a couple of hamlets loom out of the emptiness. In a village of baked mud, where the houses are domed and nippled like women's breasts, small children run out to beg for sweets.

The Baluchi drives the truck onto a paved road that shines in the sun like a ribbon of molten steel laid upon the land. To the right, far to the north, it leads to Kabul. To the left, a few miles down the road, is Kandahar. Weaving its way between bomb craters, the truck speeds along the luxurious cement smoothness. But after a few miles, the truck leaves the road again and continues on through the desert. At a place where the tracks of trucks and jeeps converge near a stream, there is a *chaikana*, a teahouse. A dull, stomping roar – bombing – begins to be audible in the near distance. With a worried look at the sky, the Baluchi races the truck on toward Arghandab. He does not want to be caught out on the open plain by the Soviet bombers.

The desert gives way to more and more settlements. The villages, empty of people, lie crushed, their domed roofs broken open like eggshells, walls crumbled and pushed over like sand castles at the seashore. To the excitement of Wazir and Varidad, familiar landmarks begin appearing. They gesticulate and point at a martyrs' cemetery. It is the first of many that appear like forested oases on this shorn and treeless land. The tall, leaning poles rise up from clumps of rock, the flags attached to them fluttering like brightly colored leaves in the breeze. The flags are green, red, white, black,

pink, orange, and blue. At each cemetery, Wazir and Varidad make
a face-washing motion with their hands, part of the Muslim prayer
ritual.

Pushing hard, the Baluchi reaches the Arghandab valley as dusk
falls. But just after dark the headlights give out and within minutes, the truck careens and comes to rest at a dangerous angle half
off the roadbed. Everyone jumps out to see what has happened.
Just in front of the truck's wheels the dirt track disappears into a
gaping bomb crater. The Baluchi saw the hole almost too late.

The journey continues on foot, with Mazen Agha leading the
party through silent orchards and bombed buildings – the latter no
longer look like man-made things, but like giant anthills. Then
the path opens onto bare ground surrounded by a low wall and
dominated by a few wattle-and-daub dwellings strangely sunken
into the ground: Mullah Naquibullah's mujahedin camp.

Slouching at the intersection of several orchards, fringed by
windbreaks of trees, the camp has been carefully constructed to
withstand the prevailing conditions of war. To prevent aerial detection, the flat-roofed earthen buildings are dug into the ground.
Windows are covered in polythene, not glass, because of frequent
bombing. At the heart of the camp is the prayer ground, the *majit*,
a square of swept earth enclosed by a decorative palisade of gray
tank shells. At each corner, large empty bomb pods, their winged
tails arching upward, serve as oversized planters for some dying
flowers. A tall wooden pole soars skyward, giving height to the
camp's field-radio antenna. The antenna wire snakes into a nearby
hut where the radio is stored; inside it is homey, with clean straw
on the floor, colorfully striped kilims covering two army cots, and
a bulging tin kindling stove.

The radio hut is where Khalilullah, the camp doctor, and Abdul
Hakim, the intelligence officer, sleep. The other mujahedin sleep
in several communal bunkhouses located around the compound.

There is also a mess hall, a cooking area, a hand-operated well, a bathhouse, a clinic, and, beyond the trees at the edge of the camp, the shitting fields.

The camp is concealed amid a welter of blasted villages along a river-fed sliver of grape vineyards, pomegranate orchards, and wheat fields. Several hundred yards away the Arghandab River courses around the nearby base of the craggy Khybara massif. On its other side lies Kandahar. Away from the river, the orchards give way to desert, a flat plain that extends as far as the base of a mountain range rising bluish and rugged from the horizon line.

The land is pitted and pocked from bomb explosions, as though great bites have been taken from it. Some of the craters are fifty feet across and filled with blue water, like sinkholes. Halfway down the slope of one lies a large black horse, its feet raised stiffly and its belly distended like an engorged tick. The trees in the windbreaks between the fields are white with dust; many have limbs shot away, exposing orange flesh, their trunks jaggedly ripped as if struck by lightning. Rockets jut out from the ground where they have landed. Many are still unexploded and with their fluted tails they look like children's arrows lost at play.

Nearby are the remains of Charqulaba, the village where Mullah Naquib was born and for which the mujahedin camp is named. Really, it no longer exists at all. Not a single dwelling remains standing, and the broken edges of the walls are softening in the wind and rain. Inexorably, Charqulaba is returning to earth. Soon, it will be no more than a hilly piece of ground where nothing grows.

Around Charqulaba, things are fairly quiet, except for the overflying bombers, and random rockets fired back and forth between Arghandab and Kandahar over the Khybara massif. The camp is half empty because most of the fighters are off serving at the Mahalajat airport front where most of the action is taking place.

Those who remain behind are either resting up from a stint at the front, awaiting their own turns to go, or still too young to fight. Some are no older than twelve or thirteen, and since Naquibullah won't let them fight until they have sprouted facial hair, they must stay behind, helping the camp cook prepare and serve the meals. Between meals, desperate to prove themselves, they spend all their free time cleaning weapons, assembling and disassembling them over and over again.

On his second day in camp Ghulam sets up his SPG-9. He points it toward Kandahar and, with a crowd of yelling and laughing fighters watching, fires it off in a thunderous bang. The afterblast creates a huge cloud of dust and shatters the wooden door of the nearest bunkhouse; it falls into pieces on the ground. This meets with a great roar of approving laughter from the mujahedin, and Ghulam smilingly announces his test a success. As for the rocket, it has landed somewhere in the city of Kandahar.

Mullah Naquib doesn't live in the camp himself, but he makes a daily appearance. He lives with his two wives and three children in one of the inhabited villages back across the river in the shadow of the Khybara. Whenever he arrives, lumbering and moon-faced in billowing black robes and matching turban, his men line up to kiss his hand and whisper ritual salutations. Naquib is huge, bigger than any of his fighters – well over six feet tall and heavily built. He also has a great sense of humor; for a mullah, he seems to spend a lot of time laughing.

Although he is only thirty-four, Naquib already carries the combined weight of his duties as mullah and as mujahedin commander. Wielding, as he does, the powers of state while also interpreting the will of God, Naquib is nothing less than a demigod to his fighters and the local civilians. Every day, from dawn until he slurs his words with fatigue late at night, Naquib receives visitors, dispensing advice and settling disputes for all those who come. The overwork shows itself in his habitual absentmindedness. After lunch he usually naps in Khalilullah's bunk. On occasion, as he prepares to return home in the late afternoon, he loses the keys to his Toyota Land Cruiser. When this happens, mujahedin are sent out to scour the trail between the camp and the car as he fumbles in his robe's deep pockets.

Naquib's near-mythical stature has evolved during the decade he has spent in the jihad. His personal prowess is fabled. In 1979, as a young soldier serving in Kabul, Naquib participated in an army revolt against the first Afghan Communist regime. As it was bloodily suppressed by loyalist troops and their Soviet advisors, Naquib fled back to Kandahar and holed up in Arghandab. He is credited with having sparked off local resistance there when he single-handedly blew away a Soviet tank with a shoulder-fired rocket-propelled grenade. Since those early days, he has come a long way. Now he is overlord of Arghandab, and his presence is felt throughout the region.

The doctor, Khalilullah, is a soft-spoken man of twenty-three. He stands out from the others by wearing the only Western dress, a brown corduroy jacket. While the other mujahedin are mostly illiterate farm boys from Arghandab, Khalilullah is the son of a well-to-do Kandahar family with its own pharmaceutical-importing firm. He joined the mujahedin at the age of fifteen, against his parents' wishes. Now living as refugees in Quetta, they are carrying on the family business with the help of several of Khalilullah's brothers. They want him to leave the battlefield and join them, but Khalilullah says his place is with the mujahedin. Once the jihad is won, his dream is to study medicine in America or Great Britain, to become a 'real doctor.'

Khalilullah became a 'doctor' after a year's paramedic-training course given by a Western relief agency in Peshawar. The other mujahedin respectfully call him Dr. Sahib. Naquibullah also regards him highly and relies on him for many things besides doctoring. Whenever he leaves the front on missions to Pakistan, he takes Khalilullah along as an advisor. And when Khalilullah isn't tending ailing fighters or the civilians who come every day to seek treatment for a variety of ailments, he updates the military log, which he files weekly to Naquib's ISI controllers. Khalilullah also operates the camp radio. For several hours every day he can be overheard in his hut above the buzzing and whistling radio static, reading aloud coded messages in the Pashto language.

Khalilullah's roommate, Abdul Hakim, is a sharp-faced man of the same age. Like Naquib, he is a native of Charqulaba, where one of his brothers died in the Soviet bombing. The rest of his family are refugees in Pakistan; only he has stayed behind. It is his job to ferret out spies among the mujahedin and the area's civilians. He has an ambiguous smile, and his eyes have an unnervingly neutral stare, as if he is measuring everything others say and do against an inner barometer for treachery.

When they have free time, the fighters leave the camp to visit friends or family living in nearby villages. Across the river, there is a bustling market selling everything from plastic shoes to oranges, road's end for the trucks carrying smuggled provisions from Pakistan. The market is full of Kalashnikov-carrying men wearing *patou*, a kind of men's shawl, gossiping, haggling, and hanging around with one another. The atmosphere is relaxed and there is little sense of urgency about anything.

The dramatic is now routine for the people of Arghandab. This is their valley, where they live and work; it also just happens to be a war zone. Even as the Soviets fly their final punishing air raids overhead, Naquib is beginning ambitious projects to revive the valley's once-flourishing agriculture. After being tentatively cleared of mines sown during the years of war, orchards and wheat

fields are being replanted. First, sacrificial flocks of unsuspecting
sheep are sent through the furrows. With a laugh, Khalilullah
describes them as 'our minesweepers.' Blueprints for the future
include the construction of new villages and the sinking of new
wells, most of which have been destroyed.

Of all of Naquib's reconstruction projects, the most symboli-
cally significant is his plan to rebuild the shattered garrison that
has traditionally been the Arghandab district's seat of government.
His men took the position following a bloody two-month siege.
The victory cost three hundred lives and left the garrison a heap of
ruins, but now, instead of the red hammer and sickle, the green
Islamic banner of the mujahedin flies from the ramparts.

The fortress sits imposingly halfway up Khybara's flanks, above
the villages and across the river from Naquib's position at
Charqulaba. For nearly a decade the government forces lobbed
howitzer and tank shells onto them from here. Seen from the van-
tage point of the fortress, the effects are devastatingly obvious.
Everything on *that* side of the river is pulped, the mud homes burst
apart, the land itself punched and abused, while on *this* side, where
the villages are tucked under the belly of the hills, virtually everything is intact.

From Naquib's viewpoint, the fortress is an ideal place from
which to exercise vigilance in the new, Islamic republic he wants to
help establish. Apart from its strategic position, it is spiritually
endowed. Next to the fortress, a small mosque marks the gravesite
of Baba Wali, a nineteenth-century holy man. Having swept away
the debris of fighting from a small garden area around the tomb,
the site's two caretakers are the hill's sole inhabitants now. Passive,
barefoot men, they spend their days making tea in a corner of the
courtyard and feeding the white doves that perch on their backs as
they sweep the ground with switches made of twigs.

He may possess a holy site, but Mullah Naquib knows there is little achievement in establishing an Islamic system of local government if there are no people to govern, and this is the case in Arghandab. Like Khalilullah's and Abdul Hakim's families, most of the valley's residents have long since fled to Pakistan. They need to come home before Arghandab regains a semblance of normality. To woo them, Mullah Naquib is counting on the support of foreign donors for his reconstruction schemes.

There are scores of Western and Arab agencies running Afghan relief operations out of Pakistan. Most are privately funded groups with humanitarian charters, but some have political agendas to fulfill as well, and enjoy government funding. For the mujahedin, these agencies amount to a supplementary pipeline for nonmilitary aid. For instance, Khalilullah's medical training was sponsored by Union Aid, a West German relief agency; the Swedish Committee for Medical Aid to Afghanistan, meanwhile, provides his clinic with medicines and a regular cash stipend.

Naquib does a fair bit of lobbying on visits to Pakistan, and it has paid off. In recognition of his status as Arghandab's de facto ruler, the foreign agencies are backing him on some of his nonlethal projects. As the channel for United Nations-sponsored agricultural-revitalization programs in Arghandab, the Swedish group has entrusted Naquib with wheat seed and cash to get replanting under way, and two thousand bags of wheat for distribution as food aid among the area's civilians.

Naquib has also begged for an ambulance from a British agency that runs an ambulance service in other parts of the country. At the moment, seriously wounded men have to be loaded into the back of a pickup and driven all the way to Pakistan for treatment. As a result, many bleed to death en route. Having an ambulance would help solve this problem, says Naquib with the flat conviction of someone who believes the vehicles are wondrous things, virtual hospitals on wheels.

As with their faith in God, the mujahedin's belief in the magical properties of the modern world's technology is as unwavering as it is boundless. It shouldn't surprise; prior to the Soviet invasion, when it was rudely awakened from its age-old Central Asian slumber, Afghanistan was one of the world's most isolated and undeveloped countries. Now, men who entered the war as goatherds sit behind the wheels of zippy Toyota pickups. Men who had no concept of man-powered flight now operate heatseeking anti-aircraft Stinger missiles and shoot down jets.

The CIA began supplying Stingers to the mujahedin in the mid-1980s. The weapons helped shift the balance of the war, as previously omnipotent Soviet MiGs and helicopters were blown to smithereens in midair. The mujahedin soon fell under the illusion that the weapons were a cure-all. This state of faith paradoxically boosted their morale while stunting their initiative elsewhere on the battlefield. The mujahedin seem to believe that by merely wielding these space-age weapons, they can overcome their own intrinsic deficiencies. It is as if, like the Melanesian cargo cultists who began venerating American pilots and their crates of K-rations during World War II, and who still await the heaven-sent goods today, the Afghans are looking to the skies for bounty, their lips seeming to move in hopeful incantation.

Mullah Naquib is the proud owner of three Stinger missiles. But he isn't going to be shooting them off any time soon, despite the daily aerial bombardments. Holding onto them is a deterrent to the enemy: Bombers no longer fly low over Arghandab, and any coming within range send off a constant stream of magnesium flares to foil the missiles. Perhaps more important, the Stingers are an important status symbol. In Kandahar, you haven't really 'arrived' as a mujahedin commander unless you possess a Stinger or two.

The Stingers have caused a rivalry between Naquib and another

Jamiat commander in Kandahar, Hajji Abdul Hadi. Hajji doesn't have any and he is jealous. One evening, at his own base near the Mahalajat front line, with several of Naquib's top aides as his captive audience, Hajji seizes the occasion to make his feelings known. He spends the entire evening complaining. 'Mullah Naquib has three,' he whines petulantly. 'Why can't I have one? Aren't I a good commander?'

Ironically, by now the entire Stinger issue is a moot point. Far from handing out any more of the sophisticated weapons, the CIA is busily trying to retrieve them, even offering to buy them back. The agency is reportedly worried that unscrupulous mujahedin might sell the missiles on the international arms market, where they will end up in the hands of Middle Eastern terrorist groups. Naquib expresses his disgust at the CIA's capriciousness. They trusted him enough to give him Stingers in the first place, didn't they? So why do they want them back now? Anyway, he says, the missiles are his now, and he is keeping them.

The more canny mujahedin commanders have always understood that one day, when the Soviets have left, the munificence flowing from the West's pipeline will begin drying up. While supplies last, therefore, it is imperative to acquire and stockpile as much matériel as possible. Whoever is best prepared stands the best chance of surviving an uncertain future, and, with skill and luck emerging even better off, as a traditional Afghan strongman complete with army, wealth, and power. For many, one way of achieving those aims is through the foreign-aid pipeline. But by coincidence, Afghanistan also happens to be one of the world's foremost producers of opium, and a number of mujahedin commanders are involved in the lucrative trade.

Although Kandahar is an opium-rich province, no evidence exists to suggest Mullah Naquib's involvement. At any rate, his role as a mullah, and a sincere Muslim at that, makes the proposition seem fairly unlikely. The Islamic code he adheres to upholds strict sanctions regarding drugs.

In Nangarhar, the Afghan province adjacent to Peshawar through the Khyber Pass, opium is as common as wheat. In fact, the two crops often grow side by side; the opium is planted in neat, rectangular patches amid the spreading wheat fields. The drug is smuggled out through the autonomous Tribal Areas lying along Pakistan's border with Afghanistan. These restive badlands are traditionally ruled by the tribes' own armies, and to keep the peace Pakistan's army stays out. If it attempted to put an end to the narcotics operations, the tribal armies could seal the vital routes in and out of Afghanistan, preventing the mujahedin and their supplies from getting through. For this reason, an implicit détente has existed between the drug lords and the Pakistani and American governments for the duration of the war. The effect of this has been a flourishing opium crop.

Several opium barons live ostentatiously in castlelike fortresses they have built at the roadside in the Khyber Pass. In the towns of Darra and Barra, renowned for making firearms, shops openly display hashish and opium for sale next to pistols and machine guns, while heroin-processing labs operate on the very outskirts of Peshawar.

During the mujahedin's assault on the city of Jalalabad after the Soviet withdrawal, much of the opium nearest to the besieged city has remained unharvested. Close to the city, where the mujahedin have dug their battle lines, the face of the land is blackening. The opium plants are dying, burning up in the sun of summer and the brushfires caused by exploding bombs and rockets. The tall stalks withering, the round spores with their narcotic juices left unscored, Jalalabad's opium is wasting away.

One morning near Jalalabad's airport, as the path he takes cuts through a patch of opium, a Hizb-i-Islami mujahedin officer named Qari is obviously discomfited. Observing the rows of poppy plants all around him as if seeing them for the first time, he points to the plants' browning stalks to show they have not been harvested by the mujahedin. If the neglected harvest isn't evidence enough that the mujahedin have nothing to do with opium, Qari goes on to blame Afghanistan's 'Communist regime' for propagating it. Once the mujahedin win the war and make an Islamic republic of Afghanistan, he says, all opium-growing will cease. 'We will forbid it, as it is forbidden by the Holy Koran.'

Some days later, Mullah Naquib shows up in Peshawar, accompanied by Khalilullah. He stays overnight at a second-rate hotel near the bazaar. Even here, Naquib is a big man. Seated on the floor of his hotel room, he fills it with his presence. Khalilullah and Naquib are on their way to ISI headquarters, to ask for more weapons. It seems that the Pakistanis have laid down the ground rules, and they intend them to be humbling. By forcing Naquib to come to Pakistan for aid, the ISI sends a message: 'You might be a big man in Arghandab, but here, where it counts, you are just another Afghan, begging for help.'

At such times, it must be hard for Naquib to be virtuous, and he could hardly be faulted if he were to fantasize about doing as so many others do, about briefly setting aside his Islamic principles – just long enough to reap some profit from the opium crop – and still being his own man at the end of it.

Balancing on the seesaw between independence of and dependence upon one's patrons is an experience shared by guerrillas everywhere. But, in Afghanistan, the superpowers raised the level of destruction and bloodshed to new and horrific dimensions by introducing Scud and Stinger missiles and MiG fighterbombers to what might have been a local affair settled by rifles shot off in the hills. During the period of Soviet involvement alone, five million Afghans were driven from their homes as refugees, another million were killed, and thirty thousand Soviet soldiers lost their lives.

As their sponsors abandon them, the Afghans may eventually sort things out between themselves, using their traditional bazaar politics, haggling and horse-trading, rather than heading for the battlefield. But they have been emboldened by their access to huge quantities of modern weaponry and the potential power it can bring; war will probably continue to be their form of political discourse for a long time to come.

In Western Sahara and El Salvador, where the guerrillas have had strong ideological aspirations and forged international ties for philosophical as well as pragmatic reasons, the changing geopolitical landscape poses common challenges. Both groups face futures in which compromises will have to be made in exchange for peace and a measure of freedom. The alternative is to remain as they are today, insurgent, true to their beliefs but kept from power, suspended forever in a state of idealistic opposition. In Kawthoolei, where the people fighting have traditionally enjoyed a measure of economic independence, the integrity of the struggle hangs in the balance as the Karen face a future in which they may be sustained not by teak but by opium or foreign aid. In Gaza, the Palestinians have forged an identity so strong they have found strength in their own condition of dependency, in seeking to undermine their enemy even as they work for him.

In the end, the lesson seems to be that when guerrillas are dependent on outsiders, they can eventually be forced to compromise. But if guerrillas can find something to sustain them — whether opium, teak, or a job with the enemy — in the land on which they fight, they can survive indefinitely. Irrespective of changing political realities, even without the original justification for their struggles, they can endure, and their wars become a way of life.

FOUR

Making War

Late one night in Chalatenango, when all the *compas* are asleep in their makeshift shelters, the army breaches the darkness with long-range weapons. Like the hand of God reaching over the mountains in an act of terrifying malevolence, three rockets scream in out of the blackness, tearing into sleep.

In the few cold seconds before they hit, the night is filled with the roar of the missiles coming in, louder and louder before exploding. The first is very close, the second, mercifully, a little farther away, and the last one a long way off. Some excited, some nervous, the *compas* emerge from their *champas* and take cover while the barrage lasts. After the third mortar, they decide the enemy is only 'probing,' and they go back to sleep. It is just a kind of hostile guessing game, one they have grown accustomed to.

At dawn the next day the *compas* arise as usual. There is little talk about the mortar attack, except at breakfast, when someone observes wryly that the first round almost hit the camp's latrine. Then, the topic is dropped as the guerrillas turn to the tasks that await them and a new day at war in El Salvador begins.

*

To make war one must confront death, and it is the routine prospect of killing and dying that makes a guerrilla's life different from other people's. In war, human life becomes expendable, and respect for it is made contingent on many factors: the war's objectives, the enemy's behavior, the physical condition of the battleground – and, perhaps most important, cultural traditions and beliefs. In the end, the value men place on human life determines how wars are waged.

'You learn to live with death, you become intimate with it,' says Augustín, who works with Haroldo on Radio Farabundo Martí. 'But the fear never goes away. If anything, you feel a stronger love for life. But, above everything else, there is a decision to surrender it at any moment for the cause.'

The collective ethos of self-sacrifice places each fighter upon the altar of revolutionary consummation, like a blood offering to the gods of war. The feeling Augustín describes is called *mística*, 'mystique' – but *mística* means much more. It is the fusion of ideological belief, camaraderie, and emotion that impels the guerrillas to continue fighting; it is the core ingredient in the revolutionary alchemy. In a poem called 'Wounds,' Haroldo puts this feeling into words.

In the worst year of the war
and in the best of the battle,
the combatant,
holding his open wrist
before his eyes, exclaims:
'My hand, I've lost it.'

But looking around him
where the warm blood

of his brothers
cries out,
he shakes himself and says:
'It doesn't matter, I'm still alive'
– and takes another step forward.

Haroldo belongs to a long line of Latin American intellectuals who have felt obliged by conscience to adopt a revolutionary cause. Tracing his earliest political involvement to a secondary-school literary group, he likes to quip that it was poetry that brought him into the revolution. His political awareness grew when he went to college.

By this time, the mid-1970s, social ferment was well under way in El Salvador, and the universities were hotbeds of dissent against the despised military dictatorship. Students, trade unionists, and church activists began demanding political reform, to which the military and right-wing oligarchy reacted by becoming more repressive.

Along with a few other young poets and writers, Haroldo formed a literary group, which met weekly in his house. After a time, they realized they were being spied upon by the police. Terrified, the group disbanded, its members drifting apart. It seemed that words had become dangerous in El Salvador.

The incident made Haroldo decide to become more involved in the burgeoning social struggle. He volunteered his time, typing manifestos and writing editorials for striking workers. Then, two people he knew and admired were killed in shootouts with the National Guard. One was an economics student, the other a poet. Suddenly they were revealed as members of a hitherto unknown guerrilla underground.

Their deaths made Haroldo think. Here were people who had defended their ideals at the cost of their own lives. Gradually,

Haroldo's own commitment to radical social change deepened, until a time came when he realized he too was willing to give his life for the cause.

Further inspiration came from Roque Dalton, El Salvador's great dissident poet and a longtime exile from his country. He was one of Haroldo's heroes. Dalton had written a poem supporting the armed struggle, and reading it made Haroldo realize that he also had the option of taking up a gun for his beliefs. For the time being, though, he saw his duty as a poet in 'lighting the flame of the struggle, to show the people the way forward.' Since those days, Haroldo has learned that in a revolution, there isn't always time for poetry. 'The organization I belong to wasn't exactly founded for cultural purposes,' he says, mocking himself.

Haroldo's final step into the hills came after he made a propaganda film about the revolutionary movement that was edited and shown abroad. Out of this project came the idea for the guerrillas to set up their own radio, to broadcast their ideas. It was arranged, but the man who was going to run it was captured, so Haroldo was asked to go to Chalatenango, where the FPL was establishing a stronghold, to replace him. Haroldo realized that this was his moment of truth. If he was to be a serious revolutionary, refusing was out of the question. He went, but he recalls weeping out of fear beforehand.

The first days were awful. He felt alienated and displaced. Also, the conditions endured by the guerrillas were nightmarish in those days, and Haroldo admits he came close to deserting twice. In the end, it was the comradeship of his fellows that stopped him. Realizing that everyone was in the same situation as he was gave him the strength to go on.

More than ten years later, he has hardened. Like his friend Augustín, he still fears death, but now his fear is dominated by reflexes conditioned in a decade of war. And Haroldo has long since reconciled himself to the necessity of killing others. He has had to. In the end, he says, 'it's either you or them.'

An old Central American adage is that there are two ways to win a war – 'por las buenas, o las males,' by good means or bad. Never forgetting that their victory depends on winning people over, not on capturing territory, the *compas* have tried to be the war's good guys. In contrast to the armed forces, the FMLN has shown clemency to its uniformed enemies captured on the battle-field, routinely releasing rank-and-file soldiers, while holding onto officers for prisoner exchanges.

Even so, the guiding principle behind the FMLN's conduct has been one of calculated pragmatism. When its political hegemony is threatened, the organization can be extremely ruthless, killing suspected informers, enforcing nationwide transport bans by blow-ing up transgressors' vehicles, dynamiting electrical pylons as part of its economic 'war of attrition.' And, in the mid-1980s, when the government sought to expand its influence by encouraging civilian candidates to run for political office in municipal elections, the FMLN responded by attacking town halls, abducting and some-times killing prospective and newly installed mayors.

As controversial as this campaign was, it achieved its desired objectives. Having wiped out the last vestiges of government rule, the guerrillas stood unchallenged by any competing political groups in many contested areas. Instead, sympathetic 'citizens' committees' were set up as fronts for the FMLN. Exploiting their unarmed civilian status and the government's belated desire to achieve international acceptance as a 'democracy,' these committees began operating more openly. Soon they took to the cities to demonstrate for the return of refugees from camps in Honduras and elsewhere.

The government eventually acceded, and thousands of refugees came back to the country, resettling in rural areas under guerrilla control. This was a major coup for the revolutionaries, for by allowing the repopulation to take place, the government was in effect conceding the existence of an FMLN civilian constituency. It also bolstered FMLN claims to being the de facto authority in one-third of the country, in its *zonas de control*, 'control zones.' After years of efforts to depopulate the countryside through its own scorched-earth tactics, this was a real setback to the armed forces.

In the *zonas*, the war continues, but the army has given up trying to maintain a fixed presence in the form of garrisons or 'civil defense' militias, nor does it mount civic action programs to win over the people. Army leaders know these are pointless. The *zonas* are the revolution's heartland, where the FMLN exercises complete political authority, and no traces of governmental authority – whether in the form of mayors, or teachers, or health workers – are tolerated. Instead, as in Las Flores, parallel systems are in place to take care of everyday needs. Here, the authoritarian policies the FMLN uses to gain ground elsewhere seem very far away. Everyone living here wants to be here. But beyond the control zones things are messier, for there the battle over the civilian inhabitants continues.

About an hour's fast walk through the hills from Giovanni's camp lies the old fishnet- and hammock-making village of Las Vueltas, the *compas'* base of operations for the area. This village is about the same size as Las Flores, but narrower, slung beside a fast creek in a deep hollow. And it has no plaza, only a wide spot where two cobbled lanes converge in front of a big white church. Its National Guard post was overrun long ago, and all that remains of a government presence is some old graffiti.

Above Las Vueltas looms a denuded mountain called La Montañona, the Big Mountain, whose flanks are so high and steep that Las Vueltas lies in shadow for much of the day. On the other side of La Montañona, the control zone ends and the so-called *zona de expansión*, 'expansion zone,' begins.

From Las Vueltas a red laterite track too rough for anything but the peasants' wooden-wheeled ox carts and their tick-infested nags winds around La Montañona's base. The track, which everyone calls the Royal Road, leads to a string of rocky hamlets – El Copinol, Ojo de Agua, El Sítio, El Zapotal – where several hundred Chalateco peasant families with red hair and white skin tend pigs and grow corn in grinding poverty. Here in the expansion zone, the *compas* don't feel secure enough to oper-ate as openly as they do in Las Vueltas or Las Flores. The police posts and army garrisons have all been overrun and the mayors chased out, but because the people have lived for years under army authority, or at least not under the FMLN's, their loyalties are still in question.

Winning over these *campesinos* is the joint responsibility of Ulíses and Diego. Ulíses, a Chalateco, is a cold, handsome man with a cowboy hat and a revolver. He walks with an athlete's nat-ural swagger and, as a former Catholic lay preacher, he has a gift with words. Diego is a Uruguayan *internacionalista* in his mid-thir-ties, a committed Marxist-Leninist who brags of 'throwing my first Molotov' at the age of fifteen. He joined the Tupamaro guerrillas and was active until, one step ahead of the security police, he fled to Argentina. When the Argentine military seized power and began its own dirty war against suspected leftists there, he sought political asylum in Sweden.

In Stockholm, Diego learned Swedish, completed a university degree, and began working for the FMLN's solidarity office. But, dissatisfied with this limited role, he volunteered to come to El Salvador. Assuming he would stay for a year, he left his wife and two children behind. Somehow, though, seven years have gone by. Increasingly, his wife's letters are irate. 'She tells me the world has changed while I have been away,' says Diego. 'She asks, "Why am I still fighting for a lost cause in El Salvador?"'

Diego isn't in a hurry to get home, however. He has taken on the Salvadoran revolutionary cause with all the fervor of a religious convert. He has an important position as an FPL political officer in Chalatenango, and tells himself that he can't leave for merely personal reasons. His life is not his own any longer, but belongs to 'the Revolution.'

Still, Diego seems an incongruous sort of guerrilla. It isn't only that he resembles a well-heeled European. With his slim physique, delicate manners, and carefully trimmed blond hair, he seems more like a café revolutionary than a real one. And, despite his AK-47 and his rhetoric about workers and peasants, Diego has some distinctly bourgeois affectations: He smokes imported Dunhill cigarettes and wears expensive polo shirts, the kind worn by tennis pros.

As different as they seem from each other, Ulíses and Diego work as a team. They coordinate their activities with Luis, a dark man who, like Giovanni, wears a moustache and a permanent deadpan expression. Born and raised in Las Vueltas, Luis is a veteran of the battles which ousted the security forces from the area. He is a hard case, the FPL's top man in Las Vueltas.

After three years of organizing work in the expansion zone, these men have assembled a guerrilla platoon that operates permanently in the area. Made up of a dozen adolescent boys and girls and led by two seasoned fighters, Carmelo and Geronimo, the squad roves constantly from community to community along the Royal Road. Its mission is to get the people accustomed to the *compas* and their ideas, and eventually, to win them over.

Ulíses and Diego are constantly roving themselves, but they move independently of the kids' unit. Every few days, they meet up. They spend much of their time gathering intelligence, adding to an already impressive dossier on the local civilians. They use this information to pressure the civilians to collaborate with them – to join their underground militia network, to pass on information about the enemy.

One hot midday in El Zapotal, Diego stops in a small shop for a bottle of warm soda. As he gulps it down, he calls out to the owner, a dour middle-aged man, that he has heard a story about him. The shopkeeper, looking wary, asks what the story is. Diego says it has to do with an incident some years ago, in which the proprietor stood up to some abusive National Guardsmen. The man shrugs and looks uncomfortable. 'So, you are on our side after all,' says Diego, smiling at the man's discomfort. 'Why have you been hiding this side of yourself from us?' He looks at the shopkeeper with arched eyebrows as if waiting for a reply. The shopkeeper grunts ambiguously, and looks away. Diego lets the matter rest there.

As he leaves the shop a moment later, Diego looks pleased. Finally he has put the shopkeeper on the spot. Until now, the man has been unswervingly aloof, and Diego wants to pin down his true sympathies. The man must now show that he is either for the guerrillas, or against them. If the story is true, he must say so. By doing so, he will make himself vulnerable to pressure from Diego to become a collaborator. But if he continues to waffle, this will be taken as a sign that his political sympathies lie elsewhere. If so, he will have to leave the zone, for no one with strong government sympathies can be allowed to remain here.

A few hours later, as Diego is walking on the road between El Zapotal and the next village, a peasant man approaches. He tells Diego he is looking for his son, a *compa*. He has heard the boy has been wounded. Diego asks the peasant for his son's name. The man tells him, and at once Diego informs him the report is true, but that his son is all right – he has merely blown off one of his fingers. Looking relieved, the peasant asks Diego to step aside for a moment, out of earshot. They stand together for a few minutes, the peasant whispering intently, Diego listening and nodding. The peasant is a civilian collaborator, giving information about what is happening in the villages that lie ahead. At length, the men part, each thanking the other, and go their separate ways.

Luis says he thinks of the expansion zone as an area full of red and white houses. The neutral or progovernment ones are white; the red ones are the guerrillas'. 'If you blur your eyes, they would all appear pink.' Gradually, the FMLN is winning the zone over.

Beyond the expansion zone lies the *zona en disputa*, the 'disputed zone.' Where the two zones meet, both sides run patrols to surveil and ambush one another, as if along a front line. In disputed zones, the army still maintains a fixed presence, and government offices remain open, but the guerrillas also claim the loyalty of some of the inhabitants. The FMLN considers these areas to have a 'duality of powers' and seeks to tip the balance of power in its favor by forcing out the military or civil-defense posts. Once these are eradicated, the area becomes an expansion zone. The task requires a combination of military action and clandestine political agitation.

Diego runs a secret letter-writing campaign aimed at demoralizing soldiers serving in the nearby disputed zone. Most of his targets are local youths conscripted from hamlets in the expansion zone. First, Diego gains the confidence of their families, learning as much as he can about them. Then he writes the soldiers personal letters, showing them he knows and is sympathetic to their problems and concerns. He urges them to ponder whether or not these problems are helped by serving in the armed forces. In the end, he hopes to get them to defect, or at least to seed enough doubt in their minds to render them ineffective as enemies.

This is painstakingly slow work and can take years to earn dividends, but it is essential to the revolution and, for Diego, very rewarding personally. Combat is absolutely necessary, but this political work, where the guerrillas conquer the hearts and minds of the people, is the war's real battleground.

In Afghanistan there are no fixed rules of war. Usually, the muja-hedin spare the lives of conscripts who surrender voluntarily, but suspected traitors or enemy soldiers who have been forcibly cap-tured in battle are often executed as security risks. Mullah Naquib himself claims to have shot thirty such men. There are some good reasons for this ferocity: In a country where one out of every fifteen people has died in the war, most of the mujahedin have lost close relatives; even more have had homes and livelihoods destroyed.

Naquib raises the subject himself one night as a gun battle takes place high up on the Khybara massif. A fat, yellow January moon rises in the night sky, and red tracer bullets flash and flicker like lethal fireflies against the massif's dark silhouette. After a long moment watching this, seemingly lost in his own reflections, Mullah Naquib says suddenly, 'Do you know what we do with all communists?'

Pausing for dramatic emphasis, he pulls a revolver from his vest – the captured Russian revolver he always carries – and, rest-ing its blunt muzzle easily against his right temple, aims it at his brain. Beaming wildly, he whispers, 'This. This is what we do. We kill them all.'

The yellow moon bursts free of Khybara and, like a luminous Chinese lantern, ascends into the black night sky. The gun gleams silvery against Naquib's head. After a few seconds, Naquib breaks the spell, laughing deeply, and returns the weapon to his clothes.

Just as they can be harsh in deciding the fate of other people's lives, the Afghans can also be stoic when it comes to their own. This stoicism comes out of their culture, in which war enjoys an exalted status, and from their faith in the Islamic idea that after death, a better life awaits. If they are to die, so be it, as long as they do well in battle and the eyes of God. They are mujahedin, holy warriors. They live to make holy war, to kill the enemy, and if necessary be martyred themselves. These are facts they accept. Most of them would have it no other way.

On the battlefield, the effect of this willingness to die is a carelessness in the way the war is fought. As demonstrated by Ghulam and his SPG-9, the mujahedin casually shoot off rockets toward cities full of civilians, and seem unconcerned about the deaths they cause. When fighter-bombers appear overhead, instead of taking cover the mujahedin climb onto rooftops to watch them as they might watch a passing flock of migratory birds. And, having taken an exposed position at the front, the fighters pray for God's protection rather than retreat to less tenuous ground. It is almost as though, until the bombs drop and the bullets strike a living target, they exist merely as abstractions. As for the objectives of their 'jihad,' it often appears that for many mujahedin the point seems to be simply to fight, rather than necessarily to achieve anything by doing so.

This abstracted approach to warfare has shown up in the mujahedin's actions following the Soviet withdrawal from Afghanistan. Contrary to predictions, the Afghan regime did not fall upon the Soviets' departure, nor have the mujahedin been able to take a city. Shifting their focus away from Kandahar, which remains in government hands, the guerrillas have launched a frontal assault on Jalalabad instead. But after advancing to the city's outskirts at the cost of hundreds of lives, they have faltered, bogging down around the government-held airfield.

Halfway between the mujahedin's forward lines and the frontier with Pakistan, the Samarkhel Experimental Farm lies where the road loops down from the gloomy brown-and-gray hills of the Khyber Pass into the hot, flat Jalalabad valley. From Samarkhel, the road runs straight on for several miles to Jalalabad's airport. In the distance, the city sprawls green and beckoning across both banks of the meandering Kabul River. Until recently, the farm's residential complex housed Soviet advisors and their families, but the Soviets are gone now, and so are the Afghan soldiers who stayed behind to defend the installations Instead, it is the mujahedin who are camped out amid the farm's ruins.

Samarkhel's pine trees are scarred by flying shrapnel, and their aromatic branches hang singed and unmoving in the dry heat. Dust raised by the traffic of war coats everything. Mujahedin lie dozing on string charpoys they have dragged out of the buildings into the cooler air of the untended gardens. Some buildings have been reduced to rubble; others have huge holes punched in them, their bricks and dried mortar spilling out in untidy heaps. The doors and windows have all been wrenched out. Inside, in the stairwells, there is a waft of death where bloodstains have been left to congeal. Despite everything, the grounds are dotted with bushes full of pink roses in full bloom.

Surrounded by wrecked masonry and reeking piles of garbage, several fighters make depth charges out of captured Soviet antipersonnel mines. They are going to go throw the depth charges in the river and see how many fish they can 'catch.' As they dismantle the mines, flies cluster unceasingly around their ears, eyes, and noses. Droning overhead, a Soviet Antonov warplane looks for bombing targets. But the fighters ignore everything as they think of the fish they are going to kill.

This morning, some newly arrived defectors are being questioned. Their leader, Esmanay, is a rugged twenty-year-old with a strong face. A brickmaker from Paktia province, he lived peacefully at home until the government army caught him and forced him to become a soldier. Eight weeks ago, he was sent to help defend Jalalabad. Last night, he and five comrades at a post near the airport seized their chance. Risking fire from both armies, they sneaked across the no-man's-land between the front lines and gave themselves up. 'Everyone wants to escape,' he says, motioning with his head toward Jalalabad. 'Even the officers.'

Esmanay and his companions are being 'researched' by mujahedin interrogators to determine whether they are genuine deserters or enemy infiltrators. Esmanay, especially, is under close scrutiny, the mujahedin eyeing him with open suspicion, listening carefully to each word he says. If Esmanay fears for his life he is careful not to show it. But he has good reason to fear. A few weeks ago, the same mujahedin faction executed a large number of government soldiers who had already surrendered. But that has been acknowledged as a 'regrettable mistake' by mujahedin leaders, so Esmanay can probably count on surviving so long as they believe his story.

All Esmanay wants is to return to his home in Paktia province. But for that, he will have to wait: Even if he passes muster, say the mujahedin, he is going to serve them as a cook. Later, if everything works out, he can go free.

Down the road, the war continues. Destroyed enemy tanks and armored personnel carriers list at the roadside. Most of the bridges have been hit, but the mujahedin simply bypass them, driving through the dry riverbeds. Where they are still intact, the bridges offer shelter to the mujahedin, who camp underneath them. All along the straight stretch of road leading up to the front, the mujahedin have their own command and supply posts, field clinics, and bivouacks. Jeeps and trucks ferrying guerrillas race up and down the road. Here and there, just off the road in small cleared patches amid the thickets, small groups of bearded men manning mobile mortars and rocket batteries hammer away at the enemy.

In one place, several mujahedin repeatedly load and fire off a BM-13 rocket launcher from behind a small knoll. The rockets take off with a blast that hurts the ears and raises a cloud of dust.

A mound of used-up boxes of rockets and shell casings grows steadily higher around the fighters, who look punch-drunk from all the noise.

There has been a lot of aerial bombing this morning, and fire has been incoming all day. On his walkie-talkie the emplacement commander keeps in contact with forward units; they are helping him direct his rockets toward some enemy tanks about eight hundred yards away. Not wanting to give away their position, the guerrillas stagger their rocketing, but even so the enemy sends some rounds back. When they come, everyone ducks below the knoll, diving into the waist-deep trench dug into its base. The incoming missiles strike the bushy ground nearby; each impact is followed by plumes of black smoke.

More rockets are fired off, and moments later, the leader gets walkie-talkie confirmation of a hit. Two of the rockets have struck a tank, he announces. The men smile, but the news doesn't ease their tension much. They sit in the trench, their eyes wide and ears perked to the sound of incoming fire, and one of them kneels in the long grass nearby, praying in the direction of Jalalabad.

In a deserted village overlooking the airstrip, there is a fortress with high mud walls, inhabited by a group of mujahedin boys. From here, the mujahedin can go no farther. Advancing is suicidal because the land is bare all the way to the runway, and sown with antipersonnel mines. As the last building between the two sides, the fortress is completely exposed to enemy fire.

The boys creep outside to a hiding place under a few scraggly pines, where they have a small mortar. Inexpertly, they fire it in the direction of the government tanks guarding the runway, then scramble back inside the fort. Their rocket's only visible effect is to attract the enemy's attention: Within minutes, to the mingled excitement and horror of the boys, one of the tanks fires back. Its first two shells screech over the parapets, but the third knocks a chunk off the outer wall, sending a shudder through the building and the boys inside.

Soon afterward, MiG fighter-bombers, perhaps called in by the tanks, fly directly overhead and begin dropping bombs. Everyone runs to stand against walls, to hug the far corners of the fortress. One boy throws himself into a latrine. Wherever he is caught, each person braces himself against the whistling suction of the falling bombs; the air is suddenly still and seems full of static, as before an electrical storm. Next, the great whooshing, the bombs erupting in bursts of red fire and black smoke; the sonic waves hurting the ears, the eyes, the brain, throwing the body up and down in a violent tremor. Dust everywhere. Then, almost as quickly, the pressure easing off, the air clearing. The people, white with dust, like statues suddenly come to life, moving around, to see what damage has been done.

After a few moments it is clear that there is only one casualty: a mujahed in his twenties, hit by a piece of shrapnel in his penis. At first, in shock, he walks around looking rueful, wincing good-naturedly at the jibes of his comrades. Then the wound starts to hurt; by the time they get him to the field clinic a few miles away, he has begun to scream.

On the other side of the airport, mujahedin sit hunkered down in dugouts on either side of the road, where an intact bridge spans a dry riverbed. Here some volunteer mujahedin from Arab countries have installed themselves. These fighters have a murderous hatred of non-Muslim Westerners, whom they consider *kafir*, or 'unbelievers,' and sometimes try to shoot. They stare with open hostility at the passing vehicle, but don't attack, apparently deterred by its mujahedin escort.

From their positions, the government's forces have a clear view of this section of road, so when mujahedin come this far forward, they simply commend themselves to God and drive at breakneck speed, gears crunching as they veer wildly around the craters in the road. Beyond the bridge, the road is clear for only a few hundred feet, because after that there are mines, and because around the next bend lies the government-held airport. A dirt track leads off to the right and through a small, tattered wood to a house. Except for the remaining foliage, the house is the only shield left between the two sides.

Here the mujahedin stay on the side of the house facing away from enemy fire. Overhead, bullets crack and whistle. Pieces of fresh green leaves cut by the bullets litter the ground. When the guerrillas venture out from behind the house, they first hold out their cupped hands to Allah in silent prayer.

The only way forward is on foot, and the fighters advance spread out in single file, loaded down with weapons and preceded by men with walkie-talkies. In the open, they move as quickly as possible, and wherever there is tree cover the men with the radios make everyone halt while they check to see what is happening up ahead. Clean gouges of earth in the brown dirt along the path show that the enemy knows where to aim.

After about a kilometer, the trail leads into a small, mudwalled village. From here the enemy's tanks are visible on the airstrip about three hundred yards away. This is the mujahedin's forward line. The guerrillas here are much younger than those farther back from the front – they're barely teenagers, and they seem heedless of the dangers they face. Fresh from Peshawar's refugee camps, they are buzzing with adrenaline from the noise and activity of war all around them.

A group of them sits in what once was the family room of a farmhouse; there is a gaping hole in one of the walls where a mortar shell has struck. A flurry of machine-gun bullets spits into the courtyard only feet away, and the roomful of boys giggles. They talk about how brave they are, about mujahedin victories past and future. They challenge one another to set out on foot and attack the tanks. When, like a giant's coughing spell, the enemy's shelling starts up again, coming closer in a series of hacking roars, the boys just laugh some more. They are young, and to them it is manly to laugh in the face of danger. They laugh because, all around them now, death holds them in a warm embrace.

The next morning, one of the boys is hit in the head by a bullet. As his friends tug at him and speak to him, urging him to revive, he gasps, his eyes roll aimlessly in their sockets, and his skin is suddenly gray. The flies, buzzing aimlessly through the bushes, now come to him and begin to cluster thickly around his face.

When a mujahed dies, his body joins those of countless others in the burgeoning martyrs' cemeteries, each with its tattered flag and clumps of stone. In the memories of his comrades and family, he will be honored as a brave mujahed, a holy warrior. They will not pity him, because he has achieved martyrdom and is now in the paradise that awaits them all. They have lost a friend, a brother, but they have gained strength and pride in the struggle, for now they have a death to vindicate. In a holy war, death becomes a combustive element, a means to an end in itself.

The *shabbab* of Gaza also believe that their violence is spiritually sanctioned, beyond reproach. Here too, the enemy is an alien occupier, non-Muslim. In the passionate battle for Palestine, this conviction is an essential ingredient, for here, unlike in Afghanistan, there is no distance between the enemies, everything takes place at close quarters.

Without recourse to arms, the Palestinians instead summon up a collective fury so intense it becomes a weapon in itself. It wells forth, producing a spontaneous violence in which so many people take part that afterward no one individual can be held responsible. Like, for instance, the killing of Amnon Pomerantz.

Amnon Pomerantz's final moments must have been especially horrific ones. The Israeli army reservist came into Breij by mistake, intending to drive into the Israeli military camp situated just outside it. Instead, he found himself driving down one of Breij's main streets. The more he drove, the more lost he became. The residents noticed him and began calling out and moving toward the car; he panicked. Wheeling the car around, he knocked down a cart carrying two children – and that was it; The crowd was all around him, smashing, screaming, and setting him on fire.

No one knows why he didn't keep driving. Mahmoud thinks that when the crowd surrounded him, the young man was so afraid he became paralyzed. This is what cost him his life. Hisham, the fundamentalist, refuses to call Pomerantz's death murder. Anyway, it isn't an Israeli's death that is at issue for him, but what the Israeli was doing in Breij in the first place. He should not have been here. He was the enemy. Still, says Hisham, the event affected him personally, because on the day Amnon Pomerantz was killed, Hisham was to have been married. Due to the Israelis' drastic reaction, however – scores of people were arrested and abused; the whole camp was placed under a strict military curfew for days – his marriage ceremony had to be postponed for two weeks.

With their brutal act, the people of Breij paid back the Israelis in kind for all the accumulated abuses suffered at their hands: all the fetuses aborted by the tear gas; all the teenagers killed by gunshots; Iyad, a fifteen-year-old whom the Israelis beat to death; Usama's aging mother, dead from a rap to the head; 'the Sheikh's' baby son, who was stepped on; all of the deaths, imprisonments, house-sealings and demolitions, and the daily petty humiliations. And Pomerantz's killers behaved remorselessly, with an extra touch of cruelty thrown in, as if to disgust their oppressors. The incident has marked Breij, making it a different place. A threshold has been crossed, and no one now doubts that the intifada is a war, even if it has a different name.

The killing has also reshaped Breij in another way. The Israeli army brought in its bulldozers immediately afterward and demolished forty-five homes and shops around the spot where Pomerantz died. The families left homeless, some three hundred and sixty people, have gone to live in the empty rooms of the old TB hospital at the edge of camp. Now, the street where the people of Breij killed Amnon Pomerantz is unnaturally broad – a brief, futile highway in the middle of nowhere.

Indeed, Breij is no longer just a place, and its inhabitants are no longer just people; they are a mosaic of interrelated histories and events, part of the ongoing Palestinian epic. Cause and effect are laid out physically upon the land; the events are held in human memory and they prompt people to further action. Like the rings in the trunk of a fallen tree, Breij's widened streets and crumpled houses have become its historical geography.

This is the heart of Palestine, in these empty spaces that mark murder and reprisal, in the hundreds of little flags of the yearned-for homeland that hang upon Breij's spiderwebbed electrical wires with all the rest of war's paraphernalia: the stones, bullets, and tear-gas canisters, all tangled up together on the black lines like children's windblown kites.

See the dirt road: This is where they killed the Israeli. Here and here – more empty spaces: This is where the people's homes stood before the army tore them down. Here is the spot where Amnon Pomerantz's car finally went no farther, and there, just around the corner, the place where the *shabbab* killed their latest spy. Directly in front is Anis's Islamic bookshop with its throbbing jihad music and fervent adolescent boys. A block away, past the slaughterhouse reeking of blood and animal guts, is Anis's house, where his father studies Islamic history and philosophy and watches his brood of goggle-eyed sons grow into men. And here, one day over lunch, he looks around at them and remarks quietly, 'It is a very dangerous time to have sons. Each one is like a loaded grenade, ready to explode.'

Here is Palestine: It exists in the instant of violence where human imagining bursts its confines, in the bravura of the riots, the beating of chests, the ululations of the women, the treacheries and executions of traitors both real and imagined, in all the tragic horrors, the heroisms, and the fatal mistakes of the people of this place. And, somehow, Palestine rises up above this squalor, because the camp and its people are at once shields, swords, and battlegrounds in the struggle for freedom; and its fate is sometimes beautiful, and sometimes ugly.

Each battlefield imposes its own conditions on the guerrillas. Like the intifada, the Saharawi struggle has had to adapt to its unusual circumstances. But while in Gaza the enemy is up close – just a few feet away – in Western Sahara the enemy is virtually invisible, almost beyond reach. How to fight such an enemy?

For the Polisario, the appearance of war has become nearly as effective as the real thing. Since Hassan's wall has prevented the Polisario's fighters from waging an effective guerrilla war, they have had to content themselves with a kind of military pantomime.

One evening, two days out in the desert from Tindouf, Moulay makes contact with a guerrilla unit that patrols a section of the wall. They arrange a visit to the front line for the next morning. All that remains to be decided is whether or not they will attack the wall; like a movable Potemkin exhibit, they are accustomed to orchestrating displays of their military prowess. This time, the guerrillas decide not to attack, but make up for it with a dramatic show of force.

In a broad wadi, several howitzer-mounted jeeps driven by turbaned fighters burst suddenly out from behind thorn trees. They drive off ahead, bouncing away over the dunes like racing sloops on a roiling ocean. Finally, coming to a hill, the guerrillas leave their jeeps and scramble up to a sniper's position at the summit. Keeping their heads low, they point across the land to the wall. There, they say, is the Moroccan enemy. But the sirocco is blowing, sand flies everywhere, and no figures are visible at all. Before long, the sirocco has obscured even the wall itself; in the end, all that can be seen through the dervish storm of sand is a smoky yellow luminescence where the sun still shines.

Men still die along the wall, nonetheless. Until Morocco agrees to a referendum that will determine the territory's future, the Polisario must show it can still cause damage. So, as the 'Saharan Arab Democratic Republic's' bevy of diplomats tries to open lines of communication with King Hassan, the 'Saharan People's Liberation Army' keeps up its patrols along the wall, occasionally charging across to engage in bouts of brief and furious bloodletting.

These symbolic assaults are the Saharawis' way of keeping the war alive, as if in a bellicose ritual or blood sport. Like a family seeking to retain the semblance of a nobler lineage than present appearances suggest, they talk of an action for months afterward, honoring it and polishing it like an heirloom. Indeed, these battles amount to precious heirlooms, material for the carefully tended oral history of a war that now exists mostly in name. Guerrilla veterans like Moulay are discernibly wistful, speaking as if their best times were behind them, back in the days before the wall made a mockery of things.

In spite of its frustrations, the Polisario has refrained from using terrorism to strike at Morocco beyond the wall. Because it pretends to nationhood, the Polisario affects the sober demeanor seemingly appropriate for a sovereign state: Its fighters aren't called guerrillas, but soldiers — and soldiers, of course, don't commit acts of terrorism. This is war with a sense of honor, fought on the battlefield.

Similarly, the lives of enemy soldiers taken prisoner are spared; the Polisario holds more than three thousand Moroccan officers and soldiers in its desert stockades. The POWs are useful. Like Moulay's war stories, which are told and retold, the prisoners are evidence not only of the guerrillas' military abilities, but also of their respect for human rights. Whenever visitors come to the Polisario's Algerian camps, the organization makes a point of exhibiting some POWs, while emphasizing that many of its own comrades captured by Morocco have simply 'disappeared.'

One afternoon, a group of sixty Moroccan prisoners of war are brought from their detention camps to a stockade where the Polisario has a museum of war booty. Ushered in by armed Saharawi guards, the prisoners file obediently out into the full sunlight of the courtyard. Most of the prisoners are young men, and appear healthy, but they move cautiously and their faces are unsmiling, diffident masks.

Today their questioners are Spaniards, a dozen chainsmoking, vociferous men and women who belong to a Polisario solidarity group from Zaragoza. The Spaniards have spent the last half-hour looking around the compound, and now they are gathered beside the piled-up debris of a downed Moroccan jet, its American manufacturers' markings still visible on a piece of the fuselage. All around the twenty-foot-high walls, garage-size niches hold captured Moroccan tanks, jeeps, and armored personnel carriers. Out in the yard, arranged in patterns of geometrical symmetry, are thousands of machine guns, mines, grenades, rocket launchers, recoilless rifles, howitzers, mortars, assault rifles — even canteens and helmets. The machine guns, assembled on their legs and oiled to prevent rusting, gleam blackly against the yellow desert sand, like deadly spiders about to pounce.

At the disposition of the Spanish visitors, the POWs stand waiting mutely, arms at their sides, like limp marionettes. Finally turning their attention to them, producing tape recorders and notebooks, the Spaniards light into the prisoners with all the glee of spiteful children. One woman begins interrogating a young Moroccan captain. He has been well treated, hasn't he? Yes, he answers politely. What about the Moroccan war against the Saharawi people, can't he now see it is unjust? Smiling uncertainly, the proud officer treads a careful middle ground in his reply. He believes the war is a means for the two peoples to come to an understanding of one another. 'First there will be the war,' he says, 'and then the negotiations.'

Gathering strength, the captain defends his right to have served in the Moroccan army, because he is a professional soldier and was only doing his duty to come and fight in Western Sahara. But by now, his questioner has turned her attention elsewhere. Soon the Spaniards wander away, and the Polisario guards escort the Moroccan prisoners to waiting trucks. The exhibition is over.

Like it or not, the Polisario is bound to its present course: talking, negotiating, and only when things seem to bog down, launching attacks on the wall. Rather like circus trainers getting wild animals to perform tricks by prodding them with sticks, the guerrillas must constantly poke and prod, measuring the distance between themselves and their enemies, always careful to avoid provoking an attack, but keeping them moving at the same time.

The war in Western Sahara may eventually lead to an understanding between the Saharawis and the Moroccans. But in Burma, forty-five years of war has not brought the Karen any closer to their enemies. If anything, the enmity between the sides has increased. Here, no powerful foreign benefactors are urging negotiations and political compromise. Each side believes its survival depends upon military victory. For the Burmans, this means conquering Kawthoolei, while for the Karen, victory would be to hang onto whatever territory they have left, and if possible, to regain what they have already lost.

When the attack on Kawmura finally comes, it is at night. First the Burmese pound the base with mortars; then the screaming soldiers charge across the killing ground.

Major Than Maung was right to be worried. Two days ago the usual afternoon mortar barrage began earlier than normal, and fearing the worst, he closed the base down. He ordered all his men into their trenches and all nonessential personnel to leave immediately. Visitors were herded into canoes and quickly paddled to the other side for their safety. By then, bullets had begun to whiz overhead; within hours the offensive began.

During the last day and a half, the barrage has increased in intensity until Kawmura is under a lightning storm of shellfire. Since the first day, no one has come or gone from the base except Major Soe Soe, who slipped across the river to join his men just hours before the ground assault. Like farmers who read the skies for weather, Soe Soe and Than Maung seem to know just what is going to happen by listening to the rhythm and tempo of the shelling.

Throughout the assault, shock waves from the battle have reverberated in Ban Mae Sot. People continue their lives as usual, but with a weather ear cocked to the explosions. Everyone wonders if the Burmese will try and cross over the Moei into Thailand as they did a few months back, to attack Kawmura from behind. As everyone says, it is the only way Kawmura will ever fall. The local Thai military commander is reputedly a KNU ally, so in spite of any deals cut between his military high command and Rangoon, he might help out Than Maung and his guerrillas.

This morning, the second since the assault began, the shelling is fierce. At the Thai army rangers' base down near the Moei River, the soldiers are jumpy, ducking whenever booms sound close by. Bullets zing into the foliage around them – wild shots coming from the battle across the river. The rangers, taking no chances, are wearing steel helmets and staying inside their sandbagged gun emplacements. Farther back, two men in jogging suits crouch in the weeds at the roadside, watching the battle through binoculars. Despite their civilian garb, they are Thai military officers, who have come to observe what is happening. If things get out of hand, they say, they will call in Thai artillery to shell the Burmese government positions. A few warning shells have already been fired.

The two officers point to the summit of the jungle hill – the Burmese have the high ground on Kawmura – where an occasional red muzzle flash indicates the position of a . 75-millimeter recoil-less rifle. Every few moments, it fires shells down on the Karen base.

More bullets come across, cutting leaves and whining suddenly overhead. It is time to withdraw from the vicinity. A pickup truck comes racing up the hill from the rangers' post, heading in the direction of Ban Mae Sot. It pauses briefly – there's just enough time to leap into it – and carries on. In the back, two Karen crouch beside a prone man. He has been hit by two bullets, one in the side, one in the shoulder. He is in pain, his face is gray, but he is conscious. With each bump of the truck, he gasps. His friends hold him steady and give him a betel nut to chew; that seems to help him. No one says anything.

Later in the day, the Thai military decides to display some force to put a stop to the Burmese offensive. From Ban Mae Sot two spanking-new, rocket-equipped armored personnel carriers head up the road toward the river. The maneuver seems to work. By nightfall, the shelling is sporadic, and finally it ends altogether. The assault is over, and Kawmura has held firm.

In the end, more than thirty Burmese soldiers lie dead in the mud of the killing ground. As usual, none have reached the Karen side. Two Karen have died. One of them, whose name means 'Full Moon Flower,' was a favorite fighter of Major Soe Soe's. Just a few hours before his death, the boy told the major he would sneak into the killing ground to retrieve an officer's pistol for him, as a trophy. Before he could do it, however, an artillery shell killed him.

The boys are going to be buried quietly in the refugee village where their families live, on the road between Ban Mae Sot and the river. Soe Soe says they aren't going to give the boys the customary full-blown martial funeral, because it doesn't seem like the right time to make 'a big spectacle.' More Karen than usual have been dying lately because of the stepped-up Burmese offensive, and sensitivities within the community are running high.

Much more than Kawmura hangs in the balance for the KNU every time the Burmese try and take the place. Kawmura has become an important test of the KNU's ability to hang onto Kawthoolei as a whole, and so it is defended as if the survival of the entire community depended upon it. With such high stakes, battles are fought with real ferocity. No quarter is given, and none is expected. Prisoners aren't taken. Enemy soldiers captured or wounded in battle are pumped for information and then killed.

This practice is officially denied. Ganemy, the prime minister's aide and advisor to the KNU leadership at Manerplaw, points out that a few enemy soldiers have surrendered, married Karen girls, and settled down in Kawthoolei. 'They are allowed to stay with us, kept under gradually decreasing surveillance,' he says. Privately, though, Karen leaders acknowledge that their fighters routinely execute enemy soldiers who fall captive. They say that the circumstances of the war itself have dictated such cruel terms, and cite the difficulties of holding prisoners as their fighters move about the jungle. Ganemy gives an example of what happens.

Three years ago, he led a nighttime raid against a government-held post on the Moei River. During the assault, four enemy soldiers were captured. As dawn broke and Ganemy's column was forced to withdraw, he had to decide the fate of the four prisoners. He concluded that they had to be killed, he says, because they had seen the faces of several local villagers who had helped him and his men. 'If we hadn't killed them, those villagers would have been dead the next day.'

But tribal animosity may have as much to do with determining the conduct of this war as any tactical consideration. The hatred between the Karen and the Burmans is centuries old, stemming from the time when Burman overlords suppressed and enslaved the Karen. To the Karen, Burmans remain the personification of evil, and to judge from the medieval cruelty displayed by the government troops, the feelings are not without justification.

In their war against the KNU, Rangoon's troops habitually raid Karen villages and take away any men and boys they find, using them as slave porters to carry huge loads of food or equipment through the jungle for them. These forced marches may last weeks, during which time the Karen are fed little, beaten, and terrorized. Those caught trying to escape – or who succumb to illness or exhaustion – are often shot. Ganemy himself was once forced to accompany Burmese troops as a porter. With another man, he had to carry a hundred-kilo sack of rice balanced on a bamboo pole. Mercifully, his ordeal lasted only three days, and yet today he still bears scars from it. On one shoulder, he shows a large, scarred ridge of flesh where the pole cut deeply into him.

Given this ongoing history of enmity between the peoples, it isn't surprising that the Karen are ruthless fighters. Their war is aimed at killing their enemy, not at winning him over. They know that the only alternative to fighting is a dismal future either as an occupied people or as refugees. Under these circumstances, the Karen's borrowed motto, 'Give me liberty or give me death,' has acquired a newfound resonance.

But the fact is, the Karen *are* losing the war. Kawmura may have held this year, but plenty of other bases – far bigger and more important ones, at that – have fallen. Kawmura's survival no longer depends only on its defenders' bravery and tenacity, but also on Thai politics. The Thais may have sold out the Karen in favor of Rangoon, but that displacement must appear to be the inevitable result of fighting between the KNU and the Burmese government, not of Thai duplicity. Rangoon's troops can do whatever they like as long as they abstain from crossing the Moei River into Thailand.

However, the border won't be an obstacle for much longer: With its revenues from the sale of Kawthoolei's teak, the Rangoon government can now buy helicopter gunships and fighter-bombers and attack Kawmura from the air. Kawmura's fall, it would seem, is just a matter of time.

Faced with such a grim outlook, the Karen know they must adopt new tactics to hit back at Rangoon. But this has only become possible recently. For years, the biggest obstacle to doing so was the Karen's own isolation. They had lived in the jungle for so long they were no longer capable of penetrating Burma's cities, for the simple reason that they didn't possess the government-issued identity cards necessary to move around undetected by police. But with the influx of students in 1988, the situation changed. Most of the students arrived in Kawthoolei with valid identity cards – and better still, they were unknown to the Burmese government. Karen leaders quickly saw the students' potential utility: They could be trained and reinfiltrated to Burma's cities, to operate as the KNU's urban wing.

This is the intended purpose of Major Robert Zan's 'Supreme

Special Command.' After studying works by Mao Zedong, Vietnam's master strategist General Vo Nguyen Giap, and Che Guevara, as well as *War of the Flea*, Robert Taber's study of guerrilla warfare, he has outlined what he expects of his commandos. 'One job is military,' he says. 'Car bombs and assassinations, things like that. The other job is political: to infiltrate and agitate inside legal political parties, to organize and divide.'

Unfortunately the first few operations haven't gone well. The last student Robert Zan sent in, carrying bombs and a silenced .22-caliber pistol with which to assassinate top government officials, has been apprehended, and is probably being tortured at this very moment. Most likely, says Robert Zan, shrugging, the boy will be executed. He is not indifferent, but he is also a seasoned fighting man, and he knows the consequences for his boys if they are caught carrying out his orders.

Robert Zan is also entertaining the idea of launching some pub-licity-seeking terrorist attacks. He doesn't feel concerned about doing damage to the KNU's reputation, because fighting cleanly for forty years has gained it nothing. 'No one even knows about us,' he says. At the very least, he reasons, such attacks will highlight the Karen's plight and hopefully, bring international pressure to bear on Rangoon, obliging it to negotiate with the KNU. The major is considering several possible targets. For instance, there are three German mining engineers stationed at a government-run wolfram mine down the border. He wonders whether taking them hostage would reap the KNU any rewards. Or hijacking a com-mercial jet belonging to Burma's state airlines. He isn't sure which is the better idea; he is still deciding. In the meantime, he contin-ues training his men.

Robert Zan's terrorist-training camp lies in the Kawthoolei forest on the other side of a small, deep river. It can only be reached by carefully balancing on foot across a bouncy bridge of felled saplings. Two farm buildings on stilts stand surrounded by a small plantation of banana, bamboo, and young teak trees. Here, the members of the 'Supreme Special Command – Promised Land' are training.

One morning his guerrillas put on a special exhibition of their skills. They are dressed in black fatigues and boots and wear burgundy head scarves that make them look like extras in a Hong Kong ninja movie. Robert Zan strides around making them sing and march, present arms and trot in place. This is the first time the group has been seen by an outsider, and he is intent on making the best impression.

The major's twelve-year-old son, Du Du, is the runt of the group. He is not much taller than his assault rifle. During formation he often falls out of step, but he keeps his eyes fixed straight ahead, his little jaw outthrust, mouth set grimly in concentration as he tries desperately to keep up with the others. Wearing a Rambo-style headband and a T-shirt with the sleeves cut off to show his puny biceps, Du Du is trying very hard to be a man. On the inside of his left arm, he has a tattoo depicting a skull and crossbones.

His son's name means 'Brave One,' says Robert Zan, and he fully expects him to live up to it. He is training Du Du to succeed him in case he is killed in battle, which can happen 'anytime.' Last season's battle for Palu, in which he was wounded himself, was the boy's trial by fire. He acquitted himself well, and now spends Mondays through Fridays at this camp; he is only allowed to come home on weekends. 'I took him out of school in the third grade to turn him into a military man,' Robert Zan says. 'I thought that if he studies now, he'll just have to fight later. Better to fight now, and learn later when there's time for it.'

But the major's grave appraisal of his son's destiny is balanced somewhat by the laughter coming from his wife. She has come to the camp for the day, and as she watches her stepson's clumsy marching movements she giggles openly. It is obvious that, to her, Du Du is only playing at being a soldier. She holds her lavender parasol aloft with one hand to protect herself from the sun; and with the other hand, cupped over her mouth, she demurely conceals her laugh.

Later on, completing the exhibition with a demonstration of his boys' explosives abilities – they study everything from plastique and TNT to gelignite and nitromethane bombs – Robert Zan adjourns to his command hut. It sits on a hill from which he has a strategic view of all approaches to the camp. Several boys stand watch around the perimeter.

Inside there is a large wooden table and two benches. On the hut's rough walls hangs the latest KNU calendar, with the Karen revolution's roster of martyrs; an old black-and-white framed photograph of General Bo Mya, Kawthoolei's head of state; and a large, insect-spattered wall chart listing the enemy's troop strength and positions. Here, Robert Zan can think and reflect. From the hut's window he can look out over the nearby hills with their rows of young teak trees. Down in the farmyard, he can see his guerrillas clowning around, his son among them.

Robert Zan knows the Karen's long-term prospects aren't good. He doesn't even know how long he can continue to count on this piece of land as a training ground. His intelligence says that the Burmese plan to target it in the next offensive, to add it to their string of victories. He holds up a Remington Model 700 with a telescopic sight. 'For killing officers only,' he laughs. It is the same weapon Motosada Mori, the Japanese sniper, used to kill the two Burmese officers at Kawmura in the last fighting season. Mori is due back in Kawthoolei soon; he is supposed to bring new sniper scopes with him, one for each besieged base, and to teach more guerrillas how to use them. If they can kill more frontline enemy officers, maybe it will slow things down. Every little bit helps.

Outside, in the late afternoon heat, the Supreme Specials lapse into playful lethargy. Some of the boys swim in the river. Others sit on the bank watching, their arms around one another's shoulders, smoking shared cheroots.

On the hike back to the pickup truck that will take her home, Robert Zan's wife walks in front, her parasol shielding her from the hot sun of afternoon. Next to her walks a young guerrilla who has a bad case of malaria and is in need of medical attention. Just behind trots Du Du. It is the weekend, and he is going home. On his back he carries a woven-reed porter's basket filled with bamboo shoots collected by his stepmother. Suddenly the major's wife stops. She stares with interest into a bamboo grove just off the trail. Getting the hint, one of the boys goes in with a long knife to collect more shoots for her. Standing in single file, the guerrillas wait. Then the boy with the knife reemerges, carrying fresh bamboo shoots for Du Du's basket, and the group walks on, lavender parasol leading the way.

Robert Zan observes the son in whom he has invested so much of his ambitions. 'I don't worry about him,' he says. 'You know why? Both my parents died in Karen territory, and my youngest brother and a cousin have died fighting at Kawmura. Besides me, I have another cousin, a nephew, and a brother-in-law, all fighting. One day, I too will die for my people and the Karen revolution. So, if my son dies, it's okay.'

As Robert Zan prepares to sacrifice his son and trains his men for terrorism in Kawthoolei's tropical somnolence, the violence he conjures up still seems abstract. The acts are to take place far away, on the other side of the mountains, outside the jungle theater of war, which is inexorably becoming a scene of catastrophe for the Karen people. But, as Robert Zan says, what else can his people do to turn back this relentless enemy onslaught in which, each year, they lose more and more territory? Soon, they will have nothing left. If the Karen and the students can take the war into Burma's cities and show that they can inflict real damage on the military regime, maybe the population can be galvanized into renewed revolt. Surely that is better than continuing this long war, even if a few innocents die in the process.

In war, death becomes the means to an end, and the people doing the killing develop a whole range of justifications for bringing it about. History, culture, battlefield conditions, political objectives, enemy behavior – all are factors that have influenced the conflicts in El Salvador, Burma, Afghanistan, Gaza, and Western Sahara.

At times, for years even, these influences may be unchanging in their characteristics. At other times they become fluid and flexible, and the wars also change. Wars, like the people who wage them, transform over time.

Whatever course wars have taken, if in the end they cannot be muted by negotiation, they become duels for survival. In the absence of talk, there can only be war. Thoughts of all else become mere frivolities in the face of death and an implacable enemy. When it becomes the means of sustaining life, violence of the kind contemplated by Major Robert Zan begins to seem less like terrorism, somehow, and more like an act of survival.

FIVE

Systems of Justice

All guerrillas impose their authority upon the people in the territories they wish to control. The systems of justice they exercise are revolutionary rehearsals of the power they hope to wield one day on a larger scale.

Each war poses similar moral and ethical challenges to guerrillas as they subject others to their will, yet the way guerrillas meet those challenges differs widely. Which laws they decide are important and how they enforce them are fundamental gauges of the guerrillas' social priorities and future intentions.

For many guerrillas a large gray area exists where the military war and the administration of justice overlap. In some places their hold over the population is tenuous, and so their imposition of authority is a major part of their war effort, a means of enforcing the people's obedience. If the guerrillas are opposed by a sector of the population, the inclination is often to use coercion, even terror, to subject the population to their will.

The mujahedin of Afghanistan give little thought to winning over the population. In this isolated and tradition-bound country,

Islam and the power of the local strongman stand virtually unopposed. If the mujahedin are militarily dominant in an area, their word is law. And usually, this means Islamic law, as interpreted by them and their mullahs.

Military crimes like spying or treason are typically handled by mujahedin parties in their own areas of control. In Kandahar, by general agreement between Mullah Naquib and the other mujahedin commanders, all serious civil crimes, such as theft, murder, and adultery, are forwarded to two elderly Muslim scholars, or *maulavi*, who run a court in a village about an hour away from Charqulaba.

This parallel judiciary has been functioning in Kandahar since the early 1980s, and amounts to a complementary division of powers between the mujahedin, as the military authorities, and the old imams, as the civic and religious leaders. The fact that some of the commanders, like Naquib, are mullahs themselves means there is a close affinity between the authorities. For instance, apart from his military duties, Naquib also arbitrates Arghandab's petty civil disputes himself.

Soon after the war broke out, Kandahar's mujahedin factions formed a *shura*, or consultative council, and unanimously agreed to create the Islamic court as a necessary alternative to the Afghan regime's own discredited judiciary. Eventually, with the government presence eradicated everywhere except in the city center itself, this alliance has come to exercise Islamic authority throughout the province, underpinning the military authority of the mujahedin at the same time.

'It is like a government,' says Khalilullah with pride. 'A government of the mullahs and the mujahedin.'

One morning, Mullah Naquib sends some men from his camp to attend a court session presided over by the supreme mullahs. The journey there is made at breakneck speed along a much-bombed road, in a green Toyota pickup that serves as the camp's ambulance. It is driven by a toothy young mujahed who plays tapes of wailing, melancholic Kandahari love songs at full blast the entire way.

The court is located in a hamlet called Pashmul. Several hundred yards away, a lone government-held hill stands like an island in the surrounding flatness. Puffs of smoke show that it is being shelled by the mujahedin.

Around Pashmul, the drab ocher fields of grape roll away, with their deep furrows and wintry tangle of leafless vines, and in the far distance, the sand dunes of the great southern desert of Registan suddenly loom up, towering hundreds of feet over the land like the crest of a golden tsunami frozen in its forward sweep.

The court has been set up outdoors, in the shade of a raisin-storage silo at the hamlet's edge. Its approaches are watched over by an honor guard of a dozen heavily armed mujahedin. Bedecked in weaponry, sporting bandoliers and even Chinese RPG-7 rocket launchers, they form a bristling gauntlet to the court. Every month the guard is rotated on a party-by-party basis, the commanders sending their best men to Pashmul.

The guards body-search all visitors carefully. Once frisked, claimants and petitioners are escorted around the back of the silo and instructed to sit on the ground. Here, about twenty people sit facing the judges around the edges of a large cloth stretched on the ground.

The two mullahs recline against pillows, with their backs against the silo's mud walls. One of them looks very old, with a long white beard; the other has a shorter, iron-gray beard. In front of them are stacked a pile of dog-eared legal texts: the Holy Koran, the *hadith*, or sayings of Muhammad, and the teachings of Imam Abu Hanifah, an eighth-century Sunni Muslim scholar.

The two judges look preoccupied. Next to them, a thin, sour-faced man with an open notebook and a pen poised in one hand stares around balefully. He is the court's scribe, a mujahedin commander who is volunteering his time. The court is busy this morning, he says impatiently; the judges have many cases before them.

Around the cloth, the Afghans' faces all bear identical expressions of mute and respectful attentiveness. Most have the knitted brows and downcast gazes of those who believe they are in the presence of superiors, like penitents at a church altar.

Today the *maulavi* are judging a dispute between two mujahedin commanders over the limits of their territories; a dispute over the division of a quantity of ammunition between two others; and some minor civilian cases as well. The cases testify to the success of the Kandahar *shura*; with such spats removed from the military realm, the bloody factional disputes so common elsewhere in Afghanistan can be avoided and resolved peaceably here.

In a résumé of the years they have held office, the judges say they have found cause to order the deaths of two pairs of adulterers, the amputation of the right hand of one thief, and the execution of eighteen murderers. On the exact numbers there is much back-and-forth talk between the judges. At one point they disagree on how many murderers they have put to death. The old judge thinks it is forty; the younger one disputes this. The records are consulted, and at length they come up with the lower figure of eighteen.

None of their verdicts have been reached lightly, say the imams, and each sentence has been carried out as called for in the Koran. ''We adhere to the Shari'a in all cases,' says the younger judge. Reassuringly, he pats the bundle of books stacked in front of him. 'All of the answers are here, in these holy books. '

The murderers were executed by the surviving relatives of the murder victims, 'by Kalashnikov.' Usually, the widow or a brother carries out the sentence, but if no relatives are available the mujahedin act as stand-in executioners. As for the thief they tried and found guilty, the judges make clear that the amputation of his hand was carried out under the supervision of no less than four mujahedin doctors. In the cases of the adulterers, their crimes were witnessed by the requisite four eyewitnesses, as called for in the Koran. There is no doubt it was adultery that took place in both instances. Three of the adulterers were duly stoned to death; one of the guilty male parties was only flogged, however, because he was unmarried. His female accomplice *was* married, so she was put to death.

Given their comparatively moderate record of handing down capital sentences, these two men are clearly not hanging judges, but simple, righteous religious scholars who deeply believe in the fairness of their methodology. And from the earnestness with which they seek to account for their harsher judgments, it is obvious they would never pronounce a verdict not countenanced by their holy books. But these imams of Kandahar were also hand-picked by the *shura* of mujahedin commanders – plucked from the mosques where they and their beloved books had been gathering dust for years – and are protected even now by a mujahedin body-guard.

Still, they insist their ethics are intact. The younger judge acknowledges 'good relations' with the mujahedin, but denies any subservience on the court's part. The judges take no money from the mujahedin, he says, even though it has been offered; instead they subsist on funds tithed to their mosques by the public. The fact is, he says, there is nothing they would love more than to return to their mosques. But they also realize theirs are holy duties, and so they have agreed to continue performing them until the jihad is won and an Islamic state officially established in Afghanistan.

At the end of this long and impassioned monologue, the elder judge interrupts irritatedly: 'Are you quite finished? It is lunchtime and I am hungry, and we have still not seen our cases!' This outburst is ignored by the younger judge, however; he apparently feels he hasn't made the point about their independence convincingly enough yet. He begins waving around a piece of paper.

It is a new edict being sent to all the mujahedin commanders of Kandahar, ordering them to 'exercise better control over the civilians in their areas of authority, and to halt the playing of recorded music.' The old men believe that the current climate of moral laxity – there has been a recent rash of thefts, and some murders, around Kandahar – is due to the pernicious influence of music. So now they are banning it. And the mujahedin are expected not only to obey the new prohibition, but to enforce it.

The news of this impending decree is somehow more chilling than all the talk about stonings, amputations, and executions 'by Kalashnikov.' Even Khalilullah looks embarrassed and uncomfortable. Kandahar is well known for its love of music, and the mujahedin are no exception.

By now the noonday sun is hot, and the sour-faced scribe is making angry mutterings. Seeing the increasingly irascible looks on his and the hungry elder judge's face, Khalilullah ends the session by thanking the judges and rising to his feet. Afterward he doesn't talk about the music ban except to say that it seems 'strict,' since most people, including himself, enjoy listening to music. But he says no more; he does not want to criticize the judges directly.

Back in the pickup, the very first thing the driver does is to insert a tape into the cassette deck and turn it up full blast. As the wailing love songs fill the car with noise, he puts his foot down on the gas pedal and grins broadly. Khalilullah says nothing, but as he stares straight ahead through the windscreen, he wears a slight, enigmatic smile.

The voice on the tape is that of Badur, an adolescent crooner from Kandahar who was martyred fighting with the mujahedin three years ago. His songs, sung in a piping, girlish soprano, are of unrequited love and the scent of flowers.

In spite of all their authority, imposing law and order still isn't a simple task for the imams. Even after the music ban, Kandahar's crime wave doesn't stop. A week after the audience in Pashmul, the old mullahs ask Mullah Naquib to apprehend a group of thieves who, pretending to be mujahedin, have robbed a truckload of sugar belonging to some Kandahar city merchants. The bandits have holed up in Hargeiz, a village at the base of the mountains across the plain from Arghandab.

Within a day, mujahedin begin arriving in the Charqulaba camp from all around Kandahar; each party sends a group of six or seven fighters. The 'sugar thieves operation' is to be a *shura*-wide effort. Mullah Naquib bustles around camp, discussing plans with the other commanders. The camp cook and tea boys work double time to provide food for all the extra mouths in camp.

Finally late one afternoon everything is ready. After a rousing assembly, like a football coach's pre-game meeting with his players, Mullah Naquib sees his men off. Rising to their feet en masse, the fighters shoulder their weapons and begin walking at a fast pace. They are going to walk all night across the plain to reach Hargeiz before dawn and surprise the bandits as they lie sleeping. As they trot off, Mullah Naquib follows them on the footpath leading out of camp, his arms upraised, urging them on in a loud and excited voice.

Not long after the fighters have gone, word comes that the thieves have cached half of their booty in a warehouse in a nearby village. Men are sent to investigate. They return after dark with a frightened Afghan civilian in tow, a local man hired by the thieves to stand watch over the stolen sugar. Brought inside the radio hut, the prisoner kneels quaking on the straw of the floor, his eyes downcast.

Sitting on one of the cots, Naquib towers wrathfully over him. Naquib wants to find out whether he knew his employers were thieves. The watchman says no, he thought they were mujahedin, that the sugar was stolen from the government. After hearing him out, Naquib scoffs at his claims of innocence and shouts at the man. The man bleats unintelligibly in submissive despair. He has been found guilty; his only hope is that Naquib spares him from serious punishment.

Luckily for him, Naquib has already decided the man is so frightened by his experience he will never make such a mistake again, but he gives him a tongue-lashing anyway, asking him repeatedly, insultingly, 'Are you a Muslim?' Then he tells the man he is going to let him go, but only because he knows and respects his father and his brothers. The man finally dares to raise his eyes from the ground. He comes crouching forward to kiss Naquib's hand. Afterward, dismissed imperiously by Naquib, he backs hurriedly out of the hut and vanishes.

The next morning, the mullah makes a trip to the warehouse. Standing around are some nervous-looking civilians who have already bought sacks of sugar from the thieves. Now Mullah Naquib wants them to return the sugar. A few men begin appearing from the warren of mud houses with hundred-pound sacks on their backs. They throw them back on the pile stacked in the warehouse, but linger, looking longingly at the sacks, as Naquib consoles them with the knowledge that they have done the right thing in the eyes of God.

By noon, news comes back from Naquib's raiding party. After reaching Hargeiz at dawn, the mujahedin surrounded the village, but instead of fighting it out, they entered into negotiations with

the gang of thieves. On Mullah Naquib's instructions the mujahedin have agreed that if the sugar is returned, the thieves won't be
punished. To settle the matter without bloodshed, they have
accepted the bandits' alibi that they believed the sugar belonged to
the government.

This is a face-saving compromise suitable to everyone: the old
imams will be pleased to see this issue resolved and out of their
hands; Kandahar's mujahedin commanders can likewise be proud
of having done justice without resorting to arms; and, of course,
the aggrieved merchants will be thankful just to have their sugar
back. Finally, the thieves can consider themselves extremely lucky
to have kept their right hands.

As the case of the sugar bandits shows, Mullah Naquib is far
from unsophisticated when it comes to exercising his authority. In
the interests of demonstrating his tolerance as well as his determination to enforce the law, Naquib has opted for compromise
rather than extreme solutions. While he is empowered by the
maulavi to invoke the full weight of the Shari'a laws, he has chosen
to be benevolent. By doing so, he has managed to come away with
everyone grateful to him – not only the sugar merchants, but also
the men he has reprieved – and the village bazaars of Arghandab
will be filled with laudatory talk of Naquib's wisdom and even-
handed rule.

Naquib's measured application of the law is appreciated by the
people, and it has earned him their respect. By contrast, after the
maulavi's music ban another mujahedin commander rampaged
through a village, confiscating everyone's radios and tape players –
more than six hundred in all – and destroying them. For many of
the affected people, the radios and tape players were their most
valuable possessions. Destroying them was not only cruel but politically stupid, for in order to curry favor with the *maulavi*, the
commander earned himself the undying enmity of six hundred

families, and also the contempt of his fellow mujahedin. Mullah Naquib, on the other hand, interpreted his duty to the imams' music ban by formally transmitting the edict in Arghandab and then ignoring it. So as to keep up appearances, he merely asks his men not to play music in his presence.

In Arghandab, the people know that if they follow the rules they will be treated fairly. There are no arbitrary punishments; nothing is meted out that is not already expected. In an Islamic land, the laws imposed by Mullah Naquib are ones the people have already learned to obey.

In Western Sahara, although for different reasons than in Arghandab, the guerrillas also stand virtually unchallenged in their control of the civilian population. Here, the chief reason is the wall. If there are pro-Moroccan Saharawis, they live on the other side. In the Algerian refugee camps, meanwhile, the control of the Polisario Front is absolute.

To govern the Saharawi refugees, the Polisario Front has ingeniously subsumed the old pre-revolutionary tribal councils, which issued laws in adherence to the Islamic Shari'a. Avoiding conflict, the Polisario has retained the old laws but gives them its own 'progressive interpretation.' There are no stonings and amputations, but a system of fines instead. The discredited old sheikhs have been given ceremonial jobs, allowing them to retain a semblance of dignity, while real authority rests in the hands of the revolutionary cadres.

So total and uncontested is the Polisario Front's control that the Saharawis claim theirs is a crime-free society. Polisario leaders say not a single homicide has been committed in the camps since their exile began, and Abba openly wishes other societies could be like theirs, not 'drugged and diseased,' as those beyond the 'Saharan Arab Democratic Republic' often appear to be.

If the Saharawis seem moralistic, it is because they can still afford to be. In Kawthoolei, a place where the Karen guerrillas have ruled their people for years with a strong moral and social code based on a hybrid of old Karen ways and British law, this system has been weakened with the worsening military situation.

The KNU is evidently inconsistent in its application of justice: There seems to be one form of treatment for the Karen, another for outsiders. The laws are also stretched when it comes to punishing KNU fighters for misdeeds. For instance, the KNU is surprisingly lenient with deserters, making them serve only one-month sentences in Kawthoolei's prisons. Such leniency is possible because the KNU actually has prisons in which to house its criminals and miscreants. The same form of treatment could in theory be applied to enemy prisoners of war, but instead they are shot.

In another inconsistency, Major Soe Soe cites the death sentence on the KNU's books as proof of the severity with which the revolution punishes narcotics traffickers. He claims that at least one drug trafficker has been executed, but waffles when it comes to the details of the case. The fact is, no one caught in Kawthoolei on narcotics charges has actually ever been sentenced to death. At Manerplaw there is a convicted heroin smuggler; not only has his sentence been set aside, but he is enrolled at Manerplaw's 'military leadership training academy.' He is also a Karen.

One afternoon, the reprieved man is pointed out by Ganemy. Slim, neatly uniformed, and with a shaved head, the man sits with a group of other young cadets gathered to watch videos on Prime Minister Saw Baw Thin's verandah. Ganemy explains that he was caught smuggling a small amount of heroin through one of the KNU's customs gates. Because he was young, from a poor family, and an addict, he wasn't sentenced to death, but given a ten-year sentence of hard labor instead. After several years' service as a porter to KNU troops on the front line, he has been given a full pardon. Now, he is going to be a KNU officer. 'He has convinced everyone of his worth,' says Ganemy, waving to the cadet with an approving smile.

The prison at Manerplaw sits on a small hill not far from the president's house at a spot where the sign on a white-painted wooden archway over the road reads, 'Give me liberty or give me death.' The prison consists of two teak cages about fifty feet long, ten feet high, and twenty feet wide, separated by a corridor where a couple of young boy guards sit cradling automatic weapons. The cages are made of massive square-cut timbers, each about four inches thick, with similar gaps between them; the floors are concrete. They are cool and dark; the men inside are barely visible. Hammocks and mosquito nets are strung up along the beams, and little bundles dangle from strings like the nests of weaver birds.

During the day, most of the prisoners are led outside for work details. There are less than ten prisoners being held at the moment, all of them recent cases. A few months ago, the fifteen former occupants were freed after they 'volunteered' to fight at the front. Two were killed; afterward, the rest were pardoned.

Charles Thada is Kawthoolei's chief justice, and it is he who decides whether people go to prison or not. A thin, languorous man, Thada lives at Manerplaw but spends much of his time traveling around KNU-controlled Kawthoolei to adjudicate pending cases. Prior to joining the Karen revolution in 1971, he was a provincial district judge and township officer. He switched sides, he says, because he disliked Burma's 'socialist administration.' The move was good for Thada's judicial career. First appointed Kawthoolei's deputy chief justice, he ascended to his present position when the former chief justice died in office.

Kawthoolei's legal system is culled from Great Britain's, but only those articles that apply to what Thada terms 'the Karen people's revolutionary condition' are implemented. When it comes to meting out punishments, the KNU has tailored the laws to suit Karen culture. For instance, there is a death sentence for murder 'by hatred,' but the penalties for murder with extenuating circumstances range from seven years' imprisonment to a twenty-year 'life' sentence. The crime of 'incestuous rape' also receives the death sentence, but if the rapist is not related to his victim, the penalty is imprisonment.

The chief justice agrees that Kawthoolei's laws are strict, but he defends them as appropriate for a people at war. Adultery, the latest addition to the list of capital offenses in Kawthoolei, was made punishable by death only in the mid-1980s, after several high-profile cases of marital betrayal began causing morale problems among frontline troops. After the law was instituted, a couple of executions were carried out; however, since then no more cases of adultery have been brought to court. Now the frontline troops are able to keep their attention focused on the war, instead of worrying about what might be happening behind their backs at home. 'Everyone who stays in Kawthoolei can only have one husband or wife,' says the chief justice. 'Excessive mistresses is death. Just one mistress is usually ten years.'

Ironically, at the same time as their own lives have become more codified because of the war, the Karen are coming into increased contact with the outside world, most especially with the promiscuous culture of Thailand, where many of the fighters' families live. Then, too, there are the several thousand Burmese students now living among the Karen; the students have their own assortment of beliefs and customs. Inevitably, these contacts have unsettled Kawthoolei's stability. Already since the student influx, the KNU has had to compromise by relinquishing its long-held separatist ambitions and joining with the students in a broad-based alliance against the Rangoon regime. But even if this move was inevitable, there are those who wish it weren't so, and who resent the non-Karen newcomers for bringing unwanted change.

As their situation gets more precarious, the Karen have become more paranoid about spies, and many top commanders are convinced that the students' ranks are riddled with enemy agents. Major Than Maung distrusts nearly everyone. The last spy he caught, he points out, was a Buddhist monk. 'The enemy uses many spies. Monks, merchants, *students* . . . even porters. We must be very careful.'

This fear of espionage is the main reason why the Burmese student camps have been located away from the Karen's own bases. One evening, Major Soe Soe blurts out, 'We have to be careful with the students, because at any moment they can turn on us. After all, they are Burmans!' His outburst shows that despite their official alliance, and for all the talk of a shared vision for the future of Burma, the Karen's distrust of their non-Karen comrades is deep-seated and continues to fester.

So far, no students have been caught spying, but they are well aware of the Karen's suspicions. They will go to great lengths to remove' the pall of doubt. One way they do this is by volunteering for dangerous guerrilla operations, like those dreamed up by Major Robert Zan. And they point to their mounting numbers of war dead as proof of their sincerity.

Meanwhile, because the KNU has left them to rule themselves in their own camps, the students have had to learn to police themselves. By the end of their first year in the jungle, Thay Baw Boe's students have erected their own 'jail,' a small hut made of driven logs built in the weeds at the edge of the camp.

The jail is the day-to-day responsibility of another innovation: Thay Baw Boe's own 'regimental police force.' So far the force consists of two sturdy youths dressed in smart military uniforms with white-shellacked belts and matching diagonal sashes, burgundy berets, and epaulettes. They keep order in the camp and escort visitors between camp and the Moei River, always at a brisk pace and with a certain amount of aplomb.

Passing by the jail one day, one of the policemen remarks that its current occupants are two students who were caught stealing a Karen farmer's corn. The detainees are serving a sentence of two weeks' imprisonment with hard labor in the camp's agricultural fields. The punishment might seem severe to an outsider, but after all, he says, it is necessary to maintain law and order. He holds up a pair of steel handcuffs and shakes them triumphantly: He was the arresting officer.

Indeed, treason and espionage aren't the only challenges faced by guerrillas seeking to establish themselves as authorities in a given area. With their Karen neighbors already predisposed to distrust them because of ethnic differences, the students cannot afford to weaken their rapport with the local community through a lack of proper discipline.

In El Salvador, the *compas* learned from early errors that they had to become policemen before they could function effectively as guerrillas. As Haroldo tells it, in the heady early days, when thousands of people were joining up, 'all types' found their way into the guerrilla ranks, and before long, there was trouble. 'We had problems with *bandolerismo*. There were people taking advantage of the fact that they carried a gun to commit crimes against the people. There were some rapes, thefts against the civilian population, and this had to be stopped.'

It was necessary to impose order and discipline so that everyone, the guerrillas and the civilians, knew where the new boundaries lay. The FMLN moved swiftly, implementing a strict system of justice, holding summary trials, and coming down hard on wrongdoers. Those found guilty of serious offenses were executed. As the FMLN has grown more powerful, lawlessness has become less of a problem, and so much of the organization's early strictness has eased as well.

Mostly, the system has worked, and in marked contrast to the government forces, the FMLN's combatants have earned a reputation for being well-disciplined. Few complaints of criminal misbehavior are made against them. But, like everything the *compas* do, the administration of justice is also a crucial aspect of their revolutionary program, and at times the line between the two is very finely drawn.

The *compas* have to be sure of the loyalties of the civilians in the areas they frequent, because a single betrayal can cost many lives. Wholesale massacres like El Sumpul and the gruesome torture-murders of suspected guerrilla sympathizers by government death squads have counted for much of the war's high civilian death toll. With these forms of reprisal posing a real and constant threat, the *compas* cannot afford to be benign in their treatment of squealers. For these reasons, the summary execution of spies and traitors – *orejas*, literally 'ears' – has long been a routine and essential part of the war effort.

One hot August day, Ulíses falls in for a march with the kids' unit in the *zona de expansión*. Today's march is from Ojo de Agua to Las Vueltas along the Royal Road. Ulíses wears his straw cowboy hat; his red kerchief is tied around his neck, and his revolver is tucked into his belt.

Halfway to Las Vueltas, the track leads through the dismal, near-deserted hamlet of El Zapotal. El Zapotal is so filthy, littered and reeking with pig excrement, the *compas* call it El Cerrotal, 'The Piggery.' At the heart of this forlorn place, a small concrete-block evangelical chapel is boarded up and plastered with the FPL propaganda unit's posters. One of them reads, YOUNG CHALATECO, COME WITH US! JOIN UP NOW! With a passing glance at the chapel,

Ulíses comments that *evangélicos* have always been 'enemies of the revolution' and that El Zapotal's congregation once harbored a 'spy network.'

Until a couple of years ago, Ulíses explains, he and Diego were assisted in their organizing work by a third comrade. The three men worked the area as a team, cultivating contacts among local civilians and trying to win them over. Each had his own special duties and areas of responsibility, and so they frequently split up for specific missions.

One night, on a visit to El Zapotal, the third man was mysteriously murdered. Because of the circumstances of his death, it was clear he had been murdered by undercover government agents. It was also obvious that his killers must have been aided by spies among the civilians in El Zapotal. The loss of their comrade was a severe blow to Ulíses and Diego personally, and it also spelled a warning to them: If the army had successfully infiltrated their civilian network, it meant not only that their work in the expansion zone was doomed, but that their lives and those of their supporters were still at risk.

It was up to Diego and Ulíses to discover the identity of the El Zapotal traitors and neutralize them immediately. They carried out an investigation, and soon enough they found the spies. The key person in the spy ring was an influential local woman – an *evangélica* – whom Ulíses knew well. She owned a lot of land in and around El Zapotal. Ulíses points up to the steep, green hills rising above the hamlet, La Montañona's foothills. 'Her land went right up to the top.'

Whenever Ulíses came through El Zapotal, he used to stay at the woman's house – at her insistence. 'She was a very bright woman. I used to argue religion with her,' recalls Ulíses with a small smile, adding that the woman went so far to gain his trust that she practically gave him one of her two daughters to sleep with. But all the time, in return for money the woman was passing information on to the nearest army garrison about the movements and intentions of the *compas*. Not only had she arranged the murder of Ulíses's comrade, but on that very night she actually met with his killers on the hillside behind El Zapotal, then guided them to where he slept.

When the woman was confronted with the evidence against her, she confessed. Soon, the rest of the spy ring was rounded up. All of the spies confessed. 'There were about eight people altogether, all *evangélicos*,' says Ulíses. 'Their network had been operating for quite a while, and besides the assassination of our friend, the information they had passed to the enemy had led to many crimes against people in the area. What's more, we found out that next they planned to kill *us* – myself and Diego.'

Ulíses then called together the entire community of El Zapotal and presented the confessed spies to them, one after the other. 'I told the people what they had done, what crimes they had confessed to, and then I let them speak on their own behalf. Afterward I asked the people what we should do with them. I told them it was their decision. But they didn't want to be the judges, they said whatever we did was fine.'

The final suspect to be presented to the crowd was the woman. 'Again the people said I should decide, but that if I let her go, *they* would be the next to die.' Ulíses shrugs. 'In the end, they all had to be executed. It was the people's wish.'

The executions were carried out immediately. First, Ulíses ordered some *compas* to go and dig graves. Once the graves were ready, he had the condemned people escorted to the burial sites. There, each was dispatched with a single bullet to the head, the most humane way Ulíses knew to carry out the sentences. He would never, for instance, kill people by firing squad, which he thinks is a terrible way to execute people. Ulíses bends his head forward and touches the back of his skull lightly with his fingertips to show where the spies were shot.

'The people around here remember that occasion very well,' concludes Ulíses. Wearing his inscrutable smile, he motions with his hand to take in the perpendicular hills, the hardscrabble pig farms of peeling and dusty whitewashed wattle-and-daub with their overgrown hedgerows of prickly pear, the few mangy curs curled in the shade, and the silent rock lane strewn with shit. El Zapotal seems utterly devoid of people except for a single thin old peasant man dressed in rags. He crouches against a wall of the evangelical church and stares silently as Ulíses walks confidently by.

A few days later, Haroldo and Justo, a companion from the Radio Farabundo Martí unit, come into Las Flores for a meeting. Holed up inside the 'popular nursery' on the plaza, with a bottle of rum in secret defiance of the FPL's alcohol prohibition, and a body-guard posted outside, they sit down and talk all night.

There is much to discuss. Earlier in the week, in U.N. arbitrated talks in Costa Rica between the FMLN and the Salvadoran government, both sides signed a document agreeing to halt 'extrajudicial executions' and other human-rights abuses. This won't halt all such actions in practice, but for the guerrillas, it means their *ajusticiamientos*, or 'impositions of justice,' as the *compas* call their summary executions, will no longer be official policy. Under the new rules, if Ulíses catches a spy, he can no longer shoot him in the back of the head.

Haroldo admits to having long agonized over the FMLN's practice of *ajusticiamientos*. 'Anyway, now we're not going to do them anymore, and I'm glad, because personally I never liked them.' At his side, Justo nods his head up and down in an expression of heart-felt agreement.

Whatever Haroldo and Justo's feelings about them, however, the fact is that in El Zapotal, Ulíses's execution of the spies has led directly to the guerrillas' unequivocal control of the hamlet. All remaining active resistance to their authority has ended, and El Zapotal's evangelical church, symbol of that resistance, is closed down as well.

Compared to the Afghans and the Karen, with their death sentences for adultery, the Salvadoran *compas* are relaxed when it comes to legislating social behavior. Far from sublimating their sexuality, the *compas* have made room for it. Perhaps this is inevitable, since in El Salvador, women fight alongside the men and are omnipresent throughout the theater of war. This close proximity between men and women in a situation where death is always imminent has had the effect of breaking down the usual social barriers, and both extramarital and casual sex are commonplace. The ruling ethos is that life is fast and hard and each person must make the most of it as well as he or she can.

There is the story of the woman who egged on the men in her squad with the promise of sex if they did well in battle. A senior guerrilla officer, Antonín, laughs as he recalls the woman called La Pís-Pís, 'The Fuck-Fuck.' 'She was something. She fought right alongside the male *compas*, and just before an ambush, she'd say to them, "Okay, *muchachos*, the bravest one gets me!" It was really good for morale, and whenever La Pís-Pís was around, the *compas* fought really well.'

Not all women are as team-spirited as La Pís-Pís, but even if they sleep around, there isn't the same stigma within the revolution for doing so as there is outside of it. 'People tend to get together and break up much more quickly in the front than in the rest of the country,' says Haroldo. 'But it's the war which has imposed these conditions. A *compa* may be killed or transferred, so relationships are many and not necessarily long-lasting. Because of the situation, there aren't the same social pressures, while the desire to be close to someone else is even more intense.'

The *compas* weren't always so socially progressive when it came to sex. In its early days, the Salvadoran revolution set forth doctrinaire and restrictive guidelines for its combatants' private lives. Intimate relationships were prohibited unless authorized by the guerrilla leaders. 'There was a time when you had to have permission just to *kiss*!' says Haroldo, only half-joking.

'Or even to *talk*!' chimes in Justo.

'But in the end, this went out the window,' continues Haroldo. 'The strict moral code couldn't last. The revolution realized it couldn't control the ass of every combatant, and so there is some flexibility when it comes to sex.'

The revolution may have rid itself of its formal sexual restrictions, but a kind of code does exist even now. Affairs are considered tolerable as long as they don't interfere with the combatants' duties. Also, the revolution expects relationships to be based on mutual sincerity. 'No aces up the sleeve,' says Justo. 'If it's just a casual thing, then that has to be mutually understood; the same if the intention is to have a mature, long-lasting relationship. '

Both men dispute the idea that liaisons formed in the bush are emotionally stunted. 'On the contrary,' says Haroldo. 'We can die tomorrow, so we give ourselves to the very core, today, as if it were the last.'

'Among guerrillas,' agrees Justo, 'love is more intense, more fully given . . .'

'We do have *some* laws,' says Haroldo. 'Like the Law of the Lake. Hey, *compa*?' He turns, grinning knowingly at Justo, who nods vigorously and begins chuckling. 'From here to the lake' – Haroldo is referring to Suchitlán, a large reservoir visible on the plain below the hills around Las Flores – 'any relationship is valid. But beyond the lake, it can be broken. If a *compa* is sent for some reason beyond the lake, like on a mission, and the other partner has to stay behind, each one can do what they want.'

'And there's also the Law of the Mountain,' adds Justo. 'If I have a *compita* here, but I have to go to the other side of La Montañona, the Law of the Mountain applies.'

'Of course,' says Haroldo soberly, 'we all aspire to stable, monogamous relationships, despite the difficulties of doing so.'

Justo shoots him an arch look. 'Speak for yourself,' he says, and both men break into laughter.

Outside, in the plaza, taking advantage of their benevolent revolution and the discretion of darkness, pairs of young male and female *compas* sit fondling and flirting with each other. It is late at night, and except for Las Flores's early rooster, who begins his screeching before midnight, the plaza is nearly silent. The only sounds are occasional flurries of excited whispers, girls giggling, and loud metallic clacks, the sound of guns slipping clumsily from the grasp of lovers onto the stones of the plaza.

The Salvadoran guerrillas may have established a kind of social equilibrium in Chalatenango, but in Gaza, no true system of justice has yet been established. This is because while the Palestinians are engaged in a common war to oust the Israelis, they are also competing between themselves for power in the future Palestinian state. Their visions of that state are violently opposed: Fundamentalists like Hisham want an Islamic state where women wear the veil and adulterers are stoned to death, while PLO activists like Mahmoud and Sami want a modern, secular democracy and a liberal Palestinian society.

The problem is that these competing visions of society already exist side by side in the overcrowded camps of Gaza. In the volatile atmosphere of the intifada, the militants wish to see their rival systems imposed *now*, by force if necessary. As the struggle intensifies, so have the *shabbab* become harsher and more ruthless.

In their latest genesis as masked and hatchet-wielding ninjas, the *shabbab* are Palestine's nocturnal enforcers of law and order, the self-appointed judges, juries, and executioners of errant countrymen throughout the Occupied Territories. Now, more Palestinians are being executed by other Palestinians than are being killed by the Israeli army. The *shabbab* seem to see spies everywhere, and an atmosphere of fear has crept into people's everyday lives.

Early one morning in Breij, Hisham goes to buy fresh bread from the market for breakfast. Twenty minutes later, he returns beaming with happiness. 'The *shabbab* have just killed a spy,' he announces. The 'spy' was an elderly cleaning woman who worked at the clinic. The ninjas killed her as she cleaned up the clinic, before it opened for the day's activity. They have killed her with axes, says Hisham. With his hands, he shows where they chopped her repeatedly on the neck.

After eating breakfast, Hisham says he wants to go and view the body. Walking up Breij's dirt streets toward the clinic, two matronly women pass by, going in the other direction. Smiling broadly, they call out to express their glee about the spy's execution. Hisham waves back, then says, 'The whole camp is very happy about this killing.'

Only six months ago, the ninjas killed the woman's son as well. He, too, had been a spy. They killed him as he prayed in the mosque. 'They tried many times to kill him,' says Hisham, 'but it was only in the mosque where they could catch him.'

Suddenly, several jeeps full of Israeli soldiers come careening into the street ahead amid clouds of dust, their tall radio aerials swinging madly. Soldiers brandishing Galil assault rifles leap out and, with heads held low, fan out to cordon off the clinic. Obviously, word of the killing has reached them. A momentary flurry of panic hits the street as Palestinian youths begin running away, and doors slam shut as people slip back into their homes.

With characteristic understatement, Hisham says, 'I don't think we can go to see the body now.'

Counting the killing of the cleaning lady, thirteen people have died violently in Breij since the intifada began in 1987. Six of these have been killed by the *shabbab* on suspicion of spying for the Israelis. Of this total, most have died in the last year. The cleaning lady's death also highlights the growing number of women being targeted as spies by the fundamentalist *shabbab* – not just in Breij, but throughout Gaza and the Occupied Territories. The phenomenon is linked to the rise of militant Islam. In Gaza especially, there is increasing pressure for the imposition of Islamic dictates in everyday life.

The swing toward fundamentalism has also been exploited by the Israelis, who have used it to their own advantage in a number of ways. The *shabbab* in Hisham's circle of friends say that one of the most effective methods used by Israel's security police to coerce devout Palestinian youths into collaboration with them is to arrest them and then produce doctored pornographic photos of their mothers, sisters, or wives. 'It is terrible,' says Fahed, a close friend of Hisham's. 'These photos show the bodies of naked women, doing all kinds of bad things, with the faces of *their* women attached. It isn't really them, but it looks like them! The Israelis tell them they will make the photos public if they don't cooperate with them.'

Naturally, the young men's Muslim sense of propriety, and their duty to safeguard the honor of their women, ensure that they will do whatever is asked of them. Fahed expresses his sympathy and understanding for the youths – for, he says, what man can resist this form of blackmail? It was its discovery of this method, he says, that made the intifada committee of Breij take a more lenient attitude toward some of the camp's unmasked collaborators.

Fundamentalists like Hisham and Fahed argue that this would-n't be happening if Gaza was a fully Islamic society. The Israelis would not have *any* photos of these Palestinian women if they were kept at home, as Muslim women should be. Although in reality they are merely the innocent pawns in a cynical game of blackmail, women are perceived by the fundamentalists to be the cause of men's weaknesses and ultimately, their downfall.

Hisham and his friends believe that precisely because women are innocent creatures, they are more corruptible than men. This is why women have to be veiled, so that the men can't see them. If they can't be seen, then men won't become aroused by them and try to corrupt them. Hiding women from public view, making them wear the veil, prevents the vicious cycle of corruption from beginning at all. 'We believe that women should have rights, but not that they should take off their clothes,' says Fahed. 'It is not man telling the women to do this, but Allah. If she disobeys Allah, she will be punished on Judgment Day.'

In fact, Judgment Day has already come. In Gaza's increasingly claustrophobic atmosphere, where everything is exploited by one faction or another for its own political gain, it becomes easy to see how young women who persist in wearing Western clothing might even be branded collaborators. After all, Western dress is a phenomenon imported directly from Israel, the enemy state. By the same token, a woman without a veil is exhibiting her defiance of Islam, which, in the context of the jihad – and to Gaza's fundamentalists the intifada has become a jihad – means she is siding with the enemy.

So it seems more than a little coincidental when, a few days later, Hisham praises the people of Khan Yunis camp for their adherence to 'Islamic values,' then remarks that a 'large number of female spies' have been killed there lately. Were they all really spies, or was their real crime that they weren't 'good Muslim girls'?

*

Walking around Breij on the morning after the cleaning woman's murder, Hisham suddenly darts to one side of the street and walks alone for a few moments. Then he crosses back over and with a wag of his head indicates a middle-aged Palestinian man walking away up a side street. 'They say he is a spy. He is always hanging around as if to hear what others are saying. So they think he could be a spy.'

If the *shabbab* decide he is a spy, the man won't necessarily be killed. His punishment will depend on the importance of the information he is found to be passing along. A kind of probation for suspected spies has been instituted in Breij; they are no longer killed out of hand. First, they are given an option: Speaking through the mosque's megaphone, they must confess and ask the people's forgiveness. Few suspects have turned down the chance to save their lives; twenty-one spies have publicly repented in this manner so far.

Mahmoud's brother-in-law Muhammad, the former prisoner whose bedroom is sealed, is a cell leader in Breij's intifada underground. Like a probation officer, he has the job of keeping an eye on the collaborators whose lives have been spared. In Mahmoud's words, his brother-in-law 'makes sure they follow the correct path.'

Muhammad's task is not an easy one. 'It is a lot of people to watch over,' he says, and the new system is not infallible. Some of the reprieved people have already resumed spying for the Israelis. Now it is up to the intifada committee to decide their fates. But this is a formality; the committee's decision is a foregone conclusion. There is only one punishment for irredeemable spies, and that is death.

The killing of collaborators is not merely a matter of the Palestinian revolution eating its young. The witch-hunt for traitors has grown alongside the rising numbers of Palestinians who have died at the hands of the Israelis. The intifada is not only street fighting between the *shabbab* and soldiers; there are also 'black' operations carried out by disguised Israeli commandos to apprehend or gun down leaders of the intifada. In such operations the Israelis' Arab collaborators are indispensable for the information they provide on the identities and activities of the targeted *shabbab*.

For the *shabbab*, therefore, it is a matter of practical urgency to root out the squealers from their midst. Of course, a corollary result of this search for traitors has been to terrorize the rest of the population into compliance with the *shabbab*'s authority. In the absence of a publicly acceptable system of law and order the *shabbab* have become vigilantes. This, too, is a first step in wielding greater power, part of a process set in motion early in the uprising, when the Unified Command demanded the resignation of all Arab policemen in the territories. The resignations created a vacuum of authority, in stepped the *shabbab*, and things have gone on from there. Now, in order to consolidate their hold over the population, the *shabbab* need to purge it of spies and traitors.

When the intifada began, the *shabbab*'s first targets were the traditional Palestinian village chiefs, or *mukhtar*s. The militant youths see these men as having served Israel's interests, as a kind of Vichy government.

Many *mukhtar*s were indeed Israeli collaborators, recruited over the years of occupation. In return for weapons, cash, and carte blanche to exercise their authority as they saw fit in their areas of jurisdiction, these individuals informed on their people and generally helped Israel keep the lid on Palestinian dissidence. The system worked until the intifada shattered the status quo ante.

To Adel, a thin, chain-smoking activist in the Democratic Front for the Liberation of Palestine, the elimination of Israel's collaborator network among the *mukhtar*s has been essential to the success of the intifada. Before the uprising, he says, the *mukhtar*s' influence infiltrated most aspects of everyday life; the simplest activities were subject to their approval. 'Let's say I wanted to build an extension onto my house. For this we need permission from the Israeli authorities. It is difficult and costs much money, so it is better not to ask, just to do it.'

The problem was the *mukhtar*. He would invariably come and demand a bribe in return for his silence about the illegal extension. If he wasn't paid, he would go to the Israelis, and they would bar the extension. If it was already built, they could destroy it.

Now this kind of abuse of authority is less common. The worst *mukhtar*s have been killed or forced to resign, and replaced by trusted men from the communities. Whoever they are, collaborators are no longer safe. 'Before the intifada, perhaps ten out of every hundred Palestinians were spies,' says Adel. 'Now, it is about two in a hundred. With the intifada, they know they will be killed, so they are not as free as they were before to do everything they like.'

In one of the intifada's earliest and most dramatic executions, in the West Bank village of Qabatiyah, the *shabbab* gathered outside the house of a known collaborator, a man particularly hated for his tyranny. They demanded he give himself up for 'people's justice.' Instead, with an Uzi submachine gun given him by the Israelis, the man shot into the crowd, killing a child. Enraged, the crowd beat and hacked him to death, then dragged him outside and hanged him from a lamppost.

To counter the Israelis' pervasive spy network, the *shabbab* have formed their own counterintelligence system. Adel uses a gang of small boys to keep an eye on suspected collaborators. 'The small boys can go everywhere. They are not noticed, so they can see everything that goes on. For example, when Israeli soldiers come, often they go into people's homes. This does not mean the people are spies, but *maybe* they are. So, if a small boy can watch from a window, or from the open door, and sees the person give the soldiers a piece of paper with one of our names on it, then we know he is a spy. And we kill him.'

One day, Mahmoud comes to Tel Aviv, the enemy city, to hang out. He brings along a friend, Hassan. Mahmoud passes for a Jew, but Hassan, who is very Arab-looking, draws many stares. He is bearded, and he has a poor man's bad teeth. He walks with the furtive slink of someone accustomed to breaking the law.

Outside of their customary turf, these boys of Breij don't try to blend in, but instead become obtrusive, aggressive, as if to draw attention to the fact that they are Palestinians. They talk loudly and roughly in Arabic, they swagger abreast along the narrow sidewalks so that passersby have to walk around them. The effect of this behavior is to alarm the Jews who notice them.

Perhaps because of the abnormally tense existence they lead in Breij, Mahmoud and Hassan walk as if they are on alert. They take in everything around them; their eyes are always searching the crowd, roving, and their bodies are taut, ready to strike or run. As they walk along, the two begin spotting fellow Palestinians among the crowd; people at first indistinguishable from those around them. It is like a game, a matter of knowing what to look for, but there is rarely anything obvious. The differences are in the way the Palestinians move, and in their eyes. They find each other out as if by instinct. The concealed Palestinians move along, their gazes moving back and forth like searchlights after dark, and then, noticing one another, letting their eyes lock in momentary recognition.

At a building site, Mahmoud and Hassan stop to speak with a group of Palestinian laborers from Gaza. Walking on, in a café on trendy Rehov Dizengoff, they strike up a conversation with an attendant who identifies himself as an 'Israeli Arab,' a member of the anomalous Arab minority living in Israel and holding Israeli citizenship. 'Yes, but are you *Palestinian?*' Mahmoud asks him repeatedly, giving the label a challenging, nationalistic interpretation. Finally, the youth says yes, and then all three relax, smile, and begin to chat.

As the day wears on it becomes clear that throughout the city many Palestinians live clandestinely in the Israelis' midst. At a sidewalk café on Ben Yehuda Street, a block from the seafront, a group of spiffy young men comes along, laughing and joking. They wear well-cut leather jackets and expensive shoes; gold bracelets flash from their wrists. They appear to be affluent young Israelis out for a good time. Suddenly, one of them, the tallest, waves and smiles, calling out to Mahmoud and Hassan. It isn't until he sits down at the table and begins speaking in Arabic that it becomes plain he is a Palestinian, not a Jew.

The newcomer is expansive, friendly, full of chat, and Mahmoud and Hassan are friendly in return, but their faces are guarded. Under the table, their legs fidget. Like Mahmoud, the newcomer looks like an Israeli. He is ginger-haired and fair-skinned, and he exudes athletic good health. But he couldn't be more different from Mahmoud in every other way.

Where Mahmoud is formal, sincere, and quite unworldly – still very much a small-town boy from Gaza – this fellow is casual, glib, and flashy. He also speaks much better English; his speech is an uncannily parroted American, right down to its intonations, peppered with slangy street expressions like 'Wow, man,' 'How's it going?' and 'What's happening?'

He has learned his English from 'girlfriends,' he says, then explains, laughing, 'I'm a gigolo.' Mahmoud and Hassan cringe with embarrassment as the gigolo, who says to call him Sammy, begins boasting of his life in Tel Aviv, living off rich foreign tourist women. He meets them in his job as a bellhop at a luxury hotel. 'I can do a British accent too.' He leers. 'And I can speak French, German, and Italian pretty good, *and* Hebrew, naturally. '

Then, catching Mahmoud's glare of disapproval, Sammy makes an effort to appear serious, and begins talking about the uprising. '. . . I don't know – I mean, if they make Gaza and the West Bank a nation, what'll we do? Where will we all work?' Then, as an afterthought: 'But someday I'd just love to have my own nation, with like my *own* flag up there, you know?'

Sammy holds one hand up as if waving a flag and laughs. His teeth are impeccable. As he speaks, his eyes take in the sidewalk crowd. He talks on for a few more minutes. He mentions that he has been arrested quite a few times, hinting that it was for intifada-related activities. Soon he gets up to go. He has things to do, he says with a wink. With a breezy 'See ya 'round!' he saunters off.

'His real name's not Sammy, it's Nahez,' says Mahmoud with a wince, afterward. 'And he's just like us, from Breij. His father is a taxi driver. Most of his brothers are in prison. He is the only one who is . . . like this. He has a wife and baby back in Breij, but he never sees them. He's not a serious person.'

Mahmoud carries on, both scornful and envious of Nahez. As 'Sammy,' he says, Nahez has lived off his wits for years in Tel Aviv, and he is certainly very clever – he's learned all those foreign languages without even finishing secondary school – but Nahez's arrests will have had nothing to do with the intifada. They were probably for being in Israel illegally. How he has managed to stay on is a mystery, but people like Nahez always find a way to get what they want.

It is obvious that the youths from Breij consider Nahez a real danger to the long-term success of the intifada. It is not possible to be a Palestinian and just want to have a good time. Whether or not Nahez actually collaborates with the Israelis, he poses a great threat. Because of the apolitical and decadent life he leads among his people's oppressors, he sets a bad example. If every Palestinian youth were to follow his lead, the Palestinian struggle for nation-hood would inevitably fail

Because of the strong reaction he has aroused in Mahmoud and Hassan, it seems just possible that one day, Sammy/Nahez may find himself on the revolutionary Palestinian underground's list of people to eliminate.

The subject of Nahez arises in a discussion some time later, in Mahmoud's house back in Breij. Jaquer, Mahmoud's tough friend from Jabaliya camp, is present. At the mention of Nahez's name, Jaquer grimaces in distaste. Then he cranes out his neck and, hold-ing one of his big, blunt forefingers out like a knife blade, draws it across his neck from one ear to the other.

By expanding the definition of what an enemy is, the boys of Gaza are setting new margins in their world. With their axes and knives, they are replacing with their own order an old, corrupt one that has served the enemy's interests. But with ever-bloodier punishments exacted for a widening number of perceived 'crimes,' the *shabbab* also risk consuming themselves – and Palestinian society – in their zeal to set the new boundaries.

In Chalatenango, the *compas* have evolved a flexible system of justice, which they and their followers have come to understand and respect. Like Naquib in Arghandab and the Polisario in its Algerian camps, the *compas* have learned that they can afford to be tolerant in some areas, so long as their overall security isn't threat-ened. For instance, despite the alcohol ban in Las Flores, the village still has one *bolo*, one old drunkard. No one knows where he gets his liquor, and he can never be seen with a bottle, but every day he can be found lurching, as if drunk, from one part of the plaza to another. But because he is the only one, the *compas* are tolerant of this fellow. They have long since ceased to remonstrate with or punish him. As if to give him the benefit of the doubt, the village joke is that maybe he doesn't have a secret liquor supply, that he is still drunk from all the booze he imbibed before the *compas* came to town.

But this is the system of justice to be found in the *zonas de control*. As shown by Ulíses's actions in El Zapotal, there is less fair play in places such as the expansion zone, where the *compas* feel less secure. There, more coercive measures are in force.

The same security principle applies in Kawthoolei as well: The KNU's administration has become less equitable the more desperate the situation has become. Indeed, as territory slips from the KNU's grasp, Kawthoolei is reverting from a 'control zone' to a 'disputed zone.' The more the war has impinged on Karen civilian life, the less independent and fair Kawthoolei's judiciary has become.

Seen in this light, the KNU's unenforced narcotics-trafficking penalties begin to take on new significance; it seems unlikely to be coincidence that just as its traditional sources of legitimate revenue are threatened, the KNU's record on narcotics sentences has become ambiguous, less harsh. By the same token, the draconian adultery law was instituted to enforce stricter discipline and political stability at a time when the war's demands began to strain Kawthoolei's domestic equilibrium. And finally there is the issue of Manerplaw's pardoned prisoners. If things were not so desperate militarily, the KNU would have no need to recruit its own prisoners as fighters and thus undermine the integrity of its judiciary.

As the KNU's political and military authority in Kawthoolei erodes, so, too, do its institutions. As the Karen face a different future, the old parameters of their society are called into question. Perhaps soon, Kawthoolei will become a place like Thailand right next door, where anything goes.

All of the guerrillas tread a fine ethical line in administering their systems of justice, and some manage it better than others.

The challenge for them is to maintain effective and ethical systems that exist independently of their own war efforts. The tendency of all of them, however, is to use 'justice' as a means of consolidating their power, to seek total control over the people whose allegiance they have won in blood.

SIX

A New Family

One of Hisham's brothers has a beautiful fifteen-month-old son whose hair color is an uncanny orange. One evening, the child is brought to the family room to be shown off.

The father dandles his son on his knee, caressing his hair, squeezing him, beaming with pride. Then he whispers something in the boy's ear, and the tot holds up his hand to make an uncertain 'V,' the PLO sign. Then he says 'PLO' out loud. The adults cheer and praise the boy, then send him off to bed, a future freedom fighter.

One of the biggest difficulties for guerrillas fighting a war is maintaining a normal family life. No matter how dedicated they are as guerrillas, the personal side of life is one in which all seek fulfillment. But for some, having a family is impossible. For them, their comrades become like the members of a new family. But in other places, like Gaza, families are an imperative of the struggle, a weapon in the arsenal of war.

Indeed, rearing large families is like a national duty for the Palestinian refugees in Gaza and the West Bank. Before the flood of Soviet Jewish immigrants that began in 1990 overturned previous demographic forecasts, the conventional wisdom had long been that, because of the huge birthrate among Palestinians, there would eventually be more Arabs than Jews in the land of Israel. The Palestinians, so the theory went, would regain their homeland through sheer weight of numbers.

Although there can no longer be such statistical certainties about the future, in Gaza, already one of the most densely populated places on earth, the Palestinians are doing their best to increase their numbers. The duty nurse in Breij's little UNRWA clinic says that a hundred children are born there each month, a figure that may make Breij's birthrate among the highest in the world.

The intifada is taking a toll, however. Alongside the birth records, the nurse also keeps a tally of intifada-related hospital cases. These include shootings, which she says average about one hundred per month; beatings resulting in broken bones; and, most distressing, a high number of abortions and miscarriages caused by tear gas or shock.

'The Israelis think that with their clubs and tear gas they can stop this revolt,' says Massoud, a Fatah loyalist in Breij. 'But it will continue. The leadership of the intifada is willing to keep it going no matter how much blood is spilled. As Gorky said, "If you want to clear the land you must get blisters on your hands – and blood as well."'

Massoud pats the head of his niece, a pretty little girl standing shyly at his knee. She is the daughter of his elder brother, who has been imprisoned for life on terrorist charges. Massoud is raising her on behalf of his brother, along with his own children. 'Anyway, we are having two babies for every one of theirs. So we can wait. We will be here.'

The Palestinians have few illusions about attaining their goals of a homeland any time soon. Even the impatient young *shabbab* know it may take many more years. They have been prepared for a long struggle by their parents, refugees already for forty years; and, born as refugees themselves, the *shabbab* have little choice but to see reality for what it is. And so, intifada or no intifada, they try to live lives that are as full as possible. Hisham, Fahed, and Mahmoud have all married since the intifada began.

For his wife, Hisham paid a bride-price equivalent to three thousand American dollars in Jordanian dinars. It took a lot of his savings, but he isn't complaining. He earns good money in his job as a construction foreman outside Tel Aviv, at the site where the Russian whores ply their wares. Hisham and his wife live in a two-story wing built onto his family home by his brothers. It overlooks the orange groves at the edge of the camp. Downstairs, a doorway leads off a high-walled concrete patio to the women's quarters. Here a veiled woman can be seen briefly as she moves past the doorway and then vanishes again: Hisham's wife. Hisham spends most of his time upstairs in the room where he studies, receives visitors, and gathers to pray with his friends.

Hisham's wife is twenty, an Arabic-language student at a college in Gaza city. A special bus transports her and some other young women of Breij to and from classes each day. Hisham met her through his own sisters. 'They told me about her. They said, "She is a very good and beautiful girl." And they were right! She tells me that she would like to volunteer her time and work for the good of the people, to become active.'

Hisham is very proud. He has made a good choice. His young bride is proving to be everything a devout Muslim man can hope for in a wife. And on top of everything else, in their first year of marriage, she has already borne him a son.

And now his close friend Anis is also to be wed. A few weeks before the wedding, though, Anis complains constantly of headaches and insomnia. Hisham laughs at him for having bride-groom's nerves. Ruefully, Anis confirms his nervousness. He has been very busy, working with his brothers to outfit a room that will be his and his bride's home after the wedding day, while trying to run his Islamic bookshop at the same time. He worries that the room won't be finished in time, he says, frowning and rubbing his jaw, which the Israelis broke some months ago.

But, whatever happens, Anis knows that he, like Hisham has made a good choice of wife. They met one another at the Breij mosque, where both teach Koran study classes – she to young girls, he to a group of boys. 'She is a good Muslim girl,' says Anis, smil-ing.

In Western Sahara too, the guerrillas have made efforts to lead normal family lives: Most fighters are married and have wives and children living in the camps around Tindouf. But where the Palestinians boast openly about their increasing numbers, in Western Sahara the subject of family size is taboo, as if it were a state secret.

One afternoon, in the sprawling Polisario camp of Dakha, the entire popular council of the Azra Bia *daira* falls silent on the ques-tion of how many people live there. They are equally mute about the average number of children each family has Finally, sharp-faced Muhammad Saleh, the council chief, says, 'We like to have large families, just like other nations.'

The Saharawis' reluctance to discuss demographics is owed to the fact that their paltry population of 160,000 people is one of the weakest links in their arguments for their own sovereign state. Naturally, the revolution wants its people to have large families, because the more citizens it can boast, the more viable a Saharawi state will seem.

As intent as they are on nation-building, the Polisario has made having families easy by helping to plan its followers' personal lives, right down to the most intimate details. Through the camps' popular committees, the Polisario not only approves marriages; it provides the bridegrooms' dowries and even assists in the naming of the children. The Polisario essentially takes over the conventional family by assuming for itself the parental role of provider and teacher. After babies are weaned, the youngest children are looked after in collective day-care centers, and at high school age, all Saharawi children go to the 'national high school.' It is located on its own, away from all the camps.

During the school year, the children see their parents every few months, and then each summer, those students with the best grades are rewarded with summer trips abroad. Abba has been a frequent minder on these trips, escorting groups to England, France, and Sweden. Finally, upon graduation from high school, there is the choice, as always assisted by the Polisario, of military service or university.

Abba isn't yet married, but he soon will be. Young people returning to the camps from university abroad don't stay single for long. Encouraged to mingle with the opposite sex in the youth clubs of the camps, most are married by the time they are in their mid-twenties.

The emphasis the Polisario has placed on family has obvious advantages. Today there is a new generation of Saharawis who know nothing but the revolution. And if there are any doubts about where their futures lie, they are dispelled by the plethora of banners that festoon their youth clubs and exhort them to sacrifice themselves for the 'fatherland.'

If the Saharawis and Palestinians continue to create and rear new families, it is because their conditions permit them to. As hard as life is, many Palestinians can still find paying work, and with their family's help, pay for a dowry and the marriage ceremony. As for the Saharawis, they are provided for. But, for the Afghan mujahedin, mostly peasants uprooted from their lands and any source of income, any thoughts of marriage and family have to be dismissed as fantasies. Many of the fighters live in almost monastic seclusion, separated from womenfolk and family life for many months at a time.

Indeed, women and children are hard to find around Kandahar, at least in the mujahedin-held outskirts; and in Arghandab, any females not locked behind the high walls of family fortresses are entirely concealed behind their full-length black *burkha*. Most others were taken away for safekeeping long ago, to refugee camps in Pakistan where their relatives and mullahs could keep an eye on them. Married mujahedin like Abdul Hakim and Mazen Agha, whose wives and families live elsewhere, receive several days leave every few months to go and visit them. Only Mullah Naquib hasn't seen his two wives and three children out of the war zone, because he says, if he is destined to die in the war, he wants them to die with him. 'Besides,' he adds, 'women have their duty in the jihad also, to cook the food and clean the clothes of the mujahedin.'

Most of the younger fighters live in a state of enforced bachelorhood because of the war. Without access to money, they can't possibly afford the bride-prices demanded of prospective grooms. Khalilullah, still single at twenty-three, is one for whom the mujahedin life has replaced all else. He and most of the fighters at Charqulaba are probably virgins. Sublimating their sexual frustrations, they throw themselves into the five daily prayer sessions with a fervid, almost calisthenic sensuality. Khalilullah wants to marry, but after the jihad. As long as the jihad lasts, he says, it isn't an appropriate thing to be thinking about.

Once, near the Charqulaba camp, a small group of unveiled Kutchi girls appear. They herd a flock of goats through the village and out onto the wide open plain. With silver bells tinkling from slender chains on bare ankles, their limber bodies swathed in vivid dresses of green, red, and orange, they strike a provocative presence in a land where the dominant culture seems obsessed with suppressing the male and female libido. And yet, as if they are beyond all temptation, the mujahedin who are present seem oblivious, looking through them as if they aren't there.

The enforced absence of family responsibilities and of the emotional ties that go with them certainly makes life easier, in one sense, for the young mujahedin. They can get on with the jihad with hardly a backward glance. By contrast, in El Salvador male and female guerrillas live together in a permissive sexual environment; while giving greater room for emotional trauma in the fighters' everyday lives, at least the *compas* can enjoy something of a personal life, and even try to build a future, while still at war.

But tragedies are commonplace: Many *compas* grieve for companions murdered by death squads or killed in battle. Haroldo, with two lovers lost to the government's killers, has been unluckier than most.

Little Good-bye Poem

To tell you
I forget you
little by little.

Look,
how you evaporate,
how I inhale your smoke
which lingers,
how the fire which burned you
dies out

Look,
how my emotions
open
and how they
recede

Look,
how you leave my dreams.

Haroldo may allude to his dead *compañeras* in his poems, but
when he is asked to talk about them, his face falls. Searching for
words, he tries to be dismissive and impersonal, but fails. 'It's a
common thing here . . . part of the experience,' he begins. 'The first
one disappeared in 1980; it was one of the things that hardened
me. It was hard to assimilate for a long time . . . Later, I was able
to. The second one –' Haroldo breaks off and looks down helplessly.
'It's a fucked-up thing . . . to lose one's companion,' he says at last.

What Haroldo is saying is that you don't get over it. His 'Little
Good-bye Poem' is bravado. No one has 'left his dreams.' Haroldo
is torn by his desire to be free, but his is the waking torment of the
survivor, and the ghosts of his murdered lovers have become
demons he can never fully exorcise.

For others, younger than Haroldo, the reality of war has not yet
impinged on the promises of a life without sadness. Jaime, the
aspiring young poet at Giovanni's camp, is one *compa* who seems to
have found the elusive 'stable, monogamous relationship' Haroldo
jokes about.

Jaime is a pale, intense young man with a strong glandular
odor, and the tremulous eyes of someone not entirely sure of himself. Around camp, he is polite and a little retiring, but in his
poetry, Jaime pours out his guts. His laboriously penned war
poems are plastered all over the noticeboard tree at the center of

camp. Most are written in the 'Ode to the Brave Martyrs' heroic tradition, but Jaime also has a copybook full of more personal verse:

I Love a Guerrilla Girl

I met you in the winter of '87.
It awoke the illusion in me that,
after all, there could be guerrilla love.

It seemed like a waking dream.
'But,' I asked myself,
'will the *compa* want me?'.
It seemed like craziness.
And with all of this,
I hadn't even talked with her
to know her ideas and her thoughts.

One day, I tried to tell her my dreams,
about what I thought, what I felt,
and about that which suffocated me.
I surprised her by telling
her that I loved her, that I loved her
with all the strength of my soul;
and I found that she, too, was
dreaming of me.
And this is how I came to love a
guerrilla girl.

Jaime 7.30.90

Jaime's 'guerrilla girl' is a *sanitaria*, a nurse, in the FPL's field hospital, which, when the army isn't around, is located not far away

from Giovanni's camp. Their first meeting was during an enemy
sweep, when all the *compas* had to hide from bombings and
ambushes and were on the run for weeks. Now they have been
'*compas*' for about three years and have a two-year-old son, 'the
result of our first month of passion,' Jaime says with a smile.

His lover took eight months off from her duties to be with the
baby after its birth, but now she is back at the front. Their son lives
with a grandmother in one of Chalate's *repoblaciónes*. 'We get to see
each other quite a lot,' says Jaime, 'But I haven't seen the *bichito*' –
the little bug – 'for seven months.'

The reason why so many relationships at the front are fleeting
ones, says Jaime, is because most of the *compas* are afraid of getting
'too close' in a situation of war and frequent death. He adopts the
slightly lofty tone of someone who feels he has found paradise first.
'But not us. Our relationship is really giving, really special,' he
says. 'It's *all* the way, for both of us.'

Jaime's eyes are bright and he is smiling as if he alone can see
something delightful shimmering in the fringe of trees. 'This is *it*.
It's our future, and something to live for.'

Several days later in Las Flores, it is about to storm. The air is
laden with electricity and the sky overhead is almost black. It is
dusty, dry, and soundless. The plaza is empty except for a single
sneezing pig, some ducks trailing broken tethers made of rags, and
some young goats, their hind legs hobbled with sticks, jerkily
hoofing it across the plaza's stones. One of them stops, leaps into
the air, and beats a sudden tattoo with its hooves against the wall
of a house. The pig moves on, stopping to sneeze again several
times before it finally disappears from sight.

The rain comes. First big thudding drops, coming sparsely, then
more and more quickly, until the rain is a torrent and everything
is wet. On the uneven surface of the plaza, pools of water form;
water roars in streams off the roof ledges, and nothing can be heard

but the deluge. In the midst of this, Jaime arrives on the stoop of the Comedor, draped in a black plastic poncho streaming with water, his hair plastered to his head. He's just hiked in from Giovanni's camp.

Jaime stands watching the rain, stamping out water from his boots. He shivers a little; the day has turned suddenly cool. There is a drumroll of explosive thunderclaps, at which he turns and says, 'All it lacks is shrapnel.' Turning back to stare out into the plaza, he murmurs, 'Only in El Salvador. Here, even the rain gives off shrapnel.' The phrase has caught his imagination, and one can see that soon it will become the inspiration for a new poem to go into his copybook.

The rain slows down momentarily, and a flash of lightning suddenly strips the plaza bare in its white light. At that instant, Jaime dashes out across the plaza to where a young woman in a green army poncho has appeared. She stands under some eaves holding a baby in her arms. It is Jaime's 'guerrilla girl,' and the baby she carries in her arms is the son he hasn't seen in seven months.

For the rest of the afternoon, during lulls in the rain, Jaime and his thin slip of a girl walk around and around the plaza. She has on a peasant woman's cheap nylon dress, and wears thick green army socks bunched up above her walking shoes. She has the long russet-colored hair of a Chalateca. At her side, Jaime beams. His AK-47 in one hand, the other around his *compa*'s slender waist, Jaime steps out wide and proud onto the plaza's stones.

Not all of the *compas* are as lucky in love as Jaime. But for most, the revolution also provides a surrogate family, replacing the loved ones they have lost, left behind, or grown away from during the war. As *compas*, they have become *incorporados*, grafted into the very body of the revolution, as in an organic union.

Carlos, the thin, gray compa who works with Olga and Adriano in the propaganda unit, is one of those for whom the revolution has replaced his genetic family. Carlos and his wife were teachers before the war. In those days, the leftist teacher's union was strongly pro-guerrilla, and consequently its members were a prime target of the death squads. They either went underground, fled abroad like Adriano's family, or joined the *compas* in the hills as fighters them-selves. Carlos opted for the hills, but his wife stayed behind. 'She didn't want to assume a clandestine identity and a clandestine life,' he says. Carlos's expression is philosophical, but sad. 'So that was it. She stayed, and I went.'

Recently, Carlos sneaked back to the capital to see his children. It was the first time he had done so since leaving ten years before. He felt safe enough, because he had aged so much in the past decade, he believed the security forces would never recognize him. He was undoubtedly right: Carlos is only forty-three years old, but he looks at least sixty.

Carlos found his children not only almost grown up, but also almost totally innocent politically. He discovered that, out of fear for their safety, his wife had kept them completely away from pol-itics. It is a cruel irony for Carlos, who has spent all these years fighting for certain ideals only to find out they are concepts his children neither know much about nor have much interest in.

'They still have no idea I'm a guerrilla,' Carlos says. For the chil-dren's safety, his wife concealed his real identity after he fled; they have grown up believing Carlos lives abroad because he and their mother are estranged, that he is some kind of businessman. His wife has maintained this fiction over the years. By following the path of revolution, Carlos has irrevocably lost the ability to influ-ence and guide his own children. Like Rip Van Winkle, he has grown old and returned home only to find that his children are strangers.

Back in the hills, the presence of Adriano – so young, creative and a committed revolutionary as well – must be a bittersweet solace to Carlos. He is a flesh-and-blood example of the son Carlos might have had if things had turned out differently, if his wife hadn't stayed behind with the kids ten years ago, and if . . .

Adriano is one of a number of the younger guerrillas who are second-generation revolutionaries, having followed their parents into the war. For them, there is no domestic trauma to overcome. In this, they are lucky. Like children raised in a hermetic religious community, they can be secure in their identities; the revolution is their birthright, their destiny.

Sandra, the *radista*, is another child of the revolution. She lives as she was raised — within the revolution — whether at home with her parents or at the front. The letters Sandra gets from them are much like those parents write to any girl of her age living away from home: full of parental advice and little instructive homilies on life. The difference is that in her letters, Sandra is told to be 'good and virtuous' not just as a young woman, but as a revolutionary as well.

For Giovanni the revolution is, in a very literal sense, a substitute for his own family. His mother and two of his sisters — one of them pregnant — were murdered; his father was castrated and tortured to death; two brothers have died fighting. Only three siblings are left out of the original seven. Some of his orphaned nephews and nieces have disappeared and are believed to have been 'adopted' by their parents' killers in keeping with the ghoulish tradition of right-wing Latin American military men presiding over dirty wars in recent years. Like him, Giovanni's surviving brother and sister are *compas*, living in the hills. 'We still feel pain,' he says, 'But we have learned to live with it. And these things oblige us to keep fighting.'

Normally dour, Giovanni relaxes and becomes downright paternal when he is with the kids in his camp, tousling their hair gently, holding the younger ones close like children, and calling them affectionately 'los cachorros de Farabundo,' 'Farabundo's cubs,' after the late revolutionary figure Farabundo Martí.

Family. That is what it all comes down to for so many of the *compas*. If they have suffered a tragedy, it lies invariably in the loss of family members. For many of them, the war has ripped out their hearts, left them reeling in its seizure of loved ones, the slaughter of mothers, fathers, brothers, and sisters.

For the kids who belong to the squad led by Carmelo and Geronimo in the *zona de expansión*, their commanders are all much more than senior officers; they are also older brothers and father figures. Carmelo is twenty-seven. A lot of these kids are fourteen or fifteen, the same age he was when the conflict began and he became involved. Now, he and Geronimo, who is thirty, laughingly call themselves the old men of the movement, and they are, because so few of the first generation of fighters are still alive.

These kids are the younger brothers and sisters of *compas* who have already fallen, or else they are the orphans of people massacred by the army in the early 1980s, when the children were still only three, four, or five years old. They have been brought up in refugee camps or else on the run as the FMLN's *masas*, and now they have come of age. For the kids, there have never been any doubts about what they would do when they grow up.

The kids come to Carmelo for advice, to complain about one another, to confide in him, to cajole him for treats and special privileges. Such and such a lady has fresh eggs, will he buy some for them? Can Elmer – one of the boys in the squad – have leave to visit his family? Can they have some money for cigarettes? In El Copinol, hearing that a video is being shown in the next village, they all come begging Carmelo to be allowed to 'go to the movies.' Indeed, much of the time, Carmelo and Geronimo seem more like camp counselors escorting kids on an outing than the leaders of a

guerrilla squad. Often, Carmelo's biggest task each day is providing enough to eat for the voracious youngsters.

Once, at mealtime, he looks them in the eyes and tells them:
'You haven't experienced real hunger yet.' He reminds them how
easy they have it now compared with how it was in the revolution's
early days. How, far from walking openly between villages and
eating corn and beans and tortillas every day as they do now, he and
Geronimo spent years having to hide in caves, venturing out only
at night to scavenge for whatever food they could find. How, one
time, all they could find to eat was the bark of papaya trees in a
farmer's field.

At other times Carmelo takes the kids down a few pegs by
reminding them that they can hardly call themselves guerrillas,
since most of them haven't been in combat yet. When Carmelo
speaks this way the kids sober right up, because he is the measure
of their own aspirations, and combat experience is what they all
want more than anything, to validate themselves as *guerrilleros*,
heroes of the people. But like true teenagers, the kids in Carmelo's
unit are more occupied with each other than anything else. War or
no war, in a group where four teenage girls are thrown together
with eight boys of the same age, sexual tension is inevitable. Out
on patrol, their adolescent moods and games set the rhythm of each
day.

Early one morning, after a Saturday night dance in the Las
Vueltas schoolhouse, the squad sets out into the *zona de expansión*.
The night before, all the kids in town – *compas* and civilians alike –
descended on the place and danced until after midnight. There
were only two cassette tapes, played over and over on someone's
boom box, but the kids were happy. It was noisy and dark, and that
was all that mattered.

As at a lot of school dances, there were more boys than girls. For
every dancing couple, there were five or six *compas* who stood

together, posing for the girls with their thumbs hooked in their belts, AK-47s on shoulders, smoking cigarettes. They kept up a running commentary about the dancers, calling out to tease their more fortunate comrades. They were watched in turn by the little kids, the *cipotes*. One group of serious little seven- and eight-year-old boys played an inconvenient game of cards in a corner of the dance floor. Still too young to dance, they at least made sure their presence was felt.

Among the kids of Carmelo's squad, the festive mood sparked by the dance lingers on well after the dance has ended. It takes them forever to get to sleep where they are bivouacked on the earthen porch of Las Vueltas's Comedor Popular. They giggle and sing and generally make a nuisance of themselves into the wee hours. Roused by Carmelo before first light, one of them turns on the cassette player at full volume. Mustering under the large stone cross on the front of the church, the *compitas* shuffle to the strains of that most euphemistic of Salvadoran dance tunes, 'Gallo Mojado' – 'Wet Chicken' – a song exalting lubricious female genitalia.

The newest member of the group is a muscular, strutting youth who joined up just five days ago. Just this morning he finally exchanges his jeans and sneakers for a pair of boots and a uniform given to him by Carmelo. The first thing he does is to roll up the uniform's shirt-sleeves to show off his biceps. Then, puffing out his chest proudly, he falls in with the others on the church steps.

Carmelo looks stern and tweaks his handlebar mustache as he waits for the teenagers to assemble. He needs to lower their excitement level, to ease them back into reality a little without dampening their spirits. First, he barks for the music to be turned off. Then, when the kids have gathered in two lines in front of him, he tells them to stand at attention, shoulder rifles, and listen carefully to what he has to say. As Carmelo drones on about their marching orders, and reminds them to be on their best behavior, the kids stare, frozen to attention, but they are only half-listening, intent as they are on looking good for the village children who have gathered to watch them.

On the periphery stands Geronimo. He nods in quiet agreement as Carmelo speaks, tousling the hair of his own young son, who lives in the village and has come to glue himself between his father's legs. Geronimo rarely says anything. Tall and ungainly, he moves slowly and speaks slowly. Even his eyelids bat slowly when he blinks. He has huge feet, wears a uniform several sizes too small, and with his slumped shoulders and bulging Adam's apple poking out from his long, thin neck, he looks like a camel dozing on its feet.

'I want you all to go slow and spread out. Stay within sight of one another,' finishes Carmelo. The squad breaks formation and begins the hike up the steep track, out of Las Vueltas to the escarpment above, and into the *zona de expansión*. The squad is accompanied by a horse. It is loaded down with jute sacks stuffed with *elotes*, the fresh ears of sweet corn just now in the full bloom of harvest. The *compas* adore *elotes*, and eat them boiled, toasted, ground into sweet tamales, or mixed with milk, cinnamon, and sugar and made into the beverage *atole*. Before leaving town, the *compas* have gorged themselves at the Comedor, the boys eating at least six boiled *elotes* apiece. Now they stuff their pockets with several more for the journey, and as the unit moves slowly out of town, most of the kids are still eating, corncobs held in their fists like pistols.

Carmelo doesn't push the kids. After only a few hours' march the group makes camp at a civilian collaborator's farmhouse on a breezy rise of land above El Copinol. They haven't made much ground, but it doesn't matter. Speed isn't important. On the contrary, in the expansion zone the unit's mission is to make its presence felt, and the best way to do that is to take things easily, talking and listening to the local people and, it is hoped, enlisting new recruits. It is slow, steady work, aiming for long-term gains. So far, it is paying off. In the first three years of organizing work the *compas* gained only one recruit in the *zona de expansión*. Now, suddenly, like a logjam breaking free, the volunteers have begun flooding in. In the past year, one has become a hundred, and now the *compas* are on their way.

The *compas* are also aided by their sympathizers among the returning refugees. In El Copinol, the unit's hostess is a guerrilla's widow, who recently moved into a farmhouse abandoned by its original owners. Its availability isn't the reason she'd chosen this site. With its strategic hilltop location and sweeping views all the way to the Sumpul River canyon, the house has long been used by the army as a command center during antiguerrilla operations. But not anymore. 'I've taken this position for the *compas*,' she says.

Like Pied Pipers, Carmelo and Geronimo lead their youthful charges back and forth through their own home villages, picking up new volunteers on each swing through. Each new kid is like gold to the guerrillas, adding to their strength. This is why Carmelo is so tolerant with those who have just joined up. As long as they are happy, and giving off a happy image to the civilians in the villages of the zone, that is the important thing.

The zone is deceptively quiet. There are no longer any soldiers stationed in the villages, and most of the collaborators have been killed or forced to flee, but the army can launch a raid anytime from its bases just over the hills. So, wherever the group camps for the night, the kids do rotating perimeter watches, and extreme caution is exercised in talking with civilians in order to keep the squad's movements secret.

Late in the afternoon, after the first day's march, Ulíses and Diego arrive unannounced at the El Copinol farmhouse. They are on a mission to make contact with collaborators in the hills between the expansion zone and the army-held towns beyond. They don't want their presence in the area known in advance, so they wait in the farmhouse until after dark before moving on. As the day fades away, a government observation plane drones far overhead in a wide circle, only to vanish again. The *compas* don't move, since as long as they stay inside the farmhouse or under its shade trees, they can't be seen.

'There goes La Chambrona [the Gossip Lady],' says one of the kids. '*Su marído* [her husband] can't be far behind.' In their effort to find humor in everything, the *compas* have given the enemy's deadly machines familiar, human characteristics. The 'Gossip Lady' relays information back to base, and if she finds a target, 'her husband' – a rocket-equipped A-37 bomber – usually arrives within minutes to wreak death and destruction on whatever lies below. The *compas* also have a name for the helicopter gunships: *avispas*, wasps, for their insectlike appearance, their irritating buzzing noise, and the 'stings' they carry.

On this occasion, however, no bombers show up, and the *compas* enjoy a peaceful sunset and supper on the breezy ridge. Soon after darkness falls, Ulíses and Diego move off on their mission, and Carmelo and his kids are left to themselves.

A couple of days later, in the hamlet called simply El Sitio, 'the Place,' Aracely and her boyfriend finally make up. They have been fighting ever since El Copinol, plunging the entire squad into gloominess with their heavy silences, sighs, and long faces. Neither looks at the other, and each has sought out allies among the other kids.

Yesterday, on the way from Ojo de Agua to this place, they marched separately; at rest stops, each sat apart from the other. The boy feigned lighthearted indifference, but Aracely was positively miserable, and in the evening she sat at a distance from everyone else, listening to love songs on her scratchy transistor radio. Finally, Ramiro, the buck-toothed fifteen-year-old who plays the fool for the whole group, tried to patch things up.

After talking awhile with Aracely's gangly beau, Ramiro came over to where Aracely sat. Loud enough for the rest of the squad to overhear, Ramiro whispered, 'He says he won't come to you. He says, "If she wants me she'll have to come to me first."' Aracely had been sitting hunched, staring stolidly at her radio. Now she underwent an instant transformation. She turned to Ramiro, her face suddenly brightening. Then, in a flash of mock anger, her expression hardened again and she hit Ramiro's shoulders and arms with lightly clenched fists, exclaiming: 'You gossip! What did he really say? Tell me!'

When the reconciliation finally comes, it happens spontaneously: Aracely comes up behind her lover as he walks past her, and she grabs him with both hands. She turns him around, her beseeching face full upon him. He crumples easily into her arms, and then both are hugging one another with pent-up passion.

At nineteen, Aracely is the oldest female present, and the other girls defer to her as they would to an older sister. The squad's *sanitaria*, nurse, she carries her meager supply of medical gear on her own back and walks quickly on her short legs. La China is a buxom, kitten-faced girl of fourteen. She is training to become Carmelo's *radista*. The prettiest of the girls, La China shows the least interest in the boys, and she sticks close to Aracely much of the time.

Anabela, fourteen years old, is the squad's *tortillera*. At every meal stop, she grinds corn, kneading the dough and slapping out tortillas. During the day's march she carries the plastic basin with the tortilla dough on her head. Anabela is also an outrageous flirt, and as a result has become the primary love interest for the boys in the squad. She often leaves her blouse unbuttoned to reveal her bra, or ties it up tightly around her breasts like a halter top, exposing her midriff. The other girls shun her, and Aracely constantly scolds her for her behavior.

The newest boy has picked up on Anabela right away and begun working her. He hovers around, whispering to her and eyeing her lustfully. She does whatever she can to inflame him, grinning at him wickedly and flicking her long hair, or, walking just ahead of him with the pot on her head, sashaying provocatively. Aracely looks on, scowling in disgust. Now and then, when she can stand it no longer, she stomps over to the girl's side and tells her off. 'Behave, can't you?' she exclaims. Caught out, Anabela stifles her giggles with one hand, and then, after a few chastened moments, returns to her old ways. All around, the boys simmer, and it seems like sooner or later there will be trouble because of Anabela.

Aracely is only trying to save the younger girl from grief, something she knows all about. When she was about the same age as Anabela is now she got pregnant, and was forced to leave the front to give birth. The *compa* who got her pregnant wasn't interested in a relationship, and so Aracely was on her own. The child, now four, is being looked after by Aracely's mother in Las Vueltas, and Aracely has returned to the front a little older and a lot more experienced.

Of the eight boys in Carmelo's charge, the only sexually active one is Aracely's boyfriend. He therefore enjoys a special leadership role among the other boys in the squad, and often wears an expression of *gravitas* commensurate with his elevated status. The others, meanwhile, still seem content to kid around with the girls and leave it at that.

Melvin, the boy in charge of the unit's walkie-talkie, is the true baby of Carmelo's unit. With large, intelligent eyes and a quick mouth, Melvin is intellectually quicker than most of his comrades, but his body is that of a puny little boy. He is thirteen but looks only nine or ten. A protégé of Ulíses, Melvin is currently teaching La China to be a *radista*. Each evening, he sits with her, trying to get her to memorize the codes. La China is very slow, but Melvin masks his frustration because he likes being close to her.

Because of his small size, Melvin is able to get away with a lot of mischief. He is constantly clambering all over La China, resting his head in her lap, combing her hair, hugging her. Usually, the girl humors him, forgetting he is nearly her own age and not a little boy at all.

Melvin is full of disarming information about himself. He likes to read and most recently finished Gabriel García Marquez's *The General in His Labyrinth*; before that, he read *The Little Prince*, which he found 'disquieting.' He says he can read fifty pages an hour, having studied for a while at a private school in San Salvador, where he learned to speed-read. He is the only son left in his family after his three older brothers died fighting with the *compas*; his mother died in a massacre; a year ago, his father died of 'alcoholic intoxication.' Afterward, he says, he and his two younger sisters came to Las Vueltas to live with an uncle, but as soon as he could, Melvin joined up with the *compas*. That was in April. It is now July. So far, Melvin's only complaint about revolutionary life is that he doesn't have as much time to read as he would like. But apart from this, he loves being a *compa*, and says he wants always to be one.

Ulíses confirms the boy's story and adds some new details. 'His family are hammock-makers,' says Ulíses. 'After his mother was killed, Melvin's father became a drunk. He used to beat Melvin all the time. For a while they were refugees in Honduras. Then they moved back to Chalatenango. The father started up a hammock-making business again, but he didn't attend to the basic needs of his kids. Melvin used to have to go and find food for his young sisters while his father slept off his binges. It was a very hard life.

Finally an uncle in the capital took them in with him, and Melvin went to school.'

When his father finally died from drinking, Melvin and his siblings were adopted by another uncle and brought back to Chalatenango to live. When Melvin joined up, Ulíses took him under his own wing and trained him as a *radista*. 'He liked it when I disciplined him, when I was strict with him,' Ulíses says. 'It's like he needed the fatherly influence. He liked to have someone pay attention to him.'

Finally, though, Ulíses sent Melvin off to join Carmelo's squad and be his *radista*. But Melvin wanted to stay with Ulíses. 'For a long time Melvin was very angry with me,' says Ulíses. 'You see, he loves me a lot. But I had to be tough with him.'

Now, a few weeks have gone by, and Melvin has settled in with the kids of Carmelo's unit. Together, they are growing up. The common experiences they have had and the life they share now gives them a bond that is perhaps greater than if they were true blood siblings.

One morning, Ramiro strips down to his underpants so that Aracely can wash his jeans in the water basin of the abandoned farmhouse where they have stayed for the night. She has offered to do him this service.

Aracely is from Las Vueltas. By the age of nine, she was acquainted firsthand with 'slaughter and *guindas*.' '*Guindas*' is the guerrillas' term for the forced marches in the early years of the war, when entire civilian communities fled the army troops alongside the guerrillas. Often, they went without food for days and hiked endlessly over mountains to avoid the army. It was necessary in order to survive. Usually the soldiers massacred any *masas* they found.

As far as killings in her family went, Aracely was lucky; she has 'only lost one grandpa and five uncles.' Finally forced to flee Las

Vueltas altogether, Aracely, her mother, and her siblings hid in the forest between Las Vueltas and Las Flores, living in *tatús*, the little caves the *compas* and *masas* dig in order to hide from the army. 'We spent our time in fear, just waiting for the enemy to find us.'

Aracely stops her washing to sit down, the soap still clinging to her brown arms. 'Those men who killed my uncles and my grandpa, they just took them and made them squat against a wall and killed them,' she says. 'I always wonder, what kind of enemies are these? I can't imagine anyone doing that. Even if they put the ones who have done so much harm to my family in front of me, I can't imagine killing them. But these people can kill even little children, knowing that they're innocent.'

La China was also born in Las Vueltas. In 1980, when she was just four, her father was murdered by the National Guard, the Guardia, stationed in those days in Las Vueltas. Her mother has told her how her father was herded with four other men to a big *amate* tree that stands by the bridge on the outskirts of Las Vueltas, then machine-gunned at point-blank range. 'My mother says Papa was still alive when they finished shooting. All the others were dead, but he was in shock, and trying to stand, poor thing, and wipe the blood off. Then those men came and finished him off with their machetes.'

La China's soft face is stretched in disgust. It is an image she cannot shake: a man, her father, rising to his feet in a wash of blood, punctured by bullets and spouting red gore, his killers walking toward him with long knives in their hands, about to stab and hack him to death. She shudders as she speaks; it is an old and recurring nightmare.

Aracely and La China compare notes on their experiences like teenagers discussing which pop concerts they have been to. 'The *guindas* I remember the most were the ones of October and November,' says the younger girl. Aracely nods. She knows immediately which *guindas* La China is talking about – naming the year isn't necessary.

After the murder of La China's father, the family went on *guinda*, fleeing for their lives. 'I remember coming down La Montañona and seeing all these shoes and sandals,' she says. 'Everyone had run away and left them . . . I remember finding a baby wrapped up in the base of a tree where it had been left in hiding . . . I remember stepping on the body of a dead woman in another *guinda*; I had to step on her to get down a steep riverbank.' After another massacre, La China can't remember which one it was, her mother found and adopted a neighbor's two orphaned children. Since then the children have all grown up together as brothers and sisters.

Aracely listens in silence to La China's stories, nodding and occasionally glancing over at the girl. Neither sheds any tears. Their only visible distress comes when they remember, indignantly, *how* their relatives were killed. They have long since learned to deal with the deaths; it is the nature of those deaths that continues to bother them.

Soon, the girls stop talking and fall silent. There is just the *whoosh, whoosh* of Aracely pounding Ramiro's jeans rhythmically on the corrugated surface of the washbasin, slurping in a bit of water now and again. Then a few other sounds – birds twittering, boots scraping on the stoop, boys humming as they clean their weapons – begin filtering through. As they do, the day seems to widen, crackling into sunlight around the farmhouse.

Having learned the hard way about the ruthlessness of their enemy, most of those *compas* with their own flesh-and-blood children have installed them away from the war zone with relatives in the cities or refugee camps; some even send their children to other countries. Although they go for many months without seeing them, the parents' solace is knowing they are growing up in safety.

Once, the whole Radio Farabundo Martí crew shows up in Las Flores. They hang out for a day at a peasant's hut just up from the plaza. It is a stormy day, and the sky is a swollen purplish blue, the color of damask grapes. A flat blanket of white clouds moves steadily overhead, propelled by the winds. The Farabundistas swing in their hammocks and watch the rain stream down from the red tiles into the surrounding mud.

They are a jocular, close-knit group, all former students, and seem as comfortable as old clothes in each other's company. Besides Haroldo, there is Justo, rangy, bearded, and bespectacled; he is the youngest of the men, at twenty-nine. Thin, intense, and very pale, Augustín, a former stage actor, is the Radio's principal announcer. He is sharp-witted and endowed with an acid tongue. Erandery is a handsome woman of twenty-four, and her lover, Richard, is a clean-faced former electrical-engineering student in his mid-thirties whom Augustín calls 'the altar boy.' Cristina is thirty-one; she joined the revolution right out of high school, in the late 1970s.

Erandery has only recently returned to Chalatenango after giving birth to a son. Normally she would have taken the ten to twelve months the FMLN allows mothers to spend with their newborn babies, but she wanted to be back in the field for the offensive against the capital that was launched a few months ago, and returned early. 'I couldn't have missed it for anything,' she says. 'I weaned my baby first, though.' Not to miss out, Augustín pulls out a photo of a tall, good-looking boy – his son. 'He's thirteen,' he announces. Then, with visible pride, he adds: 'And I'm going to have another kid in two months.'

Cristina also has a child. Now she produces a picture, one of a very young boy. She says that leaving him behind and losing the boy's father – he was killed in the war – are the hardest things she has ever faced. Her son lives with Cristina's mother in 'another country,' and it has been a full year since she's seen him. The others listen quietly but look elsewhere as Cristina struggles to keep from weeping. In the end, not a single tear appears, but her voice is hoarse and she has to stop talking. Everyone lapses into a long silence. It is eventually broken by Erandery, who exclaims wistfully, 'Oh, kids!'

'The revolution is like a family, but everyone needs their own family, too,' says Haroldo. Even after all his tragedy, Haroldo hasn't given up on love. He currently has a third companion, with whom he's fathered a young baby girl. But this time he is taking no chances: They aren't with him at the front, but 'outside,' living in safety – as is the son borne him by his first lover. 'He's almost an adolescent now . . .'

After lunch, Erandery and Richard retire to the hut's single room to lie down and be alone, while the others doze in their hammocks. Occasionally, a chuckle can be heard from the hut's interior, but after a while there is only silence.

One morning, bright with sunshine and cool after a night's rain, Luis, the commander of Las Vueltas, stands in the doorway of the Comedor and helps a young girl who is weaving a fishing net. Las Vueltas has always been known as a place where not only hammocks, but also good fishing nets are made. Strange, maybe, because Las Vueltas is so far from the sea, but that's the way it is.

Luis grins with pleasure, revealing the gap in his lower jaw where several teeth are missing. Suddenly he can be seen for the village boy he is, not the guerrilla commander with the hard mouth and eyes, with bullet wounds puckering here and there on his body. His hands become sensitive, almost feminine, as they follow old impulses to weave the net deftly and swiftly.

Luis was born around here; he knows everyone in the area, and they know him. From his command center in a house overlooking the open churchyard, Luis can look down the main street of the vil-

lage to the water spigots that sit in a line of cement troughs just in
front of the schoolhouse. There the main street curves out of town
until the roadside *amate* trees swallow it up in shade, and the over-
hanging hills come in close together to squeeze it between them.
Just out of sight there is a bridge over the road, which leads to the
provincial capital of Chalatenango. For almost ten years it has been
cut, blown up by the *compas* to prevent the army from having road
access into the valley. It was under the *amate* near the bridgehead
that La China's father was cut to pieces, where Aracely's grandfather and uncle were made to kneel and then butchered.

It was abuses like these by the local Guardia – shootings and
massacres in which two of his sisters and a brother were killed –
that made Luis take up a gun. From the moment he did so, Luis
was not able to live in the open. He survived in the hills outside of
town, on the run, like a lot of other local youths. It is only since the
last Guardia posts were overrun and the refugees have returned that
he has been able to live in the village. Even now, though, Luis
keeps his hard eyes focused on the brow of the surrounding ridges,
as if the enemy might appear at any moment.

It has been a long, hard decade for Luis. When he went into the
hills, he left behind a young wife and baby daughter. 'I had no
choice. It was a matter of survival. Those were the days when *not* to
go meant getting killed.' Luis's wife left Las Vueltas to live with
relatives in a safer town, taking their year-old daughter with her.
'After about a year,' says Luis, 'I heard she'd taken up with someone else.' Eventually, Luis also found a new mate, another local girl,
and has begun to raise a second family with her. It has been ten
years since he and his first wife saw each other.

This morning Luis is called outside by some of his men. In the
scant shade of the lone tree at the front of the church stands a
young, stocky civilian woman. She wears a bright pink dress. Next
to her stands an adolescent girl in a frilly yellow dress, little white

ankle socks, and black patent-leather shoes. A yellow ribbon holds up her long, wavy brown hair. The girl stands nervously on one foot, twisting one ankle behind the other. The woman with her holds her own hands together tightly as if to keep them from flying up all by themselves. Both are aware that they are being scrutinized, as the people of Las Vueltas stare at them from the shadows of the houses fronting the wide main street.

Luis stares expressionlessly toward them for a long moment, then walks over slowly. Everyone in the Comedor and in the houses on the far side of the church watches as Luis begins speaking to the woman and girl. Drawn from their morning game of spinning tops on the church steps, a little gang of village boys comes to eavesdrop from a few feet away. Within minutes, word filters back to the onlookers that the woman and girl are none other than Luis's ex-wife and daughter.

Soon, the three come walking over to the Comedor. The kids in Carmelo's unit who are sitting at the single wooden table get up to clear a space for them. The newcomers sit down, and the *compas* stand around watching in silence like majordomos in attendance at a public banquet. The woman smiles uncertainly and the girl wears a blank expression and fidgets. The three of them sit there in tongue-tied silence interspersed with short bursts of dry exchanges of news between Luis and his ex-wife. They are like complete strangers; nothing in their body language reveals they were ever married. 'So what year are you now – in school?' Luis asks his daughter when he finally turns to her.

The girl looks away from him to her mother and then back to her father. Looking down at her lap shyly, she tells him in a small voice that she is in the sixth grade. Luis nods, and falls silent again. He doesn't have a clue what to say next. He leans across the table and says, this time to his ex-wife, 'So, you left ten years ago, right?'

'Yes,' she nods, vigorously agreeing. 'Yes.'

At this, Luis repeats, 'So, it's been ten years, then.' He leans back in his bench again, at a loss for more words. The girl and her mother nod their heads up and down. Yes, it has been ten years.

Suddenly Luis stands up and asks them to pardon him. Without further explanation, he walks away across the main street and disappears. It is nearly an hour before he returns, by which time the girl is bored and beseeching her mother to leave in a loud whisper. When Luis reappears, he is transformed. He has been to the river to bathe. Now, with his wet hair neatly combed, smelling of perfumed soap and wearing a new uniform still with its factory creases, Luis is no longer ill at ease. His boots are new ones, gleaming blackly with polish, and his AK-47 is oiled and slung on his shoulder. Unselfconsciously, Luis poses; this is how he wishes to be seen.

The ex-wife and daughter stare; they are impressed. Now Luis looks more like the FPL commander of Las Vueltas. He sits back down, but he is still unsettled. Soon, spying Ulíses nearby, he calls out that he wants a haircut – cutting hair is a hobby of Ulíses's – and, excusing himself again, Luis walks across and plunks himself down in a chair placed outside the church. He puts down his rifle and peels off his new shirt, and there, as his ex-wife, his daughter, and all the *compas* of Carmelo's unit look on, Luis has his hair cut.

When Ulíses is done with him, Luis dons his uniform and sits back down again with his ex-wife and daughter. Now he is completely relaxed; the picture has been perfected; that the metamorphosis has taken place in full view of those he wishes to impress doesn't seem to matter: It is the final image that counts.

But by now it is late afternoon, and Luis's daughter tugs at her mother's arm to urge her to leave. Finally her mother announces that they had better be going if they are to find transport. Getting to and from Las Vueltas is difficult, as everyone knows. Luis agrees, and walks them back as far as the tree in front of the church. There he says good-bye, and watches as they walk back down the road leading out of Las Vueltas, toward the blown-up bridge, then to the world beyond.

At Kawmura, one can see them coming like unearthly apparitions against the backdrop of towering bamboo, their faces whitened with tamarind paste, taking short, quick steps in their tight sarongs, glowing cheroots protruding from their mouths like giant cigars.

They are the fighters' wives, bringing their husbands hot lunches. Some make the same trip every day, crossing the river from Thailand by standing up in a leaky dugout canoe and drawing on a wire pulley, arm over arm. If the shelling from the Burmese positions is heavy, the wives stay on the Thai side, in a stilted longhouse in the forest, a short walk back from the river, and wait for it to end.

Like the *compas* in El Salvador, Burma's Karen guerrillas have tried to ensure that their fighters are able to lead full family lives. Again, this has been easier for some fighters than for others. Here, too, there are many cases of enforced separation and personal loss, and numerous fighters for whom the 'revolution' has become a second family.

But most of the similarities end there. For one thing, in Kawthoolei the fighters actually get married, their vows sanctified by the ceremonies of one church or another. And, with their wedding vows reinforced by the adultery ban, there is no convenient 'Law of the Lake.' And, although there is a new 'girls' brigade' stationed at Manerplaw, most Karen women aren't fighters. While their men do military duty, the vast majority of women stay at home with the children in one of the six Karen refugee camps on the Thai side of the border.

However, the fighters are 'asked' not to marry until they are thirty-five. 'This is because the revolution has to assume the living costs for the families, and it doesn't have enough for everyone,' says KNU prime minister Saw Baw Thin. If fighters want to marry earlier, they can, and the KNU will help them out as much as it can, but if they have 'too many' children, they are asked to leave the front and find work to support themselves. This no-nonsense policy is another reason why many KNU families tend to have a business on the side, like Ganemy's fruit orchard, the teahouse lady's gemstone trade, or Adjutant-General Hla Htoo's rice-paddy *taungyo* up in the hills.

Clearly, the general needs his *taungyo* to help feed his large brood. About seventy now, Hla Htoo has sired seven children, some of whom still live at home in Tuvalu, the village near Manerplaw he helped found twenty years ago. Every day, he commutes to and from Tuvalu to his work at Manerplaw's 'Defense Ministry' by motor canoe.

His large stilted home, constantly full of people, is buttressed from below by the stump of a huge tree, and the smoke from a wood fire seeps up through the floorboards to ward off mosquitoes. Inside, the house is packed with the accoutrements of family life: large, old-fashioned dressers and chests of drawers sit alongside jute sacks of potatoes, rice, and onions, and in the cobwebbed rafters above, dimly lit by fluorescent light strips, there are woven baskets, sticks of spare lumber, and precariously perched cane fishing rods.

The general's grandchildren run all over the rambling place like a flurry of gnats, watched inattentively by several elderly, rheumy-eyed aunts and in-laws who sit around the kitchen area waiting for their next meal. Teenagers come and go. Hla Htoo jokes about the size of his family. 'Even when one is in the revolution, one has *needs* too,' he says, giving a lusty wink.

Indeed. Even so, some of the guerrillas have gone many years before starting their own families. David, the KNU's explosives expert, is a quiet, bespectacled man in his midfifties, and he has only been married six years. He is a neighbor of Major Soe Soe's in Ban Mae Sot and, like him, lives an outwardly settled, normal life. Many afternoons, he can be seen doing the shopping in Ban Mae Sot's crowded downtown market, walking along with his young son and daughter sitting on the handlebars of his bicycle.

David's wife is twenty-eight years younger than he is. He likes to tell the story of how his marriage came to be. 'When I joined the KNU in 1978,' he says, 'I came to Kawthoolei and then I waited for my girlfriend in Rangoon to join me, as we had arranged.' He waited and waited, but his girlfriend never came. 'Finally, after four years, I realized she wasn't coming,' says David with a sheepish smile. 'So I asked a friend here to find me a suitable bride.'

The friend began looking for appropriate matches for David among the KNU families along the border. Very soon, he told David he had found him a bride. Much to David's surprise, not only was the girl less than half his age, but his friend had already made the formal proposal on his behalf. 'By the time I met her,' says David, 'there was no backing out. So I had to marry her.'

He was 'really upset' at his friend for quite a while, David says, but in the end, it has all worked out well. The age difference does not seem to have mattered, and theirs is a happy marriage, with children.

David's colleague Major Robert Zan, meanwhile, is already on his third wife. His first marriage lasted only three months, ending when his wife was captured and imprisoned for seven years. 'I took a second wife, and when she got out, she went with another man.' His second marriage fared little better, ending in divorce after five years because he was always away at the front. 'Sometimes I was only home one month in a year,' Robert Zan says. 'She couldn't take it.' But this marriage did give him his only son, Du Du.

His latest marriage has given him two more children, both girls, and lasted ten years, so this one will probably be for good. For one thing, Robert Zan is older now, nearing fifty, and, since the fighting these days is closer to home, there isn't the same need to be far away for months at a time.

For Ganemy, the hardest thing about becoming a guerrilla was saying good-bye to his parents. All children must grow up and leave home, he knew, but this was different: He might never see his parents again. He was at university at the time. Torn with indecision over whether or not he should give everything up for the Karen people's struggle, he came home to his parents' village to make up his mind. He went out and sat in a field full of wildflowers where he had always gone to think as a boy. It was there he made his decision. Then he went and told his parents what he wanted to do and asked their opinion. 'They told me to do whatever I had to do. So I joined up.'

After five years had gone by, Ganemy managed to sneak back to his village. At the insistence of his KNU superiors, two guerrillas escorted him. Dressed in civilian clothes, disguised as traders, they hiked through the jungle to his parents' village. When they finally arrived, Ganemy realized that if he entered, he would be immediately recognized, and so instead he and his comrades hid in a sugar-cane field outside the village. For five successive nights, he crept into the village to see his parents, but then finally he had to leave. In the fifteen years that have passed since that visit, he has not been back. 'It was the last time I saw my father alive,' says Ganemy. 'Now my mother is very old and I want to see her one last time. The president thinks it is too dangerous, that I will be caught, but I want to go.'

He is in his forties now, but Ganemy still misses his mother and father. This feeling will never go away. But, after staying single for many years while serving on the front line, Ganemy recently began

a family himself. This has assuaged some of the gnawing homesickness he felt before. He and his young wife, a teacher at
Manerplaw, now have two daughters. He named their first child
Poderplaw. It is the name of the wildflower that grows in the field
outside his parents' village, where he made the decision to leave
them forever.

For David, Ganemy, and Robert Zan, it has taken years to
achieve personal happiness while also fulfilling their duties as guerrillas. Certainly, the revolution has provided them with a sense of
community, but for none of them was this enough; each has felt the
need to have his own family as well.

The Burmese students still have higher priorities than raising families. They can barely feed themselves, much less support wives and
children. The leader of the student brigades stationed near Manerplaw
is Myo Thant, a thin, bronzed man of thirty-four with a wispy mustache and a revolver in his belt. Myo Thant is a former teacher of
English history from Mandalay. 'I know that to win this revolution it
will take years,' he says. 'The younger students have difficulty thinking of such a long time, but I am trying to prepare them.'

Homesickness is one of the biggest obstacles Myo Thant faces in
his self-appointed task. Most of the students have family homes
back in Burma that are still intact, and that they can return to if
they choose. This knowledge exerts a constant emotional pull on
the young exiles, and Rangoon has cleverly tried to exploit this
feeling by declaring an amnesty to woo them back. To forestall a
wholesale exodus from their jungle camps, the Karen and student
leaders have spread rumors that returnees face torture and even execution at the government's hands. But the rumors have had little
effect. Many students have returned home; of the nine hundred
who originally fled to the Manerplaw area, more than five hundred
were gone by the end of the first year. To hang on to those who still
remain, Myo Thant has his work cut out for him.

One of his methods for keeping the students with him is to set an example of himself: Myo Thant has left behind his wife and three children. 'I've given them up for the revolution,' he says determinedly. 'Of course, I would really like them to be here. But we face many difficulties here.' If they came, he says, there would be problems providing the right food, health, and education for his sons. Also, his wife would have to stay at Manerplaw, while he would be off at the front line. In the end, the situation would be much the same as it is now. 'We'd still be apart.'

Myo Thant reasons that at least now, his wife is with her family and with her children. Then, as if banishing any lingering personal doubts about the choices he has made, he says: 'Anyway, I can do nothing else: The duty I have to my country is the same as the duty to my family, and right now my country needs me more.'

Whether or not Myo Thant's fervor is enough to keep his trainee guerrillas from defecting remains to be seen. In Thay Baw Boe camp, the problem of loneliness has led to a rash of marriages. Buddhist couples are being married by the camp's resident monks, while Christian and Muslim couples go to the nearest KNU settlement, where there is a small church and a mosque.

When they first arrived in the jungle, the students went on an austerity drive, prohibiting any marriages for at least two years. Sexual liaisons were frowned upon. But circumstances have demanded a more relaxed approach to things. Aung Lwin's lieutenant, Aung Naing Oo, ruefully explains what started it all off. 'A boy from my unit eloped with a Karen girl from the market. This could have been a big problem for us with the local Karen people. So we had to agree to their wedding.'

Since then, four more couples have been married. Two of the weddings, however, were precipitated by the group. Says Aung Naing Oo, grinning, 'What happened was that two of the couples were meeting secretly, which is forbidden. So we called a camp jury and asked them if they wanted to get married. They said yes.'

In the end, whatever cultures they are from, however committed they are to their struggles, and even after many years of warfare, no guerrillas are quite capable of sacrificing all personal desires. In all of them, there is at least the private hope for a family of their own. It is as if men and women finally become aware that ideals are fragile things, and as the only certain legacy for a guerrilla's life is the quest for their fulfillment, they seek something more tangible to mold, even as they pursue the course of death.

SEVEN

Speaking to the Gods

A clatter comes from the songbirds perched on the branches of the single tree growing in the courtyard. Hájji Din Muhammad gives out a high-pitched chuckle from where he sits, in a corner of the fortress parapet. He foresees a mujahedin victory at Jalalabad, but laughs over the notion that such things can be accomplished by men alone. 'Our work will never be done without the will of Allah,' he says. 'That is why I say, "Inshallah."'

Religious belief alone can provide the justification for a war, with men killing and dying in the service of a variety of gods and spiritual kingdoms. But among even secular groups, a kind of religiosity emerges in wartime – the military commanders becoming demigods, their dead men martyrs, even saints. It seems that all men share this need to deify themselves, to elevate their killing and dying from its mundanity on the world's obscure battlefields, to convince others as well as themselves that because their cause is imbued with a kind of divine light, it is worth dying for. It is as though men at war believe that in their wars they are speaking to the gods, or have become gods themselves.

Amid Afghanistan's war's litter, Islam has uncontestably become the law of the land. Everything about this war is religious, from the martyrs' cemeteries with their flags and sticks that rise from the bombed desert rubble like young saplings, to the invocations of 'inshallah' that precede every action, and the constant praying – and, throughout, the atmosphere given to this land by the peculiar fatalism of men for whom belief in God and paradise has replaced fear of death.

Hajji Din is helping command the Jalalabad siege for one of the fundamentalist parties. Today, in the failing light of dusk, he presides over events from this fortress about five miles west of the city. From here he has a sweeping view of the fallow fields of opium and wheat; a wide rocky swath of dry riverbed, and all around above him, the snowcapped peaks of the Safed Koh mountains. A perfect half-moon hangs, suspended in the darkening sky.

Everything is in God's hands. A few years ago, who would have believed things could have reached this point? No one. Only God can tell these things. Fifteen years have passed since Hajji Din carried out his first action against the government, when he chopped down the telephone poles on the road near his village with an ax. Afterward, he and some friends took to the hills with their old guns, and that was how the jihad began.

Life was tough in those days. 'At first, nature was as much our enemy as the Russians,' says Hajji. 'But we had to learn, and soon the trees and the stones became our friends.' Eventually, he and his fellow guerrillas came to know how they could use the harsh land to their own advantage, to ambush the enemy and then hide themselves. Now, the Russians have gone and here the mujahedin still are, with more men than before and better armed, laying siege to Jalalabad as the jihad continues.

'If the regime loses here, it will lose the war. But for us it makes no difference. As long as we are alive, we will fight. They are surrounded, so they are in jail. But we can go anywhere, we are free.'

During tea, a Scud missile comes in, a quick white flash against the blue flanks of the mountains and then the explosion. Mujahedin underlings rush to the wall to see where the missile has fallen. Hajji Din does not get up to look but remains seated, sipping his tea. He nods abstractedly when his men tell him where the Scud has hit, and then he resumes his conversation. 'People keep asking me, "When are you going to take the city?" and I tell them, "When God wills."'

Outside Hajji Din's earthen fortress, puffs of smoke and dust rise from distant hills, like dust devils whipped up by freakish winds: the impacts of tank shells missing their marks. Explosions from the ongoing battle reverberate in the background, and from overhead comes the high-pitched rushing roar of jets. The land, a beautiful tawny golden color tinged with green, is disfigured by black scorch-marks. Here and there, red flames add to the pattern.

This is how Jalalabad's outskirts appear two months into the siege, in spite of Hajji Din's triumphalist predictions. On the other side of the city, the mujahedin lines have broken and the government garrison has been resupplied. Instead of imprisoning Jalalabad's defenders, the mujahedin are trapped as they languish in exposed positions, under constant bombardment from the Afghan air force and blasted by tanks, field artillery, and long-range Scud missiles.

To make matters worse, the area is in the grip of a midsummer heat wave, and the Jalalabad valley is like a baking pan on slow broil. One day, the heat is particularly bad, at around 120 degree Fahrenheit. There is no breeze, and at noon it seems as if there is no air at all. In the shade of a tree at a guerrilla field clinic a couple of miles back from the front line, doctors and mujahedin are slumped in a stupor, waiting for the day's first casualties to arrive. On the string charpoys inside lie a couple of patients batting feebly at the flies that buzz constantly around them.

A leathery old man walks into the field clinic on foot, dressed in soiled rags and carrying a rusty milk-powder tin in his hands. Coming out of the sun to stand under the shade tree, he places the tin at his feet. The doctors, nurses, and fighters watch him from where they sit, too hot to move.

Suddenly, the old man begins babbling into the open mouth of the tin at his feet. Within seconds a writhing silver-gray cobra comes lashing out of the tin. Before he can move away, it strikes him on the wrist. With blood oozing from the punctures, he grabs the deadly snake with his uninjured hand and throws it on the ground a few feet away.

As the cobra flares its neck and starts swaying to and fro, ready to strike again, the old man stands over the snake, admonishing it in the Farsi language for biting him. Then he begins taunting it, grabbing at it with his bare hands. Again the cobra strikes, fangs sinking deep into the back of his hand this time. Again the old man grabs it, throws it down, and resumes his babbling. Droplets of blood from his wrist fall onto the dusty ground.

By now the onlookers are standing in a wide circle around the old man, keeping a safe distance away from the enraged snake. Everyone stares in fascination. One or two men are even smiling. Strangely, no one appears even slightly alarmed. 'He has the snake under control with words from the Koran,' says the head doctor, a Western-trained physician. 'He has this power from God. The poison cannot enter his body. It is a religious phenomenon.'

Eventually the old man puts the snake back in the tin and closes the lid. He stands proudly surveying his wounds, and holds out his arms to show the scars of previous bites to the assemblage. This cobra is not the first to bite him. He is a holy man, a Sufi mystic, and this is how he shows his link with God. He grins, showing a mouth missing many teeth, and holds his thumbs over the bleeding puncture marks on his hands. Clearly, he is not feeling any ill effects from the snake's poison. For a while he remains there, mumbling some long-memorized Koranic verse in a low voice.

In the distance, artillery thunders like an erratic storm. Still, no wounded arrive from the battleground, and, with the old mystic's show over for the moment, the doctors and fighters drift away to doze on their cots. They go with easy minds: Their faith in God has led them to live in expectation of miracles. No doubts about the miracle they have just witnessed trouble their thoughts. They are, after all, holy warriors, fighting God's war, and miracles are bound to happen.

Whether or not the war waged by the mujahedin is a true jihad, their Islamic faith does provide a certain cohesion to their efforts. For many fighters, the war's religious interpretation is the first one they come up with to explain their participation. Some, with crusading zeal, boast fiercely: 'First, we will liberate Afghanistan, then Bukhara,' the ancient Islamic holy city in the still-Soviet Central Asian republic of Uzbekistan. 'Allahu akbar!' – 'God is Great!' – they cry aloud when they fire their weapons, as if with this invocation to the Almighty their aim might be more accurate.

On the battleground and in Pakistan's refugee camps, the fundamentalist mujahedin are doing all they can to prepare the next generation for an Islamic Afghanistan. Toward the latter stages of the ultimately ill-fated Jalalabad siege, increasing numbers of young boys appear on the battlefield from the refugee camps around Peshawar. Pre-adolescent and completely innocent, they are being conscripted by their *madrasa* teachers to serve as cannon fodder at the flagging front line.

It is something they are prepared for from early childhood. In the village nearest to Charqulaba a dour, goateed mullah oversees a *madrasa* sponsored by Mullah Naquib and Jamiat-i-Islami. Naquib gives him free pencils, paper, and copies of the Koran. Inside the square mud-brick house, seated cross-legged on the straw-covered dirt floor, about thirty boys read aloud from Korans simultaneously, as in an old-fashioned frontier American 'blab' school. The boys just reaching adolescence are being encouraged by the village mullah to join the jihad; it is their duty as Muslims. Meanwhile, all the children are encouraged to become mullahs, and the teacher estimates that more than half his pupils will follow in his footsteps.

In their jihad recruitment drive, the mujahedin take full advantage of the customary Afghan reverence toward the clergy on the one hand and traditional strongmen on the other. As a mullah, Naquib is not only a strongman backed up by guns, he is also a figure of religious authority. His cult of personality, already well established in Kandahar, is propagated even further by Jamiat-i-Islami, which features him in its posters and party propaganda, as part of its growing pantheon of heroic strongmen.

On display in Peshawar and Quetta's refugee bazaars, pictures of mujahedin commanders are posed alongside the ubiquitous global icons of adolescent male hero-worship: Bruce Lee, Sylvester Stallone, and Chuck Norris — invincible heroes all. In one, the mujahedin commander Ahmed Shah Massoud (aka the 'Lion of the Panjshir') is depicted as an Afghan Rambo; another presents a 'through the ages' medley of bloodstained historical figures prominent in Afghanistan's long succession of wars. In another, an archetypal fundamentalist guerrilla is dressed in black: black beard, black turban, black-robed chest garlanded with a bullet-filled bandolier, (black) eyes staring and as cold as onyx; the printed message on the poster declares JIHAD IS OUR WAY.

Pir Sayyid Ahmad Gaylani is not just the leader of the National Islamic Front but a hereditary saint as well; his guerrillas carry his color portrait around with them on laminated cards. A Gaylani unit visited Arghandab during the operation against the sugar thieves, and one of the men, a grizzled and underfed guerrilla, showed off his leader's picture. He spent long moments gazing at it, proudly whispering Gaylani's name, before placing it carefully back inside his poor wallet, which he then wrapped in cloth and stowed inside his vest.

When they have such magnificent, larger-than-life characters as their leaders, it isn't hard to understand the pull of the jihad on young Afghan boys. Left behind with the women in overcrowded, sweltering refugee camps, they strain to experience life in all its glory, to seek heroism and paradise in the company of men. The jihad is their chance to do just that.

One morning, at a bunker near Jalalabad's airport, several mujahedin and two young boys watch expectantly as several MiG jets appear overhead. The MiGs begin to dive, coming in low and roaring, appearing just over the narrow trough of land separating the bunker from the airstrip – and rip past. Pulling up, they loose their bombs, and immediately the peppering smoke puffs rise from where they have hit the adjacent hillside.

No sooner have the jets gone again than a veiled woman appears on the path near the bunker. She is sobbing and yelling, her arms outstretched. The older of the two boys tries to hide. The woman is his mother, and she has come for him. He is only just thirteen, she says, and he ran away from home a few days ago to join the mujahedin. She begs the older men standing there: 'Please, let him come home to me. He is too young for war, and we need him at home.'

The mujahedin stare back at the woman, smiling at her display of emotion. Then they look away again, uninterested, their minds disengaged. They watch the smoke rise from the bombing run. The boy is here with them. It is enough; he is a mujahed now. The woman is too frightened to come any closer. Soon she realizes she has failed. Turning away, she stumbles off in the shimmering heat, wailing disconsolately.

The other boy is eleven and has come with an uncle from one of Peshawar's refugee camps, he says, 'to kill *kaffirs*,' unbelievers. He says this as manfully as he can, scowling. He looks back out toward the besieged airport, the jets, the landscape of war. There they are, the unbelievers, just over that hill, where the heart of the war lies. He might not be able to see them, but he knows they are there.

It might appear crude to outsiders, but the Afghans' Islamic chauvinism is more understandable up close. To what else but Islam can they turn, to define what has happened to their country? What else can give killing on such a scale – more than a million dead in ten years – any spiritual dimension? In a land trashed and torn by war, devoid of civilizing influences, Islam's symbols become meaningful icons for men seeking spiritual nourishment, and give them a measure of hope in the future.

In ruined Arghandab, where the presence of God is even less apparent than in most places, Islam's symbols are everywhere, erected by men who believe they will ultimately vanquish their enemies by divine right. From the green banner Mullah Naquib has hoisted onto the crumpled hilltop fortress where the holy man Baba Wali lies buried, to the fluttering flags of the martyrs' cemeteries foresting the bare desert ground, this is a land rife with religious symbols. It is also a land where the dead are more prominent than the living. To make the cemeteries, young trees are uprooted and stripped of their branches to become the grave markers for Afghanistan's martyrs. The dead men commemorated by the trees are all heroes of the holy war; unassailable status comes to those who die in the jihad.

For those still on earth, there is little need to invoke the martyrs' feats of daring in order to sustain a fighting spirit: the war continues, and, like stands of fast-growing spruce, the flag-cemeteries keep growing. The martyrs are everywhere around Kandahar, and their visible presence is a persistent call to arms.

In this spiritually oriented landscape, there is an otherworldliness to even the most mundane of daily routines, and, with their days punctuated by prayer sessions, the mujahedin resemble nothing so much as a half-wild caste of medieval warrior monks. Every dawn, Khalilullah and Abdul Hakim sit up in their bunks and, forming a silent, pious union, read to themselves from their Korans.

The mujahedin not only pray, but they find unerring guidance for all of life's aspects in the Koran or one of Muhammad's prophecies. Even the hairstyles of the fighters are presented as having an Islamic derivation. The guerrillas around Kandahar believe that the long-haired and shaven-headed look they wear are styles that were worn by Muhammad. And the black kohl adorning the eyes of many of the fighters – giving them the incongruous mien of silent-screen movie actors of the Roaring Twenties – this, too, is worn in emulation of Muhammad and his purported cosmetic predilections.

At times the adherence to Islam in all things goes to absurd lengths. En route to meet the supreme *maulavi* who impose Kandahar's Shari'a law, Khalilullah insists on using a green pen for the impending interview. He produces a green pen and says, 'Please, use my pen. Your pen is red, the color of the communists. My pen is green, the color of Islam.'

Late one afternoon after prayers with his men, Naquibullah and Khalilullah go for a walk in the fields surrounding Charqulaba. They stroll through the untended grape vineyards on bomb-cratered footpaths skirting the shady fringes of windbreaks, where farmhouses lie in chaotic tumbles of dried clay. The mullah speaks of moments of bravery, of mistakes and miracles in battle. Here –

he points – was where the Soviet troops advanced on the camp in their last offensive; here his men resisted it. Pausing at the spot where a Soviet soldier lies dead underneath the rubble, Naquib says that the Shuravi, the Soviets, were very brave, but they have never understood mujahedin tactics. That is why the mujahedin have prevailed, and why the Soviets are in retreat.

A youth rides a motorbike carefully along the path. An old man with a white beard rides on the back. It is Naquib's uncle, on his way to camp to see his nephew about something. The two men speak for a few moments. As they do, the old man's eyes keep wandering over to the formless remains of the village of Charqulaba. Finally, he chuckles and remarks how, try as he might, he can never pinpoint the exact spot where his home once stood, despite the fact that he had lived there for sixty years. Still shaking his head, he continues his journey toward the camp, to wait there for Naquib's return.

Naquib and Khalilullah walk on, soon exiting the orchards and venturing onto the uncultivated plain. The men amble slowly in the direction of the martyrs' cemetery, its telltale flags swaying like masts in a crowded harbor. The sun, a great orange ball, has begun to sink in the sky.

Suddenly the roaring of MiG fighter-bombers overhead puts an end to Naquib's pastoral reveries. The white darting jets shoot off their magnesium flares in white, fluming spurs, then bomb the horizon. The bombs hit with dull roars, and smoke mushrooms up into the blue sky. From all around comes the popping and crackle of mujahedin gunners firing futilely at the jets with rifles, machine-guns, rocket launchers, everything they have. As the drama in the sky continues, the day nears its end, and it is time for prayers.

Khalilullah and the mullah walk away toward the setting sun and, facing it, they remove their embroidered shawls and place them on the ground beneath them as prayer rugs. Then they kneel. Khalilullah's AK-47 assault rifle gleams with the last of the day's sun. The two men pray, standing, falling, and prostrating themselves in the rhythmic custom of Islam. Behind, the martyrs' flags stir on their poles with the slightest of evening breezes.

To the mujahedin in Arghandab, the hand of God is present in everything they see and do. It is almost as if, with their faith, they are endowed with vision to see beyond this life and into the next. In Palestine, too, there is this sense of the spiritual coursing through everyday life and through the violence, too, giving it texture and potency that defies standard definitions of what a war is and how it takes place.

As the world's oldest ongoing conflict, the dispute over possession of the Palestinian homeland has acquired an entirely unique mystical dimension that holds all of its participants in thrall.

For the Palestinians – as for the Jews – their land, history, and religion are inseparable, existing intertwined in a mystical sense of identity which may be irrational, but which is passionately felt. This passion in turn has propagated a richly textured folklore passed on from one generation to another, so that all the history collects in the present; biblical stories are told as if they happened yesterday, and modern tales have the quality of timeless allegory. For instance, the story told by the mother of Sami – the knife-wielding PLO militant – of the night when her father smuggled her on a donkey from the holy Hebron hills across the enemy's lines all the way to Gaza, where she grew up to give birth to sons who now fight for their lost homeland.

On the wall of the family room in Mahmoud's home, as in most others, hangs a picture of Jerusalem's Dome of the Rock and Al-Aqsa mosque, built on the spot where Muhammad is supposed to have ascended to heaven on a white horse. The image of that golden dome, floating over Jerusalem like a moon plated with precious metal, is the Palestinians' enduring archetypal symbol, hallowed evidence to their claim of an ancestral homeland, and, in its holiness, the ultimate validation of their identity as a separate people.

So desired, so hallowed is the land of Palestine that it has itself become a sacred icon to the Palestinians. Seen as proof of the people's own historical continuity, the oldest olive trees are called Romans because they have been there since Herod's time; they are treated with a caressing reverence, as if they are ancient, living relatives. Arthritically gnarled and stout with age, these trees are the mute, arboreal companions of all the Palestinian history.

Indeed, however secular their ideology, Palestinians can't ignore the spiritual dimension in their political history: The language of Islam is the element that has bonded their community through time, the watermark of genuineness on their claim to the land of Palestine. Their collective history as a Muslim people is an identity long predating their concept of nationhood. The uprising might be steered officially by a coalition of forces that includes the PLO's various factions, but the intifada's dynamism has its roots in Islam. With its promise of martyrdom and paradise, Islam alone gives a larger-than-life significance to the prospect of dying miserably on one of Gaza's dirt alleyways.

The mosque is also the spiritual fulcrum of Breij camp. Even though Mahmoud doesn't go to pray at the mosque or observe the five daily prayer rituals expected of devout Muslims, he is still, culturally, a Muslim. It is this sense of cultural identity that allowed him, for a time anyway, to claim no contradiction between secular activists like himself, and religious militants like Hisham.

For the younger, less-educated boys, like Yasir and Dasir, their feelings of Palestinian nationalism and faith in Islam are forces indistinguishable from one another. The Fatah youth group Al-

Shabibeh has provided them with political training and a structure with which to organize themselves, but it has left intact their religious beliefs. The belief that their intifada is merely the latest manifestation of an ancient war has obliged the boys to find a spiritual significance for everything they do.

The boys speak of 'fighting for the return of the holy places,' calling themselves by the hybrid label 'Shabibeh Muslims.' Even their weapons are biblical, from the *mugla* (homemade cloth slings) they use to the 'holy stones' they throw. It is as though these stones are doubly blessed: once, because they come from the Holy Land itself, and twice, because throwing them helps fulfill a prophesied national redemption. And thus, on the days leading up to a violent demonstration, the *shabbab* undergo the rituals of fasting, prayer, and the visiting of martyrs' graves. It is a cycle that lends itself to further allegory, making each day's unequal confrontation with the enemy seem like the reenactment of a biblical myth or the fulfillment of a prophecy.

For several weeks, the tension has been building in Breij. It is a fortnight since the Israelis came into the house, smashing things, stepping on the baby's foot, and driving Nasser's older brother, 'the Sheikh,' to pick up a knife and call for holy vengeance. Now the Sheikh is in the hospital. He was beaten senseless by Israeli soldiers yesterday. His family says the attack was provoked only by the shovel beard he wears, which shows that he is a fundamentalist. 'Now,' Nasser jokes blackly, 'he is the imam of the hospital.'

Tonight, the whole camp is under curfew, and Nasser's family is closeted in the house. There is an air of tense expectation because tomorrow is Friday, and in the pattern that is becoming ritual, there are to be street riots outside the mosque after the morning prayers – an assured battle with the enemy.

One of Nasser's brothers raptly watches a soccer match between the Israeli team, Maccabee, and the Milan team from Italy on the family's old black-and-white TV. Naturally, the brother is rooting for Milan. Oblivious to the game, Nasser's fat mother sits on some cushions, having her fingernails cut by a daughter-in-law. Every now and then she lets off a loud sigh of worry for her hospitalized elder son.

The Israelis have closed down the West Bank university Nasser has been attending, leaving him stranded in his overcrowded family home. Now he has become a 'born-again' Muslim. At college, Nasser, like most of his fellow students, adhered to Yasir Arafat's stated vision: that a secular Palestinian state be established in the Occupied Territories to exist alongside Israel. But now, with his education truncated, little hope of finding work, and a bullet wound in one leg from a recent street riot, Nasser's views have radicalized. He is turning inward to Gaza – and to Islam. 'Most people in the camp now see this as a religious war,' he says. 'To continue until we push the Jews out.'

In the morning, Nasser complains that he has slept poorly. Barking dogs woke him up in the early hours and he hasn't been able to get back to sleep. He is afraid the Israelis have come into the camp, which is what barking dogs usually mean. Most nights now, the soldiers come into houses and force the men outside in their pajamas, where they give them paintbrushes and pots of black paint and make them paint over the *shabbab*'s graffiti on the walls.

Some of Nasser's friends arrive; after small cups of hot, sweet tea, they all go out into the streets, heading toward the mosque. Kids stand around burning tires and acting tough, gearing up for action. Over a megaphone, the muezzin begins his melodic wailing, calling the devout to prayer. Then, like a sudden wind passed along by the boys comes the cry '*Jesh*!' – 'Soldiers!' – followed immediately by the rushing whine of jeeps.

Everyone vanishes from the streets, running down alleyways to hide inside the houses. Caught off guard away from home, Nasser runs down an alley that leads away from the main street. Darting boys appear and motion tersely to keep going. Some wait at alley junctions as sentinels until the others pass, then scramble away themselves. Everywhere is the sound of running feet and muffled shouts. Into a small olive grove at the edge of camp: no cover there, a dead end. Back into the alley labyrinth, up toward the street. But word from ahead comes back that soldiers are there too, so back down, toward the olive grove, faster now. Two women and some kids stand now at the alley's end, wordlessly dividing the arriving boys into two groups, pointing them toward the heads of other alleys where vigilant women stand waiting. Then, running, into the door of a house held open by a veiled, elderly woman in traditional dress. Once in, the door slams shut.

Sweating and breathless but safe, Nasser thanks the woman. She goes off to make tea. On the walls are framed samples of Arabic calligraphy: sayings of Hassan al-Banna, the late founder of the outlawed Muslim Brotherhood. Four cages with canaries hang on the wall, and also some decorative squares of embroidered cloth. When the woman returns, Nasser asks about them; they were made by one of her sons, doing time in an Israeli prison.

A long time passes. Silence has come over the camp. Suddenly uncomfortable, Nasser asks the woman for a prayer rug, which she brings him at once. 'I missed the prayers at the mosque,' he explains, and stands to pray. For Nasser, the act of prayer has become the essence of his Palestinian identity, reinforced five times daily. Without it, he feels adrift, weaker, somehow less of a Palestinian.

Then comes the sound of commotion, shots, and screaming, and from all around, a chilling sound that pimples the skin: women ululating. Nasser loses all sense of calm. 'The mosque! The mosque!' he yells. 'It is coming from the mosque. The *yahud*, the

Jews are killing our people!' Nasser turns and runs out of the house, heading toward the violence. Along the way, standing in the doorways and with their heads upraised like some baleful choral gauntlet, the women of Breij make their terrible sound, and Nasser runs even faster toward the fray.

At the mosque, one of the *shabbab* has tried to stab an Israeli soldier and has been shot; taking to the flat roof of the mosque overlooking the street, the boys have whipped themselves into a kind of deadly ecstasy. Blood has been spilled, and now on that flat roof interrupted by the dome of the mosque, they are ready to die. They throw down rocks and metal construction rods at the Israeli troops filling the street below, cursing them and yelling 'Allahu akbar!' It is the boys' battle cry, and it means they are willing to do anything, they can die and kill now – they are beyond reason when they shout it.

With gunshots snapping off around them, the hair-raising ululating of their women, the clouds of tear gas, the ranting of the muezzin's voice urging them on, the boys rip open their shirts, begging the Israeli soldiers to aim at their hearts, demanding that the Israelis kill them here and now.

After the mosque riot, the concrete ledge of the roof and its dome are peppered where bullets have struck them. The bullet marks remain as visual proof of the Israelis' attack on a place of Muslim worship, which is how the events of that day are remembered. As for the boy who was shot, he has bled to death and now become a true martyr. For, not only has he died in defense of Islam, he also received the fatal bullet in the very shadow of the mosque. With his blood, he has consecrated the mosque's preeminence as the nerve center of the intifada – a jihad, to believers – in Breij.

The Breij mosque has been a symbol of resistance since it was built, for Hisham and his friends in the Muslim Brotherhood built it themselves, illegally, without obtaining the necessary permission from the Israeli occupation authorities. Volunteering their own time, they erected it surreptitiously, working at night over a period of several months. Once the Israelis realized it was there, they wisely chose to ignore it, as to tear it down would have been an inflammatory act of sacrilege. Meanwhile, the fact that it stands at all is a double victory for Breij's Muslims, both as a monument to the camp's defiance, and because, in Fahed's words, 'to increase the number of mosques is to help spread the word of Islam.'

Every Friday, Fahed and Anis come to Hisham's house for the sunset prayers. Hisham's father and his brothers usually join them as well. Hisham always leads the prayers. By this time, he has not eaten or drunk all day, and his teeth and lips are pasty with a white film, his tongue thick in his mouth. Only after the prayers does Hisham eat and drink. In a room dominated by a wall-size poster photograph depicting an American creek shrouded by trees in their autumn colors, the men gather to eat. Periodically, to everyone's amusement, an electronic wall chime loudly plays a few bars of 'Rock-a-Bye Baby.' This is the cue for Hisham's brother to dash out of the room and come back with trays of food. They are handed to him by the women of the house, unseen in the hallway outside.

After supper, over countless cups of *yamsum* – camomile tea laced with aniseed – the three young men speak of their faith in God and in Islam, and of Islam's role in the war that has begun against the Jews. Fahed thinks of the intifada as prophesied by Muhammad to the Arab people. 'He said: "You will fight the Jews, and you will win. At that time, the trees and the stones will say, 'There is a Jew behind me: come and kill him.'" In other words, the Jews will have nowhere to hide.'

Fahed wears a complacent smile. 'This may appear savage, to kill every Jew. But it isn't if you understand the whole prophecy. The prophecy says that Allah first gave them the chance to be good. But, from the beginning of Creation, Allah knew they would be bad, and this is the reason for the prophecy. It is the nature of the Jew which brings about their end.'

There is no doubt in Fahed's mind that the prophecy he has quoted will one day come true. In the meantime, his faith helps him cope with the humiliating circumstances of living under occupation. By closing his eyes and believing hard enough, Fahed can almost will away the Jews and the state of Israel.

Islam has many qualities that need to be disseminated, says Fahed, not just in Gaza or the land of Palestine, but throughout the world. At present, he laments, Islam is misunderstood, as is the concept of jihad.

'"Holy War" is a term with a special terrifying significance to Europeans, especially Christians. It comes from the time of the wars between the Christians and the Muslims. To us, the jihad is something else entirely. Jihad is the weapon which you use to defend yourself if you are a Muslim. We believe that if a Muslim is fighting to bring about the rise of Islam, to liberate his land, to defend his family, this is a jihad. The man who fights for these things is a mujahed. If you are a mujahed, this means you are going to have a good position on Judgment Day, and you will go to paradise. This is important: If you believe you will go to paradise, it gives you a special strength.'

To Hisham, this belief is the secret weapon of the intifada. 'Each day we give a martyr so that things will change. Each time someone is killed it make the uprising go further, and strengthens it. The boys who opened their shirts on the mosque did so because they believed they will go to paradise. Otherwise, they would not do it. Everyone knows that when he dies he will be a martyr, and that the martyr never dies. When he is killed the rest of us are forbidden to say he has died. The Koran tells us to say he is alive.'

Fahed nods in agreement, and says, 'Killing people is not a very beautiful thing. But we are a people whose rights have been taken away, whose holy places have been taken. What do you expect these people to do? Stay at home, eating chicken?' He motions to the remains of the meal left in trays on the floor. Hisham nods in agreement. 'If it is necessary,' he announces; 'we are ready for death. We Muslims love death as others love life.'

The next morning, Anis and some of his friends gather in his Islamic bookstore. Anis shows off the shop and plays a cassette. 'Islamic music,' he explains with excitement. Last night, he, Fahed and Hisham had said that in the future *Islamic* Palestinian state, music will be banned – all music, that is, except 'Islamic' music.

Now, as the music's wild, rhythmic drumming fills the room with sound, accompanied by the soprano strains of an adolescent boy singing, Anis's eyes shine. Around him, the young men gather closer, their bodies poised, twitching with energy. Their eyes are wide, and on their faces they wear smiles. Anis grins and says, 'This song is about Hamas, the Islamic underground movement that is leading the jihad. This music fills us with spirit, and it makes us feel we can go do anything for Islam.'

Just as surely as Islam has gripped the minds of the *shabbab* in Gaza, filling it with glowing visions of the afterlife in paradise, so has the Polisario Front taken possession of the souls of the people in Western Sahara's sweeping deserts. By maintaining the trappings of Islam in its own exercise of power, the Polisario has effectively usurped the religion's role in the Saharawis' everyday lives, propagating a new and hybrid revolutionary monotheism.

Hanna is an ex-slave. Her surname, Baali, is the same as that of one of the revolution's leading families. Before the day in 1975 when the Polisario proclaimed the abolition of slavery and freed several thousand of its refugee followers from bondage, the Baalis owned Hanna. In the proprietarial tradition of slaveowners since time immemorial, they had given her their own name. Now, years later, the Baalis are her neighbors in Aoussert camp, just a few tents away.

Hanna's face is so black that its edges are a blur in the deep shade of the tent's interior. She speaks of her slave past in a shy, mellifluous voice. Hanna remembers being sold. She and her older sister, Selma, were bought by different families when Hanna was seven or eight. Their parents could do nothing about it, she says, because they were slaves, too. One day the owners of her family took Hanna with them on a trip. They said it would just be for a few days. Her father protested, saying she was too young. But they took her anyway, and sold her. The new owners told her they would take her back to her mother. After two days on a camel, she said they weren't going the right way. They beat her with sticks and told her to forget about her mother. Then they took her to the Baali family.

Hanna never saw her mother and father again. Hanna doesn't know how long she lived with the Baalis, but she thinks she is 'more than fifty' now, so it was for most of her life. During all those years, she tended their livestock and brought them water from the wells. She was married, though, to a semi-free male slave who lived with another family. Because of his status, he was allowed to come and live with her. They have had seven children. Now Hanna's husband is an old man, and spends his days tending one of Aoussert's gardens. Their children are all in the camps, except for one son who was taken away by relatives of the Baalis before the revolution. In the exodus, that family stayed behind, and today they still live on the other side of the wall, so Hanna and her husband haven't seen or heard of that son since 1975.

In 1976, Hanna and Selma were reunited. By then complete strangers to one another, they were only identified as sisters by the Polisario when each was questioned about their original families, and their stories matched up. Once reunited, they began living together again as sisters. Hanna bears the Baalis no grudge, because there is no point.

'All that is in the past. Now, we live just like the whites,' says Hanna. 'Look! We are even living right beside the whites, and our children are taught by the same teachers. It is so much more than I can express in words. I just thank God and the revolution that I now know I'm the same as the whites.'

Abba gives a triumphant look. Until now he has worn a sour expression. He didn't want to come here; he said Hanna would be embarrassed because her story dealt with the 'shameful' past, the time of injustice before the revolution. The truth is, he is also uncomfortable with her subservience and her evangelical display of emotion. They are both Saharawis, by definition 'revolutionaries,' but it is plain their comprehension of the Polisario revolution differs greatly.

For Hanna, the Polisario Front and God are as good as equal. By freeing her from a lifetime of slavery, the revolution has demonstrated the powers of a deity. An all-powerful creature of war, it can take away life and also give it back. As the catalyst to her transcendence as a human being, the revolution now possesses Hanna even more fully than the Baali family ever did. But, even though it has freed her, she has nowhere else to go. The revolution has fed, clothed, and housed her and her family. In return for these things and her theoretical freedom, Hanna has given herself in undying gratitude to the revolution, as if to a new master, and she parrots its slogans unselfconsciously and with pride. 'Now,' says Hanna, 'we have the same rights and duties as the whites in the struggle to retake our homeland.'

However much it has become transfused with the revolution, the concept of a god is still alive in the minds of ex-slaves like Hanna and some other Saharawis. But among the guerrillas, mere lip service is paid to Islam.

On the journey to the Front, the battle-scarred driver, Moulay, is the only one among his comrades who prays, and he does so discreetly, almost apologetically. Abba's expression of neutral forbearance makes it obvious that he thinks of Moulay as a kind of primitive man, a man with a pre-revolutionary consciousness. Certainly Moulay's prayer rituals don't seem to belong in the reinvented New Sahara of the Polisario Front.

But if Islam no longer has any official place, no one is saying so publicly. Islam is being displaced gradually, without fanfare, over time, and those Saharawis who cling its ceremonies and its rituals are simply tolerated, ignored. In Dakhla camp, for instance, the only mosque is closed down, officially because where it is situated – on its own in the middle of all of the camp's spread-out *wilayat* – is 'too far for the people to walk.' Now the building is being used for camp meetings instead; if people still wish to pray, they do so on the prayer grounds of their own *dairat*.

But the reality is that by reducing the judicial powers of the Shari'a judges to a ceremonial level – officiating over marriages and funerals and the naming of babies – the revolution has rendered Islam virtually irrelevant to the everyday lives of the people. But Polisario officials deny any policy aimed at curbing Islam's hold on their camp constituents. 'To fulfill the spiritual needs of the people, we've even opened schools for the study of the Koran and Shari'a,' says commander Mahfoud Ali Beiba.

The Saharawis are a very Islamic people, he goes on to say, but their faith is pure, primitive, unchanged from the days of the earliest Islamizing expeditions sent out from Arabia. 'We've never had imams here. We don't need intermediaries between ourselves and God. Faith is a practice for the individual. The Western Sahara isn't like Afghanistan or Iran.' Indeed. There is little left standing between the Polisario Front and God, certainly not Islam.

One night a ceremony is put on at Aoussert camp for the latest guests of the revolution, a group of Basque Polisario supporters. On the stage of a round brick sirocco-proof amphitheatre, a group of teenage girls ululate, sway, and sing to the rhythmic pounding of a large leatherbound drum. The audience, which also includes guerrillas and several dozen Saharawi children, is enthusiastic, for the girls are belting out traditional Saharawi rythms with new, revolutionary lyrics in the Hassaniyah dialect. In one song, originally praising the Prophet Muhammad, the words have been changed to say, 'In spite of the Moroccan invasion of our country, our will cannot be dominated.' Afterward, as in a gospel revivalist's tent, the children in the audience repeat the slogan, shouting it in a gleeful, shrieking harmony.

In one sense, Ali Beiba is right: The revolution hasn't moved *against* Islam. It has merely elbowed some room for itself in the musty hall of faith already occupied by Islam. By giving the old religious songs new lyrics, the Polisario is merely adapting, modernizing Islam to make it more relevant to the Saharawis' environment. Still, there is only room for one faith in the revolution of Western Sahara, and there is a strong sense that the Polisario is merely biding its time, waiting for the older generation to die, when the only Saharawis left will be those raised singing the Polisario's songs, fighting the Polisario's war.

The uneasy ambiguity of the Polisario's relationship with Islam becomes clearer in a desert rendezvous with a guerrilla squad, not far from Hassan's Wall. To shelter themselves from the strong sirocco blowing, the fighters huddle together inside a field tent. One of the guerrillas sets about making bread and tea on a coal fire, while the men around him discuss the role of Islam in the Saharawi liberation war – whether to them, their deaths mean they will become martyrs.

One of the fighters, a dark man with a mustache and kinky hair, says, 'The most important thing is to liberate the country.

Martyrdom is secondary. To fight for the country is a national duty, but the jihad is a personal thing, so therefore it's secondary.' Sidahmed, the platoon's lean, sharp-eyed commander, interrupts. 'Once we are martyred, we have fulfilled our duty. The duty of each of us is fulfilled either when we are martyred, or when we achieve our national independence.'

The guerrillas may have acquired a new nationalist revolutionary consciousness, but when it comes to death, they hedge, clinging to the forms of thought given them by Islam. 'Our martyrs are never forgotten, because after all, that's what each of us is here for,' says Sidahmed.

To be sure, they have been well prepared. In the Martyr Said Gaswani Baha Youth Club at Aoussert, which has rocketshell ashtrays placed around its spacious interior, the walls are covered with banners bearing the sayings of El-Ouali Mustapha Sayed – 'Luali' – the Polisario founder and its most ubiquitous martyr. IF YOU WANT YOUR RIGHTS, YOU HAVE TO SHED YOUR BLOOD, says one. And, on the bulletin board at the El Ouali Mustapha Military Training School, hidden in the dunes away from all of the camps, where the Saharan People's Liberation Army prepares its guerrillas for war, Luali can be found saying: 'Each day we are growing stronger, adding to ourselves youthful force, which doesn't fear death. This intimidates the fearful. This is life for us.'

In the tent out in the desert near the wall, the fighters become reverential when they speak about Luali. 'He is our role model,' says Sidahmed. 'He was from a poor nomad's family. He was tall, modest, and good with all people. He talked to everyone, young and old, and made them feel good. He was very nationalistic . . .'

Obviously immensely popular while alive, Luali has been elevated by the revolution to mythic proportions after his romantic early death 'on the field of honour' at the age of thirty-one. Now, as the Saharawis' own Che Guevara figure, Luali provides a heroic figure for youths to emulate. Brave, handsome, and dead, Luali with his urgings to sacrifice possesses much more resonance for the young guerrillas than do the old, traditional Koranic archetypes.

As the stories about him are told and retold throughout the desert in the nomads' and fighters' tents, and as his legend grows, Luali has come to occupy a place as prominent as that of Muhammad, and one even more relevant. Luali eternalizes the past; his example also holds the keys to the future. From his grave, Luali beckons.

In Western Sahara the language of Islam has been supplanted by the rhetoric of the Polisario revolution, but the two use the same vessel of faith. It is the hereditary piety of the Saharawis that has provided the Polisario with the means to move them forward into battle. Indeed, the struggle requires the people's devotion to the ideal that what lies beyond the horizon line of the wall and the current conflict – independence and their own state – is a kind of earthly paradise.

In Kawthoolei, as in Western Sahara, the war is also fought on a battlefield steeped in mysticism and faith. Here the Karen people's culture and long, mythologized history has given their present reality a unique spiritual dimension.

Major Than Maung has built walls around himself now, piling stacks of rough-cut teak around his once open-sided bunker. Reaching him is like ducking into a cave; only the whites of his eyes are visible at first, after you come out of the sunlight.

The major has reinforced his bunker because the enemy's mortar fire is much more accurate now, and not long ago the government forces came close to killing him. Enemy shrapnel has gouged the trunks of the nearest bamboo trees a dozen feet away. Now that he is hunkered down in his wood-and-concrete cave, there are no more dreamy, foggy jungle mornings to be viewed from bed, there is no more watching the bamboo sway and rustle in its woody, cymbalic rhythmns; but at least shrapnel can't hit him.

In this setting, it is hard to conceive of Than Maung as anything but the guerrilla commander he is. But once he was a school-teacher, and had hoped to be a preacher. The major's revolutionary initiation was an odd one. One day in 1959, a band of Karen insurgents appeared at the Seventh-Day Adventist mission school where he was teaching and kidnapped him, the other teachers, and their students. The guerrillas carried the group off into the forest and held them for a month until the local parish was able to raise the ransom money they demanded.

Even today, remembering the ordeal makes the major agitated. Throughout it he was in fear for his life; apparently all the hostages were threatened with death if the ransom wasn't paid. Finally, he and the others were freed, he says, with the guerrillas' apologies and the explanation that the kidnapping had been planned in the mistaken belief their mission school was government-run. They were sorry for their error, and now, Than Maung was free to resume his normal life.

But things weren't the same for Than Maung afterward. The experience had unsettled him. Before, he had always been very innocent about politics, but the month he spent with the guerrillas had opened his eyes. By talking with them and reading the pamphlets they gave him, he learned a great deal about his own people's history of oppression at the hands of the Burmans. Within a year, he joined up with the guerrillas himself, and now, somehow, thirty years had gone by. 'Maybe it's God's will that I have become a soldier instead of a missionary,' he muses. 'Maybe when the fighting is over I'll go back to do God's work, but that depends on God's will.'

The major hasn't given up the faith. Every night he listens to Seventh-Day Adventist shortwave broadcasts out of Guam, and on the weekly Sabbath, an American pastor travels up from Bangkok to deliver an open-air service for the major and his fellow disciples in Kawmura.

From his cot, the major motions toward the overgrown ghost town at the heart of Kawmura, off limits now because of its exposure to shelling. Once, he says, there were three places of worship: a Protestant church, a Buddhist temple, and a mosque. But now, with each rainy season, the rotting shells of Kawmura's churches recede farther from view beneath the growing tangle of jungle foliage.

It is claustrophobic in the bunker; there is nowhere to sit except on the major's bed, and it is hot and airless. Stepping out the other door, into a patch of bleaching white sun, there are thirty human skulls. The skulls are artistically placed on stakes between one and three feet in height and jammed into the earth on either side of a narrow footpath. The major wanders out a few seconds later. Blinking in the sunlight, he sees the skulls and says, 'Some of them are captains, some are sergeants and soldiers.'

The skulls belong to the enemy soldiers killed in the last suicide assault across Kawmura's killing ground. 'The enemy don't take back their dead,' says the major disapprovingly. 'Their bodies are just left there. Some are near our own front line, and there are many more we haven't been able to reach.'

To retrieve these trophies, his young guerrillas sneak out at night into the death ground and bring them back, along with any IDs they find. Collecting skulls is like a sport. Each skull is placed on its own stake, and the major keeps the IDs. With them, he keeps a tally of how many of the enemy have died; he calculates that a hundred have fallen in the three attacks launched since May. It is now September, and the rainy season is ending, so he expects another human-wave assault any day.

'We can expect anything from the Burmese. We know they're

capable of dirty deeds. They don't respect international law.' The major strolls among his garden of skulls, appraising them. Then something stops him in his tracks. In the gaping nose cavity of one, someone has stuffed a half-smoked cheroot. The major looks dismayed. Kneeling, he removes the offending article from the skull and throws it on the ground. Straightening up again, he surveys the rows of skulls and looks satisfied. Once again there is a clean, artistic geometry about the cranial arrangement. Once again everything is back in order, exactly as it should be.

The skulls don't bother him. 'They do bother some of the Burmese students, though,' he says, smiling. 'And little children. They are afraid at first. Then they come and touch them. Then, after they see them for a while, I don't know what happens but they aren't afraid anymore . . . and they become very ready to fight.'

The major turns away and goes back inside his bunker. In Kawmura's heat, the crickets shrill. Barefoot guerrillas pad quietly by the major's garden of skulls. There is a regular flow of foot traffic to and from the trenches at the front line a hundred or so yards away. Inside, in the darkness of his bunker, the major chews his betel nut and stares out at the white light of day.

The major's behavior is perhaps explained by the Karen's unique syncretic blend of animism and Christianity, which predates the influences brought by the British colonizers and is one of the keys to the Karen national identity. In the early nineteenth century, American Protestant missionaries found the Karen extraordinarily receptive to their message. The Karen found in the Bible stories many parallels to their own mythology, sparking a widespread belief among them that they could be one of the lost tribes of Israel. Also, the Karen saw the schools, churches, and industries established by the missionaries as a means of improving their standard of living and becoming less dependent on their traditional Burman overlords.

The missionary influence has been profound, yet Christianity hasn't displaced the Karen's own animist beliefs and practices. Covered in tattoos designed to protect themselves from evil spirits, the Karen attend church services in clean, pressed clothes – some wear Karen national costume, others Western dress – completely at ease with the exotic duality of their lives.

There is in this devotional tendency of the Karen an endearing earnestness. Every afternoon in his home, Major Soe Soe, a Catholic, leads a prayer session with his family and staff. It is a time of day which is sacrosanct, and if visitors arrive at this time they are met by whispering aides who simply point upstairs, put a finger to their lips, and motion for them to sit and wait. In Kawthoolei, people's faiths, whatever they are, are respected.

The Burmese students, too, are deeply religious, and whether Catholic, Baptist, Muslim, or Buddhist, they have taken their faiths with them into the war. In fact, for most of them it was their moral outrage more than any coherent political convictions that brought them into the jungle in the first place. What the army did – killing students, their own people, in the prodemocracy demonstrations – was evil and has now to be resisted, the perpetrators punished for their crimes. Next, the system has to be changed so such killings can never happen again.

The Thay Baw Boe camp leader and Baptist activist Aung Lwin communicates his language of revolutionary social transformation in a Marxist vernacular, but since it is based on the radical Catholic philosophy of liberation theology, it is profoundly religious in nature. To Aung Lwin, the struggles for religious redemption and national democracy are one.

In his story, similar to the Saharawis' tales of their exodus into the desert, the students' flight into the Burmese jungles was the rite of passage for a spiritual rebirth. Recalling the nightmarish trek across the rugged Dawna Range, Aung Lwin searches for a

Biblical analogy and finds 'Abraham wandering in the desert.' To him, the Karen villagers who helped the lost and hungry students on their path to freedom were true Samaritans.

Indeed, guided as he is by his belief in a Christ who wars on behalf of justice, Aung Lwin has turned each stage of their experience into a kind of *Pilgrim's Progress*, something almost beautiful, much greater than the wretched existence that it often is. And by doing so he has infused his followers with the high ideals of their enterprise. 'It is no coincidence, I think,' says Aung Lwin with a mystical smile, 'that our first guns were bought with money we made from caroling house-to-house during our first Christmas in exile. Christ helped us find the means to fight, because our cause is just!'

Just as for many students it was their religious beliefs that determined their decision to take up arms, now, succored by the similarity of their ordeals to biblical parables, they can reassure themselves that their experiences fulfill a preordained spiritual challenge; through them, they can achieve goodness for themselves and for their country.

Enhancing the sacramental connotations of the students' transformation into guerrilla fighters is the presence in their midst of Buddhist monks. They joined the students because their consciences demanded it. Now, if the camps are attacked, they say that they too will pick up guns to fight; several have already begun military training. Meanwhile, they continue to live as monks, their iridescent orange robes in the drab surroundings making them appear like ornate birds of plumage, only momentarily alight in a long passage. For the young, malarial students, struggling to sustain the idealistic fervor that has brought them this far, the monks' presence is a reaffirmation of faith. As hard as life is at present, it enjoys a certain divinity and holds out the promise of metaphysical reward, if not in this life, then in the next.

*

Just as Aung Lwin has used the deeply religious cultural heritage of most of his followers to give their struggle cohesion and strength, so have the FMLN's *compas* found a useful receptivity to their social revolution among the Catholic peasants of the Salvadoran countryside.

One afternoon a heavy rainstorm breaks over Giovanni's camp. It is preceded by a series of loud thunderclaps, like bomb explosions, and then the rain comes down in a cool gray torrent. Sitting it out in the smoky darkness of the adobe cookhouse, Santiago gnaws on a roasted corncob smeared with salt and fresh lime juice, and tells the story of his own revolutionary conversion. Before the revolution, like so many other Salvadoran peasants, he worked as a day laborer to make his living: as a ditch-digger, as a bricklayer's assistant, and as a coffee picker in the annual coffee harvest.

During one picking season, Santiago went to work on a plantation owned by the Guirola family, one of the oligarchic 'Fourteen Families' whose military-assisted hold over El Salvador had been absolute until the war began. This was the early 1970s, before the *compas* had begun the armed struggle, but already *campesinos*, peasants, were 'disappearing' in the countryside. Santiago soon found out why.

'I found out from the workers that *el señor* Guirola, the plantation owner, was one of the Pactados.' The Pactados were a secret cabal of oligarchs who had made a pact with the devil, Santiago explains. 'The devil made them rich in return for turning one human over to him each week. And the workers said Guirola was one of them.'

Santiago had to find out if it was true. So, one night he waited at midnight in the shadows by the great front gate of the Guirola hacienda. After a time, the Pactado emerged – Santiago interrupts himself to imitate the creaky turning of a key in the gate lock, and the clip-clop of a horse's hooves – from the gate. He sat astride a great white horse with a peasant slung over the saddle in front of him, inert as a side of bacon. His dogs were with him. The dogs were big and black, with gold teeth and earrings, and wore ties.

'There to meet him was the devil – a tall man breathing smoke – who asked him in a deep voice: "Well, do you have what you owe me?" And the man on the horse said, "Yes, here it is," and handed over the *campesino* he had brought, and the devil took him off, carrying him on his shoulder.'

Santiago swears he witnessed this chilling encounter, and that every detail is true. When he looks back, however, what bothers him the most wasn't that the Pactado legend was true. That was no surprise. 'It is well known among all the peasants of El Salvador,' he says. What shocks him is that the oligarch's dogs were better fed than the workers.

'Look you!' Santiago exclaims, angry at the memory. 'The injustice of it! The dogs were fed veal, and what did the workers get? A single soggy tortilla!'

He might actually be fighting in a revolutionary movement that espouses Marxist-Leninist principles, but for Santiago it is easier to conceive of the 'class enemy' as an ally of the devil. His belief that he saw this Faustian midnight transaction himself is a testament to the power of myth, but, more important, it places Santiago's own conversion into the familiar moral realm of good and evil. After all, he has seen the enemy, and the enemy is none other than the devil himself.

The peasant guerrillas see life as a moral tale: Men are divided into those who are good, and those who are evil. This is the fertile earth in which the FMLN has worked to recruit new fighters for the revolution. That task has been aided by the politically active clergy who accompany the guerrillas and their flock in the hills.

The parish priest of Las Flores is a Basque Jesuit, a practitioner of the revolutionary doctrine of liberation theology, and his order is viewed with open enmity by the armed forces. The fact is, the priest himself is lucky even to be alive. Six months ago in the capital, soldiers acting on the orders of a colonel murdered six of his fellow priests.

One Sunday, the priest shows up in Las Flores in a state of restrained agitation. He walks into the grubby little shop next to the Comedor Popular and asks for a bottle of Fanta. A couple of *compas* and local villagers are there, eyeing the paltry selection of merchandise, and chatting. Handed his soda by the shopkeeper, the priest takes a swig, lights a cigarette, and starts talking.

He has just come from the military garrison in Chalatenango. He's been there to complain because the army has shelled a civilian hamlet two miles down the road. The shelling went on for a day and night, and it was, he says, 'only a miracle of God' that no one was hurt or killed. The shells fell very close by. It was not the first time this has happened, either. Five months ago the same hamlet – one of the new *repoblaciónes* – was hit by army mortar fire, and a family of five was killed. That was bad enough, but this time there were no *compas* around, so the army had no conceivable excuse for the latest attack.

When the barrage finally ended, the priest went to the source of the shelling, the Chalatenango garrison, to find out what was going on. There he asked to see the colonel, the commanding officer. After a long wait, he was ushered in to see the colonel. As he recalls what happened next, the priest shakes his head in angry indignation. 'I still can't get over it. Do you know what happened? I walked into his office and very politely, I told him about the shelling and asked him what he planned to do about punishing those responsible. And you know what he said ?' The priest sweeps the room with his eyes. 'Nothing at all. I mean, nothing! He didn't even open his mouth, or register that I had spoken to him! At all!' The priest wears an expression of disbelief.

'Finally, I asked him if he had heard me, and he still didn't answer. We both sat there for the longest time. I didn't know what to do, what to say. He simply never spoke! So, finally, I just . . . walked out.'

The priest finishes his warm Fanta and folds his arms, meditatively shaking his head from side to side. The shopkeeper and the *compas* listening are expressionless, blank. No one says a thing. At length the priest pays for his drink and leaves the shop, walking across the plaza to the church, to prepare the Sunday service.

Hearing of the colonel's blatant animosity is no surprise to anyone. It was the use of silence as a reaction to the priest's complaints that was so unique. Usually, army officers go through a pretense of hearing their petitioners out, promising to investigate, and to punish any wrongdoers, and so forth – and then do nothing. That is expected; at least a kind of ritual protocol is observed. But the colonel's telling silence – of course, he himself ordered the shelling – casts a pall of foreboding over all those who hear the priest's story.

The incident doesn't augur well for the future safety of Las Flores and the other *repoblaciónes* taking root in the area with the priest's help. An engineer by training, he is trying to get civic projects under way in the devastated zone: roadworks, bridge reconstruction, electrification, and the digging of new water wells. The priest is convinced that a rebuilt economic infrastructure will ensure the survival of the reborn communities. He has the cooperation of the FMLN, and officially of the government, but in practice the army is doing all it can to sabotage Chalate's revival; the shelling is just one of its methods.

In Las Flores, meanwhile, the guerrillas are encouraging the priest's efforts by engaging in some civic action of their own. One day in the plaza, not long after the priest's visit, the members of Giovanni's propaganda unit have arrived and are hard at work. The mysterious sand pile in the basketball court is shrinking, as Conejo and some of the others shovel it into a wheelbarrow, then cart it off toward the church. There they are mixing it to make cement; they have almost finished repairing the crumbling front porch and steps of the nuns' house next door. While they spread and smooth the cement, they leave their AK-47s leaning against the cracking walls of the church.

Across the plaza, Adriano has drawn cartoon figures in pencil all over the green-painted façade of the little kindergarten. With the help of a young female *compa*, Olga is painting them in with bright colors. Little boys and girls hop and scream delightedly about, smearing the dripped paint on their fingers.

In the afternoon, when they finish at the kindergarten, Adriano and Olga move across the plaza to the whitewashed side wall of the church. Standing on a ladder and watched by the plaza's gaggle of kids, Adriano sketches out a large mural. It shows an idealized Las Flores, topped off with a quotation from the book of Isaiah that significantly features the phrase 'building a new people.' The image of a Marxist guerrilla painting a biblical quotation on a church wall underscores the hybrid nature of the Salvadoran revolution, embracing Catholics and Marxists alike within its ranks. This unlikely union is explained by Justo, who says, 'The majority of the masses are religious, and the revolution has had to respect that.'

The church-revolutionary synthesis has developed to the extent that religious figures like the late Archbishop Oscar Arnulfo Romero have become leading revolutionary icons. This is because of the historic role played by priests and nuns in Central America's revolutionary struggles. These clerics, like the emblematic Romero, have adopted liberation theology as a means of bringing about social justice. It could be argued that, by urging the poor to fight their way out of misery and injustice, this breed of clerics has served as the guerrillas' recruiting officers.

Accurately or not, that is how the armed forces have always seen it, and in the early years of the war their death squads went after the clergy under the slogan 'Be patriotic, kill a priest.' Tragically for the murdered nuns and priests, there has been sufficient philosophical coincidence between themselves and the guerrillas for right-wing conspiracy theorists to perpetuate the myth of an unholy guerrilla-clergy alliance.

In reality, the FMLN's relationship with the church has always been highly complex, and not always smooth. In its position as the war's moral arbiter, the church wants to see an end to the war and the establishment of a more just society. But more than anything, it wants the killing to stop. In order for that to happen, it has urged the two sides to accept compromise and reconcile their differences in peaceful dialogue. The FMLN meanwhile, has taken the attitude that if it can't get what it wants through negotiations it is perfectly willing to continue the war until it does.

Liberation theology is a useful tool with which to organize and unite devout peasants to fight for revolution, but the FMLN is still a Marxist-led organization. Even if many low-level guerrilla cadres still believe in God, most of their leaders do not. Inevitably, the leaders' attitudes exert a powerful influence on the rank-and-file *compas*; as a result, more and more *compas* are professing their atheism.

In Las Flores, it is mostly only the villagers who attend the weekly church services given by the priest. The *compas* hang back on the periphery, respectful and protective but uninvolved Their studied atheism also extends to simple everyday gestures. Traditionally, Salvadoran peasants who pass one another on a country road have always said 'Adios,' 'Go with God.' By contrast, the *compas* say 'What's happening?' – *never* 'adios.'

In an uncanny echo of Polisario commander Ali Beiba, Augustín of the Radio Farabundo Martí crew says there is no secret agenda by the FMLN to stamp out the piety of its peasant followers. 'It's just that they've had to face the facts of life,' he says. 'The people have lost their faith because of the pragmatic realities of life in war.'

In fact, much as the Polisario Front has usurped the role of orthodox Islam as the linchpin in its people's lives, so too have the FMLN's canons replaced those of traditional Catholicism for many of its followers. The workaday ideology of the Salvadoran revolution is a curious admixture of Marxism, Catholicism, and local folklore, some of it undoubtedly contradictory, but cobbled together in a comfortable and unresolved amalgamation that seems to work. In the end, the FMLN's fusion of beliefs is a moral, rather than an ideological alliance, but it is no less potent for that. The FMLN has something else going for it, as well: the power of armed might. The FMLN, not the church, possesses weapons, and therefore the perceptible means to change things.

Every day the war continues, something happens to lay bare the shaky foundations of the old faiths and make people cling to the new totems even harder. Each story further fuels the evolving revolutionary folklore taking hold in the hills. One story, which has acquired the symbolism of a religious parable, deals with an episode that is supposed to have taken place several years ago.

On the *compas'* network of secret trails in the mountains there is one little-used path that leads through a deep forest, skirting a river that tumbles down through the mountains. For a couple of years, all the *compas* who were sent through there emerged from the forest scared out of their wits, telling stories of having seen a witch. Matters finally reached the point where none of the *compas* would go there, and the guerrilla high command could do nothing to convince them to. Reasoned explanations that witches simply don't exist fell on deaf ears. Finally, the high command sent out an investigating commission to explore the haunted forest.

There, in the forest, the guerrilla explorers found a woman who was half-wild, naked, and filthy, living in a cave like a beast. She could not speak, but only grunted unintelligibly. With her in the cave were the bones of hundreds of small rodents, birds, and snakes that she had eaten over the years; there was also the mummified body of a human infant. The *compas* took the woman back to camp, where in time she was coaxed back to health and lucidity. Eventually, she regained her power of speech as well, and it was then that the *compas* learned her story.

It emerged that several years before, to escape an army massacre in which everyone else in her family was slaughtered, she had run off into the woods clutching her newborn child. Near a stream, she found a cave, where she hid, coming out only after dark to hunt for food. But her breast milk soon dried up, and her infant quickly dehydrated and starved to death. Afterward, she lost her mind, but her instinct to survive remained intact, and she stayed on in the cave, becoming 'the witch in the woods' to the terrified young *compas* who glimpsed her fleetingly. Today, the 'resurrected' woman is alive and well, living in a guerrilla camp somewhere in the mountains.

As new archetypes replace the old, the revolution's own heroes and martyrs are pushing aside Catholicism's panoply of dusty saints. Archbishop Romero, as yet unacknowledged by the Vatican, is already sanctified by popular acclaim amongst the FMLN's *masas*. In their churches he is depicted in Christ-like manner, with a radiant golden halo around his dark head. And, there is Chalatenango's own local hero, Dimas, who is reminiscent of Luali in the Western Sahara.

Remembered for being a good military commander – yet sensitive and humorous, 'a true revolutionary spirit,' says Augustín – Dimas is sorely missed by his comrades. Since his death, the revolution unabashedly seeks to mythologize his positive qualities, enshrining them forever as its own spiritual property. Now, as the result of a propaganda campaign overseen by Olga, Adriano, and Carlos, the burly visage of Dimas stares out from flyers affixed to a thousand trees and lampposts throughout Chalatenango's hills.

From beyond the grave, Dimas demands revolutionary vigilance with his immortal challenge: '*Compañero*! Are you totally ready to pulverize the enemies of the people?'

In the end, all guerrillas are crusaders, people imbued with a belief that there are things worth dying for. And, whatever they believe in – Islam, Christianity, 'democracy,' Marxism-Leninism, or simply, a world where things are either good or evil – they are fighting to fulfill ideals greater than themselves. In the meantime, as they fight on, the guerrillas have themselves become larger than life figures, the saints, gods, and martyrs in a world of their own creation.

Afterword

My journeys through the insurgent world coincided with a series of historic events that profoundly altered the global political landscape, and that had a direct effect on many of the guerrilla movements I spent time with. The precipitous collapse of the Soviet bloc brought an end to the long Cold War, and with it, an end to the subsidies by Moscow and Washington that had fuelled many of their proxy conflicts around the world. Suddenly bereft of sponsorship for their wars, many guerrillas sued for peace.

In January 1992, the FMLN guerrillas signed a United Nations brokered peace deal with El Salvador's government, formally ending the country's twelve-year-old civil war. In exchange for promises of amnesty and government reforms, the guerrillas agreed to lay down their weapons and enter politics. Over the years since then, the FMLN has evolved into a mainstream political party. In March 2004, Shafick Jorge Handal, the onetime Salvadoran Communist Party chief, stood as the FMLN's presidential candidate in El Salvador's latest general elections. Although Handal lost, it was by a narrow margin, and the forty-three percent of the votes he won showed that El Salvador's guerrillas had come a long way since their days in the hills.

But El Salvador's social and economic problems have not ended in peacetime. It remains one of Central America's poorest and most violent nations, plagued by a proliferating criminal gang culture that specializes in murder, kidnapping, car theft, and drug trafficking. Many of the gang members are the sons and daughters of returned refugees, unemployed former soldiers, and demobilized guerrillas. Not everyone has been able to adjust to lives without *mistica* in the postwar reality.

In 2002, a friend in El Salvador informed me that 'Justo,' one of the *compa*s I had spent time with in Chalatenengo, was in Spain, teaching university workshops in 'wartime journalism.' I learned that Justo's old comrade, 'Haroldo,' had also returned to civilian life, giving up his pseudonym and reclaiming his true identity as the poet and writer Miguel Huezo Mixco. In late 2005, we resumed our contact with one another via e-mail. At the time, Huezo Mixco was earning a living with the U.N. Development Program in San Salvador.

I asked Huezo Mixco how he felt about his years spent as a guerrilla propagandist. 'I feel proud of having been part of that process,' he replied steadfastly. 'I acknowledge that the sacrifices for the country were immense, not only in material but also in human terms, and that what has been achieved seems very little today. Only with time, I think, will we be able gain a perspective on that struggle and what it meant. Whether or not its effects endure, and whether more justice and freedom can be achieved, no longer depend on that struggle, but on what we're able to build now, with other tools: those of knowledge and sensitivity, of positive values.' The Salvadoran revolution, in other words, was over, but Miguel Huezo Mixco hadn't lost his *mistica*.

*

In the Western Sahara, the Polisario and Morocco signed a cease-fire agreement in 1991. Afterward, a specially created United Nations peacekeeping force was dispatched to monitor the agreement and to organize a referendum that would decide the future status of the territory. But disagreements between the Polisario and Morocco over the question of who is eligible to vote, on either side of Hassan's Wall, have repeatedly stymied the United Nations negotiators, and the referendum has never taken place. The death of King Hassan II in 1999 and his succession by a reformist heir, Muhammad VI, brought early hopes of a break-through in the impasse, but this has not occurred. At the heart of the problem lies Morocco's continuing insistence that Western Sahara is an 'integral' part of its national territory, while the Polisario, just as adamantly, argues for the Saharawis' right to 'self-determination.'

There have been some goodwill gestures on both sides, including prisoner releases. Beginning in 2000, the Polisario began releasing its Moroccan POWs. One of the men freed in 2003 had been a captive for twenty-eight years, making him the longest-held political prisoner in the world. In August 2005, despite continuing concerns over the fate of several hundred 'disappeared' Saharawi civilians and Polisario fighters, believed to be in Moroccan custody, the Polisario released the last of its Moroccan POWs, totalling 404 men.

In April 2004, after Morocco's rejection of a peace plan, a frustrated Kofi Annan threatened to withdraw the United Nations peacekeeping forces unless one side or the other was willing to show compromise. But his deadline slipped by, the U.N. mandate was renewed – as it has been every six months for the past fifteen years – and the cold war of talks and threats has continued, with very little change occurring on the ground.

Just as when I visited them in the late winter of 1989, the

Saharawis in the Polisario's desert camps remain in limbo, the citizens of a guerrilla nation-in-waiting.

Burma itself – or 'Myanmar,' as it was renamed by the military regime – is largely the same repressive place that it was at the end of the 1980s. The standoff between the country's unelected rulers and pro-democracy activists continues, a situation that, along with the junta's persistent human rights abuses, has kept Burma high on the list of international pariah states. Burma's leading political reformer, Aung San Suu Kyi, has spent most of the last two decades under house arrest, but continues to advocate nonviolent dialogue as the best means of securing a peaceful transition to democracy. Much of the Burmese hinterland, meanwhile, remains under the de facto control of a diverse array of ethnic factions and opium-trafficking warlords, some of whom are believed to enjoy mutually lucrative relationships with Burmese military commanders.

Not long after I left Kawthoolei in the autumn of 1989, the Burmese military regime bought a billion dollars' worth of weapons from China and embarked on a nationwide offensive against its ethnic insurgents. By the mid-nineties, almost all of the insurgent groups, except for the KNU, had signed cease-fire agreements with Rangoon. In 1997, after signing important gas extraction and cross-border pipeline deals with Thailand and several foreign corporations, Rangoon's military launched a sustained assault against the Karen, and virtually obliterated them as a fighting force. The KNU's few remaining bases fell, including Kawmura and its headquarters at Manerplaw. Thousands of guerrillas and their families fled into Thailand, swelling the Karen refugee population there to an estimated one hundred thousand.

By then, most of the Burmese students who had joined the Karen in Kawthoolei were long gone. Those who had not already deserted, succumbed to cerebral malaria, or death on the battlefield soon found their way into boarding houses and camps in Thailand, or sought sanctuary in other countries. Some of the Karen guerrillas I knew have found new lives abroad. Ganemy, the prime minister's adviser, is now reported to be living in Australia. Major Robert Zan, who apparently continued to train his Karen and student cadres as 'terrorists' well into the 1990s, finally left the Kawthoolei battlefield for a new home in Minnesota.

For two or three years after my last visit to Kawthoolei, I received Christmas cards from the Japanese mercenary sniper Motosada Mori. Then they stopped. For years I wondered what had happened to 'Moto.' Then, in 2004, in a magazine for mercenaries, I read an unconfirmed account that he had been killed fighting in Kawthoolei and been buried there.

In January 2004, a KNU delegation headed by General Bo Mya traveled to Rangoon, where he signed a cease-fire agreement in exchange for the regime's promises to hold a national convention in which all of Burma's ethnic groups were represented, and to draft a new national constitution. While he was in Rangoon, Bo Mya's hosts threw him a banquet to celebrate his seventy-seventh birthday. To all intents and purposes, the long Karen insurgency was over.

In Gaza, the first Palestinian intifada ended in the early 1990s as direct talks began between Israel and the Palestinians, raising hopes for a lasting settlement to the Israeli-Palestinian conflict. Sweeping concessions were made by both sides, such as the PLO's recognition of Israel's 'right to exist,' and Israel's reciprocal recognition of the PLO as a legal political party. The Palestinian Authority, a virtual government headed by Yassir Arafat, who was permitted to return to his homeland for the first time since 1967, was set up in the

Occupied Territories of Gaza and the West Bank. It was only a matter of time, it seemed, before there would be a Palestinian state.

But a final peace deal was not secured, and in September 2000, a 'second' Palestinian intifada began. This time, however, it was not a resistance waged by *shabbab* throwing stones, but by Palestinian fighters using automatic weapons, and, increasingly, by young suicide bombers sent into Israel's streets to kill themselves and as many Jewish people as they could at the same time. The great tragedy of the lost opportunity for peace in the 1990s meant that a new generation of Palestinians grew up with no hope of a future. For a distressingly large number of them, death in a 'martyrdom operation' came to seem a worthwhile destiny. Their bombings took place in restaurants, on crowded streets, and on passenger buses, and have caused horrific carnage. Many hundreds of Israeli civilians died in the new bloodletting.

Israel's response, under the leadership of the hard-line Prime Minister Ariel Sharon, was to hit back with unmerciful harshness. It became routine for Israel to send in its tanks and helicopter gunships to retaliate for attacks on Israeli soil; destroying the homes of suicide bombers, assassinating Hamas leaders with missiles and bombs, and unapologetically shooting on sight anyone who seemed suspicious. Like their Palestinian counterparts, the latest crop of Israeli soldiers were much more callous and prone to violence than those who had served in the first intifada. Among their three thousand-odd victims were over five hundred Palestinian children. They also killed several foreign human rights activists and journalists, apparently on purpose. One of them was a twenty-three-year-old American girl named Rachel Corrie. She was run over by an Israeli army bulldozer in March 2003, as she stood in its path in a symbolic attempt to prevent it from demolishing a Palestinian home in the Rafah refugee camp in Gaza. Two weeks earlier, in Breij, where I spent so much time in the first intifada, the Israeli army killed eight people, including several civilians, while carrying out a raid to arrest a Hamas leader. One of them was Nuha al-Magadmeh, a Palestinian woman in her ninth month of pregnancy, who was crushed to death when the Israelis dynamited the house next door to hers, and the wall of her home collapsed on top of her.

The terrorism of the new intifada also brought an end to the comings and goings of most Palestinians between Gaza and Israel. As pernicious as it was, Israel's 'black labor' system, which so many Palestinians depended upon for their livelihoods, has all but ended. Israel has resolved its shortage of labor problem by importing contract laborers from countries like China, the Philippines, and Romania. In 1991, with a population estimated at 750,000 people, Gaza was one of the most overcrowded places on earth. By 2005, its population had swollen to nearly 1,400,000.

In spite of all the violence – or, perhaps, because of it – the sketchy outlines of the future Palestinian state are beginning to take shape. After a long and tense standoff with Yassir Arafat that ended only with his death, by illness, in late 2004, the Israeli government began to reengage with the Palestinians. Once negotiations resumed with the newly elected Palestinian leadership, the violence of the second intifada was reined in significantly. Additional security was enforced through physical separation, as Israel erected a huge concrete wall along its self-imposed borders with the West Bank. (A few years earlier, Gaza had already been fenced off from Israel, while its traditional rights to road passage to the West Bank through Israel were suspended in 2000.) As Palestinian villages and towns were isolated from one another in a series of territorial enclaves, however, the wall appeared to have been designed not only to separate Palestinians from the Israelis, but from each other as well. Many Palestinians began to fear that when the Israeli occupation finally ended, they would be the inhabitants not of a homeland, but of a prison.

In September 2005, Israel finally withdrew its military forces from Gaza, ending thirty-eight years of military occupation. As part of the move, Israeli troops also evacuated the inhabitants of several Jewish settlements that had been built there, then destroyed the installations they had left behind. Gaza was now 'free,' but, like the rest of Palestine, from which it was disconnected, it was a territorial island, linked to the outside world only via its land border with Egypt on the Sinai Peninsula. There was talk of an eventual solution to the problem of Gaza's link with the West Bank: a 'secure road' that would cut through forty kilometers of Israeli territory but would run at a depth of twelve to twenty feet beneath the surface, like an open tunnel. The route would give the Palestinians access to one another, but also keep them firmly isolated from the Israelis.

A great deal has happened in Afghanistan since the summer of 1989, when I spent time with the Afghan mujahedin during their siege of Jalalabad, but I recall with clarity the encounter I had with the eleven-year-old boy on the battlefield, who told me he wanted to 'kill kafirs.' In those days, in Afghanistan, the definition of a kafir shifted from person to person. Formally an 'unbeliever,' an infidel, I knew that the term also included foreigners – people like me – who were killable because they did not share the faith of Islam, or merely because they looked different. Although I was standing right next to him, the Afghan boy was too young and unaware to realize that I could easily have fit the bill.

A day or two after my encounter with the boy, my mujahedin escorts evacuated me urgently from the frontline after a group of 'Arab jihadis' sent a scout to sniff around the hilltop fortress where I was staying. The jihadis were religious volunteers from Arab countries who had come to fight alongside the Afghans. I had not sought out contacts with them, even though they operated out of a nearby camp, because they were said to be unfriendly to Westerners. The jihadi scout spoke with one of the Afghan sentries. He told him that he and his comrades were looking for kafirs to kill, and thought they had seen one – *me* – with the mujahedin in the fortress. The sentry lied to the Arab, telling him that he was mistaken. There were no kafirs there, he said, only Afghan mujahedin. The Arab went away, but, according to the sentry, who came inside immediately to warn us, he had looked unconvinced.

Upon hearing this news, my Afghan companions became extremely alarmed, and said that it was only a matter of time before the Arabs sent back a larger force of armed men to find me. Moving quickly, they made me conceal myself with a turban and a wraparound Afghan *patou* blanket, and then they placed me between them, all heavily-armed, in the backseat of a Jeep. We set off within minutes. The only track that led out to safety passed directly in front of the Arabs' bivouack. The jihadis stared angrily as we passed, but did not open fire, apparently because I was with their local allies.

It was several years before I heard the name Osama bin Laden, but I eventually learned that he was in Jalalabad that summer, and that those jihadis had been his men. Somewhere, probably based not all that far from where he was during the summer of 1989, Bin Laden and his fellow jihadis are still hunting kafirs, but now their battlefield has expanded to encompass the whole world.

The siege of Jalalabad was an abject failure. Several thousand lives were lost in the process, including those of many of the young boys I met on the front line, adolescent volunteers from the refugee camps in neighboring Pakistan. Three years later, the mujahedin finally seized power in Kabul, and then, predictably, proceeded to fight over it, reducing much of it to rubble and killing tens of thousands of civilians in the process. With the mujahedin's rise to power, meanwhile, my old host in Argandhab, Mullah Naquib, became the supreme commander of Kandahar. After a chaotic tenure of just two years, however, he handed the city over to the armed religious students known as the Taliban, who in 1994 swept into the country from their madrasas in Pakistan, bent on restoring law and order and imposing Islamic justice. By 1996, they had seized Kabul, imposed a strict Islamic tyranny on the country, and soon welcomed back Osama bin Laden, who had been living in the Sudan for the previous few years. Bin Laden returned to his old haunts in Afghanistan, and began preparing his terrorist organization, Al Qaeda, for its global 'jihad' against the West.

With the attacks on New York and Washington, D.C., on September 11, 2001, the insurgent world – in a devastatingly real sense – finally became part of all of our lives.

Two weeks after the attacks, I journeyed back to Afghanistan for the first time since 1989. I spent three months traveling across Afghanistan before, during, and after the U.S.-led military campaign against the Taliban. A few days before the New Year, I reached Kandahar.

The Taliban had vanished from the city by the time I arrived. The newly arrived American military troops had occupied a base at the airport outside town, and small groups of heavily-armed, bearded United States Special Forces commandos roved around in pickup trucks and wearing Afghan clothing. Otherwise, Kandahar did not seem to have changed much since 1989; it was still a poor, beaten up, and dusty city. Here and there lay the collapsed remains of buildings that had recently been bombed by the Americans. I found Mullah Naquib living at his new home on the northern outskirts of the city, next door to the sprawling walled complex where the fugitive Taliban leader, Mullah Omar, had lived until very recently.

At the time of my visit, Naquib was keeping a rather low profile. The Americans and their Afghan allies who were now in control of Kandahar suspected him of having helped Mullah Omar escape from the city before they arrived. During the war, a couple of weeks earlier, as the American and anti-Taliban forces had closed in on the city, the Taliban leader had agreed to surrender peacefully after handing the city over to Naquib. But sometime during the night before the surrender was to have taken place, Mullah Omar, several other senior Taliban leaders, and most of their fighters had mysteriously vanished. After a halfhearted attempt to hold the city with his own militia, Naquib had stood down and retired to his house, claiming to be 'tired of politics.' He professed to have no knowledge of how Mullah Omar had escaped.

Naquib looked much the same as I remembered him. He was still big and burly, but his beard now had some streaks of gray in it. He greeted me in a modest receiving room of a house in his compound where there were gunmen lounging around in his flower garden. Naquib did not remember me, but said he did after I had refreshed his memory with some stories about my stay at his camp in Arghandab. He smiled. He was delighted, he said, to greet 'a friend from the days of the jihad,' and I accepted his invitation to accompany him on a visit to the old base camp the next day.

Naquib's flamboyant aide-de-camp, Mazen Agha, was there too, and when I greeted him, his face brightened with recognition and he gave the same high-pitched whinnying laugh I remembered from years before. But Mazen Agha had a weathered and somewhat dissipated air about him, I noticed, and he was no longer dressed so splendidly as before.

When I returned to Naquib's house the next morning, he ushered me into a large white, luxurious Toyota Land Cruiser. I saw that he had several identical cars parked there, and I complimented him on his fine possessions. He beamed proudly and confided, 'I have ten of them; they were Mullah Omar's.' Naquib winked mischievously. As we drove past the destroyed compound of his former neighbor and began climbing the hill toward Arghandab, Naquib started fiddling with the dials of a CD player built into the dashboard. As a romantic crooning melody filled the car with music, Naquib smiled contentedly. I asked Naquib if the CDs had been in the Land Cruiser when he had taken possession of it. 'Yes,' he replied.

'So,' I said, 'are you saying that the man who banned music for his countrymen liked to listen to it himself?'

He shrugged and said, 'So it seems.'

Naquib remained silent for a moment, then, with another of his winking looks, he quipped, 'What is life without music?'

Acknowledgments

First, I must thank the guerrilla organizations that gave me their trust. In Afghanistan, the Jamiat-i-Islami; in El Salvador, the Frente Farabundo Martí para la Liberación Nacional; the Karen National Union of Burma; and the Frente Polisario in Western Sahara. In Gaza, my access was secured less formally, through individuals rather than political organizations.

People who helped me in the field include Khalilullah, Ghulam Azrat, Mazen Agha, Muhammad Shoaib, and Wali Khan (Afghanistan); Haroldo, Justo, Matilde, Giovanni, and Carmelo (El Salvador); Mahmoud, Ahmed, Sami, Yasir, Dasir, Hisham, Anis, Nasser, and Usama (Gaza); Ganemy, Robert Zan, Lydia, Soe Soe, Aung Naing, Pang, Moscow, Ying Sita, and Robert Tuja (Burma); and Abba, Moulay, and Foulan (Western Sahara). Most of these people are guerrillas – indeed, many of the names I give are false ones – and can be found in the pages of this book. Beyond this, what they all have in common is the invaluable assistance they lent me during my forays, in a few cases at considerable danger to themselves.

There is another group of people, none of them guerrillas, to whom I owe thanks for their help and friendship during my work on this book: Alberto Barrera, Robert Block, Rebecca Brian, Patricia Codina, Tony Davis, John Gunston, Rex Henderson, Chris Hooke, Arna Mer Khamis, Mary and Muhammad Khass, Michelle Labrut, Donatella Lorch, Nancy McGirr, Douglas Mine, James Nachtwey, Robert Nickelsberg, Abu Hani Obeidi and his family, Tina Rathbone, Nick Richards, B. M. Rolfe, Vanadia Sandon-Humphries, Charles Siebert, Alessandra Stanley, Nohad Al-Turki, and Rafael Winer.

With her informed and encouraging eye, my mother, Barbara Joy Anderson, herself an author, was a special help during the writing, as was my brother, Scott Anderson, and my good friend Francisco Goldman. As always, my father, John William Anderson, provided me with the benefits of his wisdom.

Henry Ferris was an early advocate for this book, as was Kate Parkin. At a crucial time, Deborah Schneider looked after my best interests and kept her faith in me. I am very grateful to Amy Hundley for her invaluable editorial insights, to my agent, Sarah Chalfant at the Wylie Agency, and to Ursula Mackenzie at Time Warner, for deciding that *Guerrillas* should be reborn as an Abacus Original. Special thanks to Tim Whiting, Rachel Ludbrook, Caroline Hogg and Kerry Chapple, for helping to make that happen.

Finally, I thank my wife, Erica, for her singular patience and unstinting support throughout the three and a half years it took me to complete *Guerrillas*. In my long and repeated absences, in the infectious hepatitis I brought home to her from Chalatenango, and in many other ways, the guerrilla world became almost as much a part of her life as it was of mine, and yet she never once complained.

Now you can order superb titles directly from Abacus

☐ The Fall of Baghdad   Jon Lee Anderson   £9.99

The prices shown above are correct at time of going to press. However, the publishers reserve the right to increase prices on covers from those previously advertised, without further notice.

──────────────── ⬭ABACUS⬭ ────────────────

Please allow for postage and packing: **Free UK delivery.**
Europe: add 25% of retail price; Rest of World: 45% of retail price.

To order any of the above or any other Abacus titles, please call our credit card orderline or fill in this coupon and send/fax it to:

Abacus, PO Box 121, Kettering, Northants NN14 4ZQ
Fax: 01832 733076   Tel: 01832 737527
Email: aspenhouse@FSBDial.co.uk

☐ I enclose a UK bank cheque made payable to Abacus for £ . . . .
☐ Please charge £ . . . . . . to my Visa/Access/Mastercard/Eurocard

☐☐☐☐☐☐☐☐☐☐☐☐☐☐☐☐☐☐☐

Expiry Date ☐☐☐☐   Switch Issue No. ☐☐

NAME (BLOCK LETTERS please) . . . .

ADDRESS . . . .

. . . .

. . . .

Postcode . . . . Telephone . . . .

Signature . . . .

Please allow 28 days for delivery within the UK. Offer subject to price and availability.

Please do not send any further mailings from companies carefully selected by Abacus ☐